A HANDS-ON, EASY-TO-USE GUIDE TO EFFECTIVE ORGANIZAT...

D0959846

DESIGNING AND USING ORGANIZATIONAL SUR... practitioners with a clear and practical work... implementing successful organizational surveys... consulting experience, authors Allan H. Church and Janine Waclawski present a concise seven-step model that covers the entire survey process from its conception to evaluation and—perhaps more importantly—to making the results meaningful and achievable for the future of the organization. Their highly pragmatic approach pays special attention to the political and human sensitivities inherent in the process and clearly shows how to overcome the many potential barriers to conducting a successful survey.

"In my view, this book is simply the best, A to Z resource for organizational survey and assessment practitioners available. . . . A fresh and lucid perspective that inextricably links theory and practice. Comprehensive and practical, the seven-step process approach provides a closed-loop blueprint for designing and implementing organizational surveys that work!"
—SALVATORE V. FALLETTA, MANAGER,
GLOBAL HR RESEARCH, INTEL CORPORATION

"The many tools that Church and Waclawski offer alone make this book a treasure chest. . . . A considerable array of figures, examples, and samples that are helpful to the experienced and inexperienced practitioner (and consultant), including sample scripts and content for communications and focus groups."
—DAVID W. BRACKEN, PARTNER,
MERCER DELTA CONSULTING, LLC

"A great primer on organizational surveys. Church and Waclawski integrate into their approach to surveying both the science of the field and the art of practice in dynamic organizations. . . .Will provide valuable discussions among even the most seasoned professionals as well as insight for those just starting out in the field."
—KAREN B. PAUL, MANAGER,
HR MEASUREMENT SYSTEMS

Jacket design by Brenda Duke

HUMAN RESOURCE MANAGEMENT

JOSSEY-BASS
A Wiley Company
350 Sansome St.
San Francisco, CA 94104-1342

www.josseybass.com

ISBN 0-7879-5677-5

9000

9 780787 956776

Designing and Using Organizational Surveys

Allan H. Church
Janine Waclawski

Foreword by Allen I. Kraut

Designing and Using Organizational Surveys

A Seven-Step Process

JOSSEY-BASS
A Wiley Company
San Francisco

First Jossey-Bass edition published in 2001. This book was originally published in 1998 by
Gower Publishing Limited, England, under the title *Designing and Using Organizational
Surveys* by Allan H. Church and Janine Waclawski.

Jossey-Bass is a registered trademark of Jossey-Bass Inc., A Wiley Company.

Jossey-Bass books and products are available through most bookstores. To contact
Jossey-Bass directly, call (888) 378-2537, fax to (800) 605-2665, or visit our website at
www.josseybass.com.

Substantial discounts on bulk quantities of Jossey-Bass books are available to corporations, professional associations, and other organizations. For details and discount information, contact the special sales department at Jossey-Bass.

 Manufactured in the United States of America on Lyons Falls Turin Book.
This paper is acid-free and 100 percent totally chlorine-free.

Library of Congress Cataloging-in-Publication Data

Church, Allan H., date-
    Designing and using organizational surveys: a seven-step process / Allan H. Church,
Janine Waclawski.—1st ed.
        p. cm.—(Jossey-Bass business & management series)
    ISBN 0-7879-5677-5
    1. Employee attitude surveys. I. Waclawski, Janine, date- II. Title. III. Series.

HF5549.5.A83 C483 2001
658.3'14'0723—dc21   00-011967

HB Printing   10 9 8 7 6 5 4 3 2 1   FIRST EDITION

The Jossey-Bass
Business & Management Series

Contents

Tables, Figures, and Exhibits

Tables

Figures

Exhibits

Foreword

This book will serve as an excellent primer for executives and practitioners who are about to embark on an organizational survey. In a careful, step-by-step fashion, the book covers the many decisions that have to be made to do an effective survey. At the same time, *Designing and Using Organizational Surveys* will be an effective review and checklist for even the most experienced survey researchers.

It is hard not to be impressed with the clear thinking and lucid writing that Allan Church and Janine Waclawski have brought to their work in this volume. They cover a wide array of topics and do so in a way that demonstrates a lot of practical experience and fine academic training; it also reflects the deep thought they have given to the topic.

The authors take little for granted as they systematically guide the reader through all the important choice points along the way toward doing a survey. This comes out right away in their "starting with the end in mind" and then systematically proceeding to show how to get to that desired end. In the case of a survey, that means being clear on why one wants to conduct a survey. What strategic purposes are to be served? What goals are to be achieved? This awareness is key to getting commitment to the survey from senior management and employees. It also helps one to specify what kinds of data should be gathered and where organizational "helps" and "hindrances" may lie in wait.

For the authors, this understanding and goal setting is the first step in their seven-step program for effective surveys. The other six steps follow a logical process to the end desired by nearly all practitioners: to see the survey used effectively. It is this orientation that is so consistent, compelling, and attractive to me. Every step of the process is aimed at producing a first-rate survey that will actually be used. The continuing emphasis on doing a survey that will result in real action is a distinctive feature of this book.

At the same time, the authors have made the book useful and easy to read. One device I particularly like is the checklist provided at the end of each chapter. This serves as a useful chapter summary, and even as a practitioner's checklist while doing a survey. For a lazy reader like myself, it is an easy way to jump ahead to the conclusion of each section and decide whether or not to go back through the details (I always did).

Another technique that the authors use is to devote a full chapter to each of the seven steps. This lets the reader move to sections of his or her own interest in a logical (if not sequential) way. I think this is especially important for those of us who would like to refer back to particular sections from time to time.

Each section is full of fundamental materials as well as very sophisticated insights and suggestions. For example, in the chapter on putting together a world-class survey, they review the basics of writing good questions. But the authors also detail a technique used only by advanced practitioners: the use of a survey team (or steering committee) to get the benefit of diverse thinking and to gain the energy of an involved group of potential allies and advocates in the organization.

Fortunately, the authors don't assume that we know a lot about all aspects of surveys. As an example, we are treated to a brief history of surveys and their use before we even get into the seven-step process. From this short introductory section, we get a sense of the role that surveys play in organizational life today, as well as their potential for improving effectiveness.

In a reader-friendly manner, Church and Waclawski review the major issues to be confronted at each stage. More important, they lay out the options available, along with the pros and cons of each decision. These options make up an excellent discussion on much of what is known about doing surveys well. The authors' academic knowledge, as well as their survey experience, shines through here. Moreover, while they let us know what they would advocate, the authors are not doctrinaire with their advice.

As a result, we get skillful guidance through the other six steps in conducting an effective survey. These cover putting together a high-quality survey questionnaire, communicating to the organization, administering the survey effectively, processing and interpreting the results, transmitting and reporting the findings, and translating the newly learned information into meaningful action.

Based on my own experience, I can see that the authors have accumulated a long list of the mistakes and misjudgments that are common in doing surveys. These are the sorts of errors that most practitioners recognize in hindsight and never commit again. The readers of this book will be in a much better position to avoid such errors. Moreover, they will have effective alternatives.

Although other survey researchers in industry have had extensive experience and insight into doing effective surveys, few have set down a comprehensive and thoughtful account of their knowledge. Allan Church and Janine Waclawski have done so in this book, and their contribution to the field will be widely recognized. I believe we are indebted to them for their aid in moving the field forward and up to a higher level of excellence.

New York
January 2001

Allen I. Kraut
Professor of Management
Zicklin School of Business
Baruch College, CUNY

Acknowledgments

For those of us who are unaccustomed to or uncomfortable with the art of giving praise well, the acknowledgments page is perhaps the most difficult part of a book to write. This may seem like an exaggeration, but it is nonetheless true. The difficulty stems from not knowing the right words to use when saying thanks. The ability to sum up all of one's feelings of gratitude in a few simple lines takes a combination of eloquence and feeling. To say thank you to a mentor, friend, or colleague in a way that sounds both intelligent and genuine is no easy task. With this said, we would like to try and express our appreciation for those who have helped us along the way and hope that our simple words will do them the justice they deserve.

First and foremost, we are especially grateful to W. Warner Burke. Warner, more than any other person, has helped us attain the collective knowledge and experiences that led to the development of this book. Over the years, he has given us innumerable opportunities to acquire, enhance, and refine our skills in the organizational survey arena.

We want to thank the many unnamed clients, including those not described in these pages, with whom we have worked over the years and from whom we have learned a great deal.

We would also like to thank Dale Crossman for suggesting us as potential authors for this project and Denis Kinlaw, who reviewed our initial book proposal and worked with us on the first draft of our introductory chapter.

A hearty round of applause goes to our graduate students in the Organizational Psychology Program at Teachers College, Columbia University, for being sounding boards for much of the material contained herein. We wrote the first version of the book while simultaneously developing and delivering our first class on the subject of data-driven methods for organizational change. Our students proved to be an invaluable source of feedback and inspiration, which was so important in shaping the final manuscript. Their intellectual curiosity, frequent requests for greater detail and clarity, and probity in giving us feedback about the quality of our content worked together to produce a much better product. Moreover, many of the suggestions for improvement those students made in the classes after the first year have been incorporated into this new edition.

We would also like to thank our proofreader, Mary Zippo, for her work in copyediting the initial drafts of this manuscript. Mary's remarkable ability to read and reread the same chapters over and over again without falling asleep or being driven to physical violence is testament to her professionalism.

We also owe many thanks to Allen Kraut, not only for very graciously agreeing to write the Foreword for this new and improved edition of our book but for providing us with useful feedback about its contents. Moreover, Allen gave us the opportunity to hone some of our thoughts for the final chapter by asking us to serve on a panel with him that was focused on the importance of survey action planning.

And speaking of people who have given us opportunities to refine our thoughts on action planning, we would like to thank several members of the Mayflower Group—two of whom are Karen Paul and Kevin Nilan—for inviting us to present on this very same topic at one of their annual meetings in Colorado Springs, Colorado. In addition to enjoying the fabulous location and great company, this meeting gave us a chance to refine our thoughts on the subject of the often-asked question, What happens after the survey results go out? On a related matter, we would also like to thank Dave Bracken for his kind review in *Personnel Psychology* of the first edition of this book (which was published in 1998 by Gower Ltd.), and for motivating us to expand some of the concepts discussed and improve its contents as well.

Last but certainly not least we are forever indebted to Julianna Gustafson, our editor at Jossey-Bass, for her interest and enthusiasm in bringing the book to the United States and letting us make the necessary changes and improvements for this new and improved edition. We hope the book serves many people well for many years to come!

Pound Ridge, New York   Allan H. Church
January 2001   Janine Waclawski

The Authors

Allan H. Church is director of organization and management development at PepsiCo, Inc. He specializes in designing customized multisource feedback systems and large-scale diagnostic surveys for organization development and change. Previously, he was employed at PricewaterhouseCoopers, LLP, in the Management Consulting Services line of business. Prior to that, he spent nine years at W. Warner Burke Associates, Inc., and three years at IBM in the Personnel Research Department and the Communications Research Department. He is an adjunct professor at Columbia University and a distinguished visiting scholar in the College of Business, Technology, and Professional Programs at Benedictine University.

Church received his B.A., with a double major in psychology and sociology, from Connecticut College and his M.A., M.Phil., and Ph.D. in organizational psychology from Columbia University. He has published more than ten book chapters and more than one hundred articles in academic and practitioner publications; his work has appeared in the *Journal of Applied Psychology*, *Public Opinion Quarterly*, the *Journal of Occupational and Organizational Psychology*, *Personnel Psychology*, *Journal of Applied Social Psychology*, *Group and Organization Management*, *Human Resource Development Quarterly*, and *Consulting Psychology Journal*. Along with David Bracken and Carol Timmreck, he is coeditor of *The Handbook of Multisource Feedback* (Jossey-Bass, 2001). Church currently serves as editor of both

The Industrial-Organizational Psychologist (TIP) and the *Organization Development Journal;* he is associate editor of the *International Journal of Organizational Analysis* and OD Forum Field Editor for the American Society for Training and Development (ASTD) publication, *Performance in Practice.*

Janine Waclawski is a principal consultant in the Management Consulting Services line of business of PricewaterhouseCoopers, LLP. She was formerly a principal at W. Warner Burke Associates, Inc., for eight years. She has also worked for IBM in corporate personnel research and for New York City for the director of training in the Department of Investigations. She specializes in using surveys and multisource feedback for organizational change and executive development. In addition to her full-time consulting work, she is an adjunct professor at Columbia University; she has been an instructor at Hunter College in New York City.

Waclawski received her B.A. in psychology from the State University of New York at Stony Brook and her M.Phil. and Ph.D. in organizational psychology from Columbia University. She received the prestigious ASTD Donald Bullock Memorial Dissertation Award for her research on large-scale organizational change and performance. She has published more than twenty articles, with a primary emphasis on data-driven methods for organization development and change in a wide variety of journals, including *Consulting Psychology Journal, Group and Organization Management,* the *Journal of Occupational and Organizational Psychology,* and *Quality Progress.* Currently, she is the editor of *The Real World*—a quarterly publication in *The Industrial Organizational Psychologist (TIP)*, which has a circulation of more than 5,500 professionals. Being actively involved in several professional organizations, she is on several journal editorial boards and has been an invited speaker, panel chair, and discussant for many national and international conferences.

Introduction

Welcome to the information age. Although we may not like to think of ourselves as a collection of data points just waiting to be identified, gathered, and quantified in some controlled fashion, in large part that is what we are. Each of us comprises an endless supply of information, from the factual (date of birth, gender, ethnicity, religious background, education) to the attitudinal (preferences, dislikes, opinions). This is how various information systems perceive, understand, and ultimately define our existence.

Of course, the fact that our databases are continually growing and changing over the course of our lifespan makes it all the more difficult to understand ourselves. This process of understanding, however, through information gathering (data collection) and interpretation is one of the primary roles of organizations today. For many organizations these data—our individual and collective experiences as human beings—are among the most important sources of information to be harnessed. In fact, many e-businesses and Internet firms (even the more traditional organizations with their eyes on e-commerce) today are basing their corporate strategy around the prevalence of such information. Moreover, these data are the basis and lifeblood of such data gathering strategies as polling (on political preferences, television viewing preferences, and current topics), administering undergraduate and graduate record examinations, conducting the national census, and using targeted marketing for various products. Rest assured that if you are watching a particular program on television, any advertisements shown have been targeted at your segment of the marketplace. In today's burgeoning information society, understanding the effective use of data collection and interpretation through survey methodology in organizations presents one key means of increasing our understanding of the human experience.

In the organizational context, surveys play an important role in helping leaders and managers obtain a better understanding of the thoughts, feelings, and behaviors of their own employees and of their customers. In fact, surveys are among the most widely used techniques in contemporary organizations for gathering data from a large number of people in a short amount of time. More than 70 percent of U.S. organizations today survey their employees, either on an annual or a biannual basis (Paul and Bracken, 1995). The trend toward survey use appears to be going up rather than down (Kraut and Saari, 1999). For example, although the Mayflower Group—one of the elite survey consortia populated by the top-ranked organizations in their respective industries—contained only fifteen charter members at its inception in 1971, the group boasted a membership of forty-two in 1995 and a growth rate of 40 percent since 1985 (Johnson, 1996). Similarly, presentations and research at professional conferences on surveys and their applications have been consistently popular over the years. Moreover, in the 1980s and 1990s organizational surveys have moved from being the sole province of institutions that are academic (for example, the Center for Applied Social Research at Columbia University) and research-based (for example, the Census Bureau and Gallup) to either internal organization development (OD) and human resource development (HRD) functions or external consulting firms versed in applied research methods such as those made up of industrial-organizational (I-O) psychologists.

The popularity of the survey process in organizations can be traced in large part to two main factors: (1) people usually like surveys and (2) surveys are easy to conduct.

As for the first point, surveys have a broad-based appeal and carry an implied sense of legitimacy. And they are viewed by many people as being a democratic, fair, and typically confidential means of assessing a wide range of opinions. Although prior experience with poorly implemented organizational surveys may have left some people disillusioned (we will return to this issue in a later section), most people like the idea of being asked their opinions, thoughts, and ideas. It is human nature.

As for the second point, surveys do compare favorably with other methods in ease of use and basic effectiveness. For example, one-to-one interviewing, observing, and holding focus groups have not escaped either practitioners or those commanding organizational budgets. Large-scale survey efforts are not cheap, but they are considerably less expensive and more reliable than any other approach currently available. Furthermore, depending on the use to which the survey effort is directed, the costs may seem trivial in light of the value of the information obtained.

Despite the inherent popularity and widespread use of survey methods in organizations today, practitioners are still in need of guidance regarding how to effectively implement and manage the entire survey process—one that continues to grow and develop. In fact, organizational surveys and ways to base action on survey results continue to be popular subjects at professional conferences, workshops, and survey consortium meetings (see, for example, Waclawski and Church, 1999, 2000). In short, although it may appear to be relatively easy to generate some interesting questions, send them to people, and ask for their answers, the survey process is a highly complex and situationally dependent one that is in need of careful management.

Many factors must be considered before a survey can be used as an *effective* tool for the organization. Some of these are as follows: obtaining the necessary resources and political backing to obtain support from the organization, developing questions that appropriately reflect the specific purpose to which the survey effort is directed, understanding the nature and content of the communication process, working through resistance and feedback, interpreting the survey's results in a meaningful and effective manner, and working with those results throughout the organization.

Many good books have been written about the specifics of survey research and its methodology—its sampling schemes, item construction, response theory, and multivariate analysis. However, these books are not usually designed to provide the organizational practitioner with a clear, concise, and pragmatic working guide for how to go about doing a survey. This book is intended to fill that void. In short, our aim is to supply HRD, I-O, and OD practitioners with an easy-to-use, practical, hands-on guide to conducting successful organizational surveys.

In contrast to the more academic resources, this book was written primarily for the organizational practitioner who wants help in conducting surveys. Therefore, wherever possible we have made use of real situations and learnings from actual large-scale survey efforts conducted in organizational settings to enhance our points. This book should prove most useful for anyone involved in the use or implementation of large-scale organizational surveys, including professionals in human resource management, organization development, communications, training and development, and I-O psychology, as well as leaders and managers working with others to implement surveys (or the results of such efforts) in their own organizations.

First, however, let us define what we mean by the term *survey* and describe the type of surveys to which we will be referring throughout this book.

What Is a Survey?

A *survey* can be loosely defined as any process used for asking people a number of questions (general or specific) to gain information. The information can be factual or attitudinal, or it can be designed to assess an individual's beliefs or judgments (Schuman and Kalton,

1985). On the surface this definition seems acceptable. It carries with it basic elements of a survey; many different types of data collection could be classified as such. For example, a series of telephone interviews conducted in a particular locality asking homeowners about the quality of their refuse collection would be considered a survey under this umbrella, as would a questionnaire distributed at the copy machine regarding the quality and reliability of its performance. Some authors would agree with such classifications, but this definition of *survey* is far too broad to be considered useful here. Given this book's concentration on the HRD, I-O, and OD practitioner, we have chosen to define our use of the term *organizational survey* as follows:

SURVEY: a systematic process of data collection designed to quantitatively measure specific aspects of organizational members' experience as they relate to work.

In most cases, this type of organizational survey involves the use of a standardized questionnaire (either in paper or electronic form) containing a series of items and associated response scales. Such a survey could also be conducted using an automated telephone system, also known as a voice response unit. Although individual interviews could be conducted as well, that would fundamentally defeat the advantages of the large-scale approach. Aside from the obvious emphasis on organizational members and settings contained in the definition, a number of unique elements should be highlighted.

First, we are concerned primarily with a *systematic process* for conducting surveys. This is not to say that a simple opinion survey could not be quickly thrown together and administered, and yield meaningful findings. It can. More often than not, however, some important element is missed, and the results end up being obtuse or uninterpretable, or the questionnaire is administered to the wrong sample or possibly even contains the wrong items. Any survey effort, whether large or more moderate in scale, should be taken seriously by those administering it. It certainly will be by those being questioned. This means that some type of planned, systematic approach should be adopted, and attention should be paid to effectively managing each of the main phases of the survey process.

It may seem simplistic, but remember that the purpose here is *data collection designed to quantitatively measure* something. Although we will try not to inflict on the reader all the statistical terminology that normally accompanies such an emphasis, the quality of the specific questions included on the survey instrument and the manner in which they are displayed and administered both have an effect on the quality and quantity of responses returned. For example, the level of detail obtained for a question using a 3-point scale (for example, agree, neutral, disagree) will be vastly different from the same question using a 7-point scale that uses more gradations in meaning. Sometimes these effects simply offset each other and are worth knowing about only to be informed, but in other cases some simple changes can have a drastic impact on the information received. A case in point: a simple wording change in a survey item from "generates creative solutions" to "creates solutions" alters the meaning of the statement completely.

Another issue related to data and measurement is how emphasis is placed on quantification. More specifically, although survey efforts can contain many different types of questions (scaled items, write-in comments, forced-choice options), the value of a large-scale survey effort is that it provides a significant quantity of responses from people on the *exact same question with the exact same response options*. That means the question must be clear; then it is relatively easy to interpret, work with, and analyze the resulting data. To sum it all up, there is an old adage in the survey (and consulting business) that says, "You get what you measure" or, more crudely put, "Garbage in, garbage out." In the application of organizational surveys, these sayings hold true as well.

The phrase *specific aspects of organizational members' experience* in the definition refers to the type of information or data to be collected, which brings us back to the purpose of the survey effort itself. The following questions highlight the different kinds of topics that can be assessed in a survey:

Are you interested in knowing whether employees feel empowered in their jobs?

Do you want to know which types of communication systems are most and least effective for communicating different types of messages?

Are managers behaving in ways that reinforce the new mission and vision of the organization?

How satisfied are employees in their jobs?

What are the barriers to enhancing employees' performance?

Do employees at all levels of the organization understand and commit to the stated mission or vision of the company?

What are employees' perceptions about compensation and benefits?

Do employees think that organizational changes are occurring too quickly or not quickly enough?

Is the current organization structure one that facilitates the completion of work?

What is the perception of the organization's senior leadership team?

This list contains only a small sample of the types of questions that can be included in an organizational survey. The potential list is limitless; in fact, it is only constrained by the experience (for example, content knowledge, background, formal education, and prior work with surveys) of the survey developer and the scope of the project.

We discuss ways to identify survey objectives in the first chapter, but the message here is that people behind the survey effort need to be clear about (1) what kind of information they want,

(2) how they want to assess it using a questionnaire methodology, and (3) what they intend to do with that information when it has been collected. All this has a significant bearing on the specific aspects of the survey.

Based on this brief list of possible topics for an organizational survey, it should be clear to the reader that surveys, even as we have defined them here, can serve a multitude of purposes in organizations. This is due, in large part, to the variety of sources from which our contemporary approach to conducting and using surveys developed. The following section provides a brief history of these sources and influences, followed by a more detailed discussion of the general uses of organizational surveys in contemporary organizational life.

A Brief History of Surveys

Given the popularity and widespread use of surveys in most organizations today, it may be surprising for some people to note that surveys (as we know them) were not used extensively in organizations until the post–Second World War era. The use of surveys to assess employees' thoughts and opinions, which seems quite straightforward and natural today, evolved as an offshoot of a variety of factors, which we discuss later. Until recently, however, survey techniques and usage resided primarily within the academic, military, and political realms. Nevertheless, the basic premise of survey methodology has existed for a very long time. In fact, if we consider the more general survey definition previously discussed (a survey is any process used for asking people a number of questions, general or specific, to gain information), it is apparent that surveys have existed since the beginnings of formal language. The first recorded use of surveys, for example, dates back to the ancient Egyptians, who are credited with the establishment of the census process for counting the number of inhabitants (Babbie, 1973). We also know that the Romans used crude survey techniques to find out how many people and of what types lived in their great cities.

Despite its ancient heritage, the survey as a formal methodological approach for collecting data in organizations did not gain widespread acceptance until the 1950s. One of the most significant contributors to the contemporary use of survey feedback is the early and groundbreaking work by researchers such as Samuel Stouffer and Paul Lazarsfeld. Their efforts are generally credited for the acceptance, popularity and, above all, quality of surveys today (Babbie, 1973; Higgs and Ashworth, 1996). These researchers concentrated on developing and refining survey methods and analyses to improve empiricism in the social sciences. Their contribution to the field can be traced to their use of survey methods to examine significant social issues of the time, such as the effects of the Great Depression on people's well-being, the status of blacks in the 1930s, the effects of McCarthyism, and the effects of social factors on the formal presidential voting process. These individuals examined various social, political, and economic factors in America using a large-scale survey technique. Lazarsfeld is also credited with establishing the first academic center for survey research—the Bureau for Applied Social Research at Columbia University (Babbie, 1973).

Surveys have been used throughout the development of western civilization to gather many different types of information, from people's socioeconomic status, annual income, and place of residence to their opinions about political leaders, religion, capital punishment, and consumer preferences. Before gaining prominence and widespread exposure in organizations, these tools were used extensively (and still are, for that matter) in three different arenas: political, economic, and social. Table I.1 shows a breakdown of the different types of survey data collected that reflect common emphases and applications for each of these three domains.

Many of these types of surveys are still commonly used today. For example, the U.S. election process (at the city, state, and federal levels) is in fact a *very* large-scale survey. Most people are eligible to vote, but only a certain sample usually participate (by vote) in the election of a given representative. This response set or sample is

Table I.1. Different Types of Survey Data.

Political	Economic	Social
• Public opinion polling	• Census	• Attitudes and opinions
• Voting processes	• Market or product research	• Leadership
• Election polling	• Advertising testing	• Religious values
• Party affiliation	• Economic behavior	• Social issues

then used to determine which official will represent the entire population. Furthermore, at the federal level the construction of the electoral college mandates that each state receive a certain number of electoral votes, depending on the size of its population (based on census data). Similarly, many business organizations, such as IBM, have extensive research functions, with literally hundreds of professionals devoted to the sole purpose of surveying and analyzing market trends among current users and potential buyers of their products. Collecting data on people's responses to new advertising campaigns is also a common practice among such organizations, particularly given the exorbitant costs associated with running such spots on national television and in popular magazines and newspapers. Last but not least, the social sciences are anything but inactive in the area of current survey usage, both with respect to examining social issues (the province of many sociologists) and to the various organizational and related social psychological applications.

Contemporary Use of Surveys

These days a number of organizations base their entire existence on their survey practice. A. C. Nielson and Arbitron, for example, are two of the largest private sector survey firms that use surveys to estimate television viewing audiences (Rossi, Wright, and Anderson, 1983). Similarly, academic institutions such as the National Opinion Research Center (NORC), as well as popular media surveys like the CBS–*New York Times* poll and the Gallup organization, have done a great deal to promote surveys in the eyes of the general public. Many management and organization consulting firms today specialize in conducting or providing advice regarding organizations' surveys, many of which have been founded or are populated by HRD, I-O, and OD professionals who have left their internal positions in survey departments in the past.

Many factors have served to increase the acceptance and usage of employee survey approaches in the world, but the birth of the Mayflower Group—a consortium of forty-two blue-chip companies—in 1971 (Johnson, 1996) marked a significant turning point in the history of organizational survey research. This professional group was developed specifically to advance the practice of opinion surveying in organizations by sharing best practices and normative data among firms. This highly unusual (in the business world at least) process of sharing information has led to the establishment and maintenance of a database for benchmarking purposes across organizations. The formation and continued existence of this consortium has shown the willingness of (and the trust required for) companies to exchange potentially sensitive information—a positive trend, given the continued competitiveness of the world marketplace. The participation at various times by highly profitable and well-respected companies such as IBM, Sears, Xerox, 3M, Merck, Johnson & Johnson, GTE, and Du Pont, just to name a few, not only demonstrates the importance attached to survey research in top-tier organizations but serves to place a seal of approval on the survey process in general. It also sets an example for other companies to follow. In fact, in the last few years another group of cutting-edge technology firms, including Cisco, Intel, Dell, Unisys, Gateway, IBM, Microsoft, NCR, Nortel, Sun Microsystems, and SAP, have formed their own consortium called the Information Technology Survey Group (ITSG). The consortium is aimed at sharing leading-edge survey practices in high-tech companies (http://www.itsg.org).

Although the approaches to survey and data-feedback methods are somewhat more advanced in these companies (Waclawski, 2000) compared with many more "typical" organizational approaches, a host of challenges must always be overcome in any survey effort. For example, although speculating about future trends and applications is always questionable, even when employees are responding to surveys on their personal digital assistants (PDAs), cell phones, or some new and as yet unforeseen information and communication tool, many of the central problems inherent in designing, delivering, and using the results of an effective survey will remain the same. In short, it is clear that surveys themselves, both in and out of organizations, are here to stay.

Surveys in Contemporary Organizational Life

Why do surveys continue to be so popular in organizations? One of the likely reasons is the diversity of applications to which the results and even the process of a survey effort can be directed. For the HRD, I-O, and OD practitioner, surveys provide a myriad of possible uses and can sometimes simultaneously serve a number of different objectives. Some of the more significant categories of uses include

- To understand and explore employee opinions and attitudes

- To provide a general or specific assessment of the behaviors and attributes inherent in employees' day-to-day work experience

- To create baseline measures and use these for benchmarking various behaviors, processes, and other aspects of organizations against other either internal or external measures

- To use the data for driving organizational change and development

Each of these applications will be described in greater detail. It should be noted before continuing, however, that the categories are not mutually exclusive. In fact, survey efforts usually involve a combination of these different objectives.

Traditionally, and in their early use in organizations, surveys had been concentrated on assessing the opinions, attitudes, and beliefs of organization members. Early applications of this approach involved attempts to gauge workers' knowledge of and interest in potential unionization efforts, among other topics. However, more contemporary examples of this type of objective include measuring such individual and personal beliefs and feelings as employee satisfaction, empowerment, organizational commitment, autonomy, work–life balance, pride in the company, and perceptions of fairness and equity in standardized policies, systems, and procedures.

Other types of questionnaires have been designed to measure more involved and detailed topics such as rankings of employee assistance programs for desirability (given a list of types from which to choose), opinions of the quality of training and development programs, reactions to various messages and strategic initiatives, and external perceptions direct from the customer or client of product service or quality. All these types of data can be extremely useful for planning at every level, from the senior most strategic perspective to the extremely tactical implementation of a compensation and benefits program at a local department level. The one caveat, especially with the measurement of employee opinions, is that one needs to *be prepared to openly acknowledge and ultimately attempt to deal with the issues raised.* One of the most difficult problems that survey administrators face is finding a "bad" outcome on an important item (for example, employee motivation or morale), only to realize that no one in HR or senior management wants to take up the issue with employees. This "duck and cover" approach to dealing with survey findings often results in the alignment of many negative forces against any current and future survey efforts that might be undertaken.

A second type of survey objective concerns the assessment or measurement of more specific behaviors and conditions that exist in organizational life. Most survey efforts are a combination of this and the opinion approach; however, assessment surveys differ in that they involve identifying certain observable, behavioral tendencies that can be accurately rated by employees. Because the assessment of behavior involves the observation of various individuals engaging in these behaviors, this type of assessment typically involves questions pertaining to the actions of immediate managers, functional, divisional, or business unit managers, and senior managers and executives. We discuss the details of developing and using different types of items in a later chapter, but here are some sample items of this nature:

Please rate the extent to which . . .

Senior management is consistent in word and deed

Senior management communicates with employees at all levels

Your manager awards and recognizes people in your work unit

Your manager provides you with the information you need to do your job

These types of data are intended to provide more specific and actionable information than the opinion perspective alone. Attitudes and opinions are helpful; however, they are not as easy to act on at the individual level. You cannot say to a manager, for example, "Make your employees feel more satisfied" without knowing what conditions will lead to employee satisfaction. Through the use of surveys and data analysis, one can identify what types of specific behaviors or working conditions need to be changed or reinforced, which will ultimately lead to that employee feeling more satisfied. This is a somewhat subtle distinction but a very important one nonetheless. In many ways, these two types of survey objectives represent the distinction between a survey that simply captures a picture of the present state and one that can be used for diagnosing problems and effecting significant organizational change.

Another popular use and objective of survey methodology is its contribution to the benchmarking process. Benchmarking is a means of comparing survey results from one's own organization with some predetermined measure (benchmark) to identify relative strengths and weaknesses. Many practitioners think of benchmarking in terms of external indicators, but it is also acceptable to use survey data as an internal benchmark, both with respect to other functions, divisions, and work processes at the same point in time, as well as over time through the use of repeated survey administrations.

In its simplest form, for example, a company can use an initial effort to establish a baseline measure against which future survey results can be tracked. Therefore, a benchmarking survey can be used to assess improvement or decline over time on the specific areas it has been designed to measure. Similarly, by incorporating a range of responses for the highest- and lowest-performing units (for example, departments or work teams) suitable for comparison with the present level of results, the survey client can gain an immediate understanding of the areas in which he or she excels relative to the rest of the organization and those that could benefit from additional support and learning through the exchange of best practices from within.

In addition to internal benchmarking, many organizational members are interested in knowing how their individual and collective data compare with those of other organizations. These external indicators can range from the most competitive firms within their own industry to companies in entirely different industries but with similar types of processes or those facing similar issues. When using competitors within the same industry for benchmarking purposes, survey clients are typically interested in knowing how they rate with respect to their competition on certain areas of organizational functioning. In other words, they want to know how they rate against the competition in the areas that they feel are necessary for success. When using organizations in different industries as points of comparison, the purpose is often to see how one's own company fares outside its industry as an indication of its overall competitiveness, irrespective of industry type. Given the increasing tendency for organizations to span national boundaries and compete in different markets, this approach has more credibility than it once did. The previously mentioned Mayflower Group represents one such type of comparison. Members in this group receive norms on a number of standard items that are classified by and across industry type.

Perhaps of most concern to HRD, I-O, and OD practitioners is the use of organizational surveys for the express purposes of organizational change and development. Practitioners have long acknowledged that data-based feedback is one of the most powerful means of effecting change (Nadler, 1977); recent studies based on individualized multisource feedback methods have supported this contention (Atwater and Yammarino, 1992; Church, 1994a, 1997, 2000; Church and Bracken, 1997; Church and Waclawski, 1998a, 1999; Furnham and Stringfield, 1994; Van Velsor, Taylor, and Leslie, 1993). During the 1990s the use of survey data for organizational change became increasingly popular, and a number of external consulting firms have now begun to specialize in these services. The basis of the questions themselves is often similar to or the same as those described earlier. However, there is a fundamental difference in this approach in that the survey process is seen as only a part of a larger change initiative involving other (complementary) methods. Furthermore, the survey questionnaire is seen as both *a means of communicating what is important to the organization*, particularly if some aspect of behavior change or a change in strategic direction is required, and *a way to identify, link, and leverage key variables that lead to desired end states in the organization* (such as increased morale) to those who cause or drive them. This type of analysis, although complex to conduct and interpret, represents perhaps the most powerful and potentially effective application of survey results. In effect, individual opinions and assessments of workers' behaviors are used to identify and drive those organizational changes that will have the greatest impact on future behavior and success. Surveys, if concentrated on this objective, can provide

HRD, I-O, and OD practitioners and organization leaders with important information about employees' perceptions of change and their readiness for it, as well as many other issues that can affect the success or failure of large-scale change initiatives (Church, Margiloff, and Coruzzi, 1995; Waclawski, 1996a).

The Seven Steps to Effective Organizational Surveys

If we have made our point so far, it should be clear that although most anyone can participate in a survey effort, a number of significant issues and complexities must be managed if the outcome is to be a positive one. In the following text you will be introduced to the seven steps, or phases, involved in implementing an organizational survey. Figure I.1 shows the stages. Following is an overview of what each of the steps entails.

Step One (Pooling Resources) focuses on the process of pooling resources in the early stages of a survey. As in any sizeable organizational initiative or intervention, one must always begin by laying the appropriate groundwork with all the right people. Gaining substantive input and cooperation from all key parties is never an easy task, but without the appropriate support and resources, most survey efforts fall short of expectations with respect to impact. In order to satisfy the needs of important constituencies and the ultimate end users of the survey, involvement early on is crucial.

In this chapter we discuss how to set the stage for a successful organizational survey effort, including the following: (1) how to set clear strategic objectives regarding the purpose and uses of the survey process itself, (2) how to obtain commitment from senior management as well as the rank and file of the organization, (3) how to identify and overcome negative energy or apathy due to prior experiences, (4) who should be involved in the data collection effort, (5) what specific types of information are to be collected, (6) what types of additional information (for example, demographics or organizational characteristics)

Figure I.1. The Seven Steps to Effective Surveys.

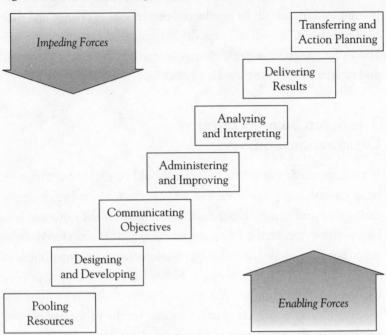

should be collected and at what levels, and (7) how to prepare the organization for the survey effort.

This first stage in the survey process comprises building alliances, support, commitment, and energy for the survey effort before it can really begin. In our experience it is this stage, more than any other, that will determine the ultimate success or failure of the survey effort with respect to its perceived viability as a worthwhile endeavor. In other words, organizational initiatives are often judged (fairly or not) by those people who stand behind them and those who do not.

Step Two (Developing a World-Class Survey) concentrates on the second stage in the survey process—the fundamentals of the survey instrumentation itself. In this chapter we look at characteristics of the questions, the content, the response options and scales, the layout or presentation, and the formal instructions, to name a few topics. After a brief comparison of the pros and cons of using existing standardized instruments from other sources versus creating a customized survey tool, the discussion turns to the issue of design. Through examples and descriptions of prior research and experience, the survey practitioner is guided on the importance of the following: (1) using teamwork to build high-quality survey instruments; (2) gathering, identifying, and working through key issues that need to be assessed; (3) drafting a survey instrument; and (4) piloting and refining it for final administration. By the end of the chapter, practitioners should have a better understanding of how to write items that (1) concentrate on specific issues, (2) are clear and easy to respond to, (3) avert the typical problems often found in new questionnaires, (4) are free of jargon and cultural biases, (5) are methodologically sound, and (6) are appropriate for the level and type of readership at which they are directed.

The issue of response options or scales is also addressed, as are the pros and cons of using write-in comments to help augment and add spice to the more quantitative data. The use of frameworks, models, or organizing themes for the survey instrument to enhance respondents' understanding of and interest in completing the survey is also discussed, as are the benefits of exploring potential linkages ahead of time with other existing (or impending) organizational measurement or change initiatives.

In Step Three (Communicating Objectives) we turn our attention to one of the most simple-to-understand yet difficult-to-implement concepts in the survey process: communication. In this chapter we start with another old adage: "communicate, communicate, communicate." Many practitioners, managers, and leaders for that matter would agree with this sentiment, but few in our experience actually follow through on the edict. And yet it is one of the basic aspects of an effective survey process. In this chapter we look at the importance of communicating the purpose, objectives, and content of the survey initiative clearly and effectively to those involved in the data collection effort—the employees completing the survey. Of course, this means gaining agreement first among those in power as to what the expected outcomes of the survey effort are. It also means laying the necessary groundwork to ensure that people agree with the survey's objectives and that they understand how the data are to be used, as well as issues of confidentiality. Thus, after a brief introduction and overview of the contents, processes, roles (CPR) model of organizational communication, this section explores each of the phases of communication in a survey effort from first contact to the formal information and messages provided with the survey instrument.

We also discuss general guidelines for communicating to employees, understanding the strengths and weaknesses of various mechanisms for sending messages, and seeing the need to balance the amount of information given so that it is neither too much nor too little. Also covered is the need to manage the informal communication system—the grapevine. In some organizations, this can be a more powerful means of making or breaking a survey than anything the senior leadership or even the immediate manager says.

Besides these larger issues, the cover letter and the accompanying instructions on the instrument (how all these messages come together for the respondents) are discussed in this section. Although clear communication in and of itself will not save a bad survey effort, poor communication can kill a good one.

Step Four (Administering the Survey) covers what is for some the most mundane and for others the most stressful part of the survey effort: the formal administration process. In this chapter we discuss the details involved in carrying off a successful administration. This includes everything from the importance of establishing a clear, comprehensive, and reasonable project plan with appropriate milestones, checkpoints, and buffer areas for making up lost time when dates begin to slide (as they invariably do) to holding your internal or external clients' hands and allaying their fears and concerns regarding the process and the inevitable glitches.

We also cover the specific methods of and options for the administration itself. For example, what are the pros and cons of mailing the survey to each employee with return envelopes versus having mass administration sessions in large auditoriums with proctors? Who should complete the survey first? What types of data collection methods should be used? Organizational surveys typically conjure images of paper-and-pencil questionnaires with optical scan response forms, but with the advent of the information age (not to mention the popularity of the Internet and the prevalence of local intranets) a variety of alternatives for collecting survey data are now available. Some of these are as follows:

- Transmission of responses to a computer by pressing keys on a telephone (also known as voice response units)

- Individual computer-disk-based methods in which a response is made on a computer, and the disk is sent to someone else for processing

- Various e-mail-based surveys that either have respondents reply directly in the body of the note or via downloadable templates or executables attached to various programs (such as Lotus Notes or Microsoft Excel) that are submitted to a central server once completed

- Fax-back surveys for which paper responses are scanned automatically

- Internet, intranet, and related on-line, Web-based response systems that capture the survey data immediately and often interactively

These alternatives are often exciting, particularly to those who are either enamored of computer technology or bored with the more traditional methods, which have strengths and weaknesses. We highlight those where appropriate because of their effectiveness and usefulness in certain situations. Although electronic survey methods are increasing in popularity, both in terms of practice and as an applied research topic, pencil-and-paper methods remain the most commonly used in organizations, for reasons that will become clear in our discussion. Step Four also covers the importance of having a continuous learning and process improvement orientation to working with surveys in organizations. This involves making effective use of feedback from the organization, particularly in the early stages of administration, to adjust and adapt the process to make it optimally effective in a given situation.

Next, in Step Five (Interpreting Results) we move to one of the most potentially complex and consequently misunderstood aspects of survey work. Once all the data have been collected, it is time to put them into that black box, as our clients sometimes call it, and analyze the results. Most people, especially those with advanced degrees, can calculate an average value from a series of responses without having done a good deal of previous survey work or having had experience in applied research on large-scale data sets. But it is a more difficult and refined skill to pull all the results together into a cohesive yet statistically supported story about what is occurring in an organization. Many different stories and themes always emerge in any survey of a large population. However, we are concerned here primarily with the first wave of analysis—the one presented first to the survey client or the senior management organization (other types of subsequent analytic work will be discussed in Step Six). Such an effort requires the practitioner to identify the main issues and important relationships among a mass of data in what is often the shortest timeframe of the entire survey effort. This happens because once the survey has been sent out and people start responding, everyone wants to know the results as soon as possible. It can take five months to develop the appropriate questions for use in the questionnaire itself, but the time from final data collection to the first reporting process must be only a few short weeks for the results to be meaningful and have the appropriate credibility upon which to take action.

Moreover, in some organizations results are expected in a matter of days, or even overnight, as in the case of survey efforts at Federal Express. The point is that *appropriate* timing is everything. Time and time again we have seen a senior management team receive their initial top-level results (the big picture) shortly after final administration, only to be so disturbed by the findings that they asked that we withhold the feedback from employees for several months. In cases like that, delay makes the results far less relevant and more lacking in impact when they are finally communicated, not to mention the impact such actions have on the credibility and utility of future survey efforts. In this section we discuss such topics as how to make a compelling story of a large collection of numbers with and without advanced statistics, how to balance expectations with realities inherent in the data, how to work with normative and benchmarking data to assist in interpreting the results rather than becoming the focal point, and how to use write-in comments to enrich the data and presentation. The use and abuse of the benchmarking process is discussed in greater detail in this section as well.

Step Six (Delivering the Findings) is concerned with the delivery of the survey results to organizational members, both in various forms and throughout different levels. In this chapter the emphasis is on picking a strategy for delivering the feedback to all those involved. This strategy, often described as a roll-out process, is conducted on a gradual management-level-by-management-level basis. It is important to note that the approach advocated here places a greater emphasis on the appropriate delivery of results vis-à-vis helping organizational members work with their data interactively to promote understanding and plan for change rather than on quickly supplying everyone in the organization with a copy of their results without interactive coaching support. The former is primarily an OD approach and has the potential for catalyzing energy for improvement; the latter is what we refer to as "the desk drop" and will only be as effective as the motivation level of the individual to whom the results are given.

In some ways this stage represents the second half of the analysis process, whereby the data are reexamined at lower levels and for specific groups, functions, departments, comparisons, or segments to look among similar or different stories in their specific findings. For example, in a large-scale organizational survey it is possible not only to provide reports for every department with a certain number of people responding but to provide a report that compares how several different departments rated one another on service quality and cooperation internally. A simple presentation of results can easily be undertaken without the benefit of subsequent interpretation, but to maximize effectiveness the roll-out process should involve some degree of interpretative assistance built into the framework of the delivery vehicle itself. Of course, the timing as well as the complexity of the information delivered must also be carefully managed for the results to be meaningful. Just as waiting too long to provide any feedback is problematic, so too is "dumping" (for example, through a desk-drop approach) the entire results of the survey on all employees in some overly complex and underinterpreted fashion so that no one can understand what it all means. We have seen that happen in well-intentioned but misconstrued attempts to be entirely open in their survey communications.

Other issues with respect to feedback delivery to be covered in this section include tips for making formal presentations that have an impact, using organizational models and frameworks for describing linkages or relationships among key variables of interest, resisting when requests for additional data threaten the ethical integrity of the confidentiality norms established at the outset of the survey process, and knowing how to present good and not-so-good data in ways that recipients can accept.

Finally, Step Seven (Learning into Action) centers on the last stage of the survey process. Many clients and practitioners pay little attention to this phase once they reach it, feeling instead that when the survey is done and all the feedback is delivered, it can be forgotten. The fact is that this stage can make or break the survey effort. Even the best planning, the most well-constructed questionnaire, the most appropriately conceived and implemented administration process, the best analysis, and a variety of staged feedback reports will not be enough to make a survey effort effective to the organization if the data are not used to drive change and improvement in the system or in people's day-to-day behaviors. Thus, in this chapter we discuss the importance of follow-through, including attention to common barriers to effective action planning, as well as a detailed comparison of four approaches to making full use of survey results to drive change in an organization. Regardless of the objectives of the survey effort itself (for example, to gauge employee opinion, to assess behavioral tendencies, to communicate and reinforce the culture, to target areas for change and development initiatives), it is of paramount importance that the results be used by recipients to make decisions and take actions that will ultimately affect the organization's future. We are concerned here with planning for action, identifying areas for intervention and improvement, enlisting and involving others in the process, measuring progress over time through resurvey efforts, and linking survey results to other key measures of organizational performance. If the organization does not take ownership of the results, the data will have no meaning and therefore no impact. This occurs with many surveys in today's organizations. It can also happen to new survey efforts that fail to receive adequate support from senior management and other key opinion leaders in the organization at the outset; these efforts become lame ducks. It can also happen to survey systems that have been in place for years, where engaging in the survey has created a routine process that employees do not trust, respect, or pay attention to but is nonetheless used by management as a "dipstick" for gauging employee opinion. Step Seven describes how to prevent this type of entropy in the survey process.

1

Step One: Pooling Resources

Silence is the most perfect expression of scorn.

George Bernard Shaw

Two of the most important components of an effective organizational survey effort are involvement in and commitment to the process. Many senior managers (and some HR and OD personnel as well) would like to believe that conducting a survey is a relatively simple task and therefore should not require much effort beyond deciding what questions to ask. However, the fact is that if a survey has not been (1) endorsed by organization members early in its implementation and (2) integrated and linked into the existing framework of corporate initiatives and directives, it will fail to make a significant impact. This means that very early in the life of the survey effort, as with any large-scale organizational initiative, an appropriate level of support must be obtained from key players in the organizational hierarchy.

Because these individuals need to be highly visible and strategically placed, they are typically either senior-level managers or high-potential employees being groomed for future leadership positions. Often labeled *champions* (Ulrich, 1997) of a given initiative, these proponents serve three necessary functions with respect to the survey process and can help establish the groundwork for building commitment and involvement. A survey champion provides:

- Direction and leadership regarding the importance of the survey effort to the larger organizational system and its relationship to existing core business initiatives

- Resources in terms of staff, time, and money to support the various aspects of implementation (for example, development, administration, analysis, integration, action planning, and follow-up improvement interventions)

- Validity, credibility, and significance to the entire survey process for all organizational members

The first stage in designing and implementing a world-class survey process (pooling intellectual and political resources) is centered on two subprocesses: (1) identifying the primary objectives and integrating framework of the survey effort and (2) building the needed alliances, support, commitment, and energy among people in the organization to support the successful attainment of these objectives. Once again, although it may seem like a simple and obvious idea that this type of large-scale intervention needs to be grounded in the broader strategic fabric of the organization and receive visible and vocal support from key players to be truly effective, it is nonetheless an idea that is often overlooked. Many organizations attempt to pursue a survey effort because of the vision of a small group of individuals in the OD or HR function (and even with the backing of the most senior human resources person in the organization) only to have the entire project put on hold by top management in anticipation of a more "appropriate" time to conduct a survey. In other cases the survey project may move forward but ends up being forced on the organization without the proper alignments and support; therefore, it is doomed to have little or no (or perhaps even a negative) impact in the long run.

A significant amount of groundwork with respect to relationship building and managing strategic integration is needed at the start of any survey effort, regardless of whether the survey is intended to be used as a one-time diagnostic tool or as part of an annual change management measurement system for organization development and improvement. As consulting professionals we have found that more and more organizations are involved in many different and often competing initiatives of which a new (or revived) survey effort may only be a small part. Navigating this phenomenon, which has been called midstream consulting (Burke, Javitch, Waclawski, and Church, 1997), involves integrating goals, processes, and resources across initiatives to help bridge the gap. Thus, for the survey to be perceived by organizational members as an effective mechanism (and perceiving is believing with respect to this type of initiative), it must be built into *and* around the existing organizational reality. Organizations are indeed social systems comprising many interdependent components (Katz and Kahn, 1978); this means that in order to effect change in one area, other areas must be considered and possibly changed as well. A survey conducted without concern for other variables in the organizational system is likely to produce only isolated and limited results.

The Burke-Litwin (B-L) model of organizational change and performance (Burke and Litwin, 1992) provides a good example of how such interdependencies operate (see Figure 1.1). The figure shows that from a systemic perspective the higher-level factors of senior leadership, the overall culture, and the mission and strategy of the entire company exert a driving force on the day-to-day actions of managers, the formal organizational structure, and its operating systems (for example, rewards, communication, selection, promotion, and training). These factors, in turn, affect people's experience in their jobs with respect to the climate in their work group, levels of individual motivation, and the extent to which needs and values and task requirements are met.

The reader is directed elsewhere (see Burke, Coruzzi, and Church, 1996; Burke and Litwin, 1992; Burke, 1994; Church, Waclawski, McHenry, and McKenna, 1998) for a more complete discussion of the B-L model for organizational diagnosis and intervention planning. No single facet of organizational existence exists alone. The

Figure 1.1. The Burke-Litwin Model of Organizational Performance and Change.

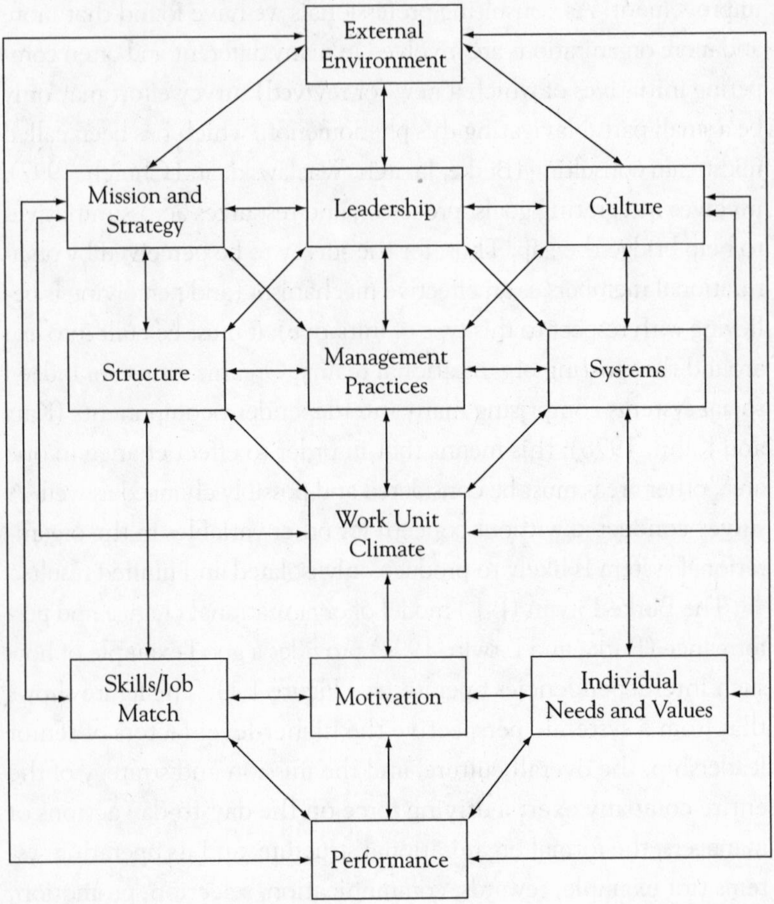

Source: Burke and Litwin, 1992, p. 538. Used by permission of the *Journal of Management*.

interrelationships and interdependencies among people, systems, and initiatives must be considered when planning a world-class survey process.

The remainder of this chapter explores how to set clear and strategic objectives for the survey, how to involve organizational members in the process and thereby generate support and commitment, and how to work through apathy and negative attitudes and prepare the organization for the survey roll-out. In short, this step concentrates on how to ensure that the survey does indeed become a fully integrated initiative.

Setting Clear Strategic Objectives

We know from the social and organizational change literature (for example, Beckhard and Harris, 1987; Lewin, 1958) that an important early step in any change initiative is the identification of expected outcomes or the desired end-state of the process. This is the driving force behind the increasing popularity of future search (Weisbord, 1995) and whole system methodologies (Bunker and Alban, 1997), wherein large groups of people are brought together in real time to build commitment to a shared vision of the future and a means to obtain it. For any large-scale initiative, including an organizational survey effort, to be successful it must have a set of clear and measurable objectives that have immediate relevance and are linked strategically to the organization as a whole. Once these outcomes have been established, the means (and obstacles) by which to achieve them can be identified for those implementing the process.

Conducting a survey effort is like embarking on a journey. Before you start out you must choose a final destination. You can certainly just start traveling without an end point in mind, but you will not know where you are going until you get there; it may turn out that when you do finally arrive, you're not in a pleasant place to visit after all. Thus, having identified a desired destination for your trip, in order to find your way there you need a road map or guidebook, or at least a plan for how to obtain the necessary directions as you get closer. It can be very frustrating to know where you want to go but to have no idea of how to get there. There also needs to be a marker or a signpost at the other end that lets you know when you have reached your final destination.

Following this analogy, if we consider the survey as a means for getting where we are going, then we need first to establish the des-

Figure 1.2. Fixed Factors Influencing Survey Effectiveness.

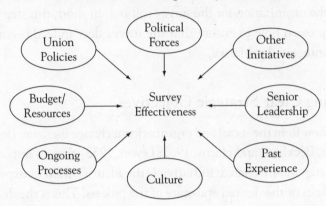

tination—the core statement of purpose of the survey—a simple, clear explanation of why the survey will be conducted.

At first glance this may seem like a clear-cut and straightforward thing to do. However, as with many complex organizational issues, hidden agendas and political issues can become part of the process (see Figure 1.2). The impact of these fixed factors can be minimized or sometimes even used to enhance the total process if the goals and objectives of the survey are clearly and formally stated, and agreed upon by all constituents involved. This, of course, is why the question, Who are the key constituents? becomes important as well.

We have seen these political issues at work many times in organizations and in many different ways. One poignant instance occurred, for example, in an employee opinion survey effort conducted in a large financial services organization after several acquisitions had occurred. This organization had in the previous year acquired at least half a dozen smaller competitors in an attempt to consolidate its position in the marketplace as the local retailer of choice. From the point of view of our client, who was the vice president of human resources, the formal objectives of the survey itself were to (1) assess the general state of morale in the organization as a result of the recent changes, (2) examine the extent of differences inherent in those employees who had been acquired from various sources versus those who had been with the company prior to these actions, (3) use the results for follow-up organization improvement initiatives, and (4) establish a baseline for future assessments (for example via resurvey efforts at time 2, time 3, and so on, or as an annual process).

After several meetings with various internal constituent groups, including the second-in-command of the organization and the chair of the organization's diversity committee, it became apparent that the survey was intended to serve other purposes as well. For the second-in-command, who was championing the effort and serving as a figure-head in the organization, the survey would provide a means of communicating his new agenda and interest in employees in preparation for his impending move into the chief executive officer (CEO) position the following year. He intended to use the results to drive his changes, many of which had already been planned in advance, through the organization. The chair of the diversity committee, however, was interested in exploring trends in employee attitudes and perceptions by various subgroups related to his agenda such as gender, ethnicity, religion, age, marital status, single-parent responsibilities, and so on. He intended to use the results to secure funding and support for various diversity programs. By uncovering, exploring, and integrating such issues into the survey design and implementation process at the outset, we were able to incorporate specific questions and demographic items into the measurement process, which allowed the data that were eventually collected to be used for these additional purposes. If we had not been aware of these issues and made the additional design changes in the questionnaire initially, the data would have been limited and therefore problematic and less useful and meaningful for these two important constituents, one of whom was our survey champion in the organization.

So what are the most important components of setting quality survey objectives? The list to follow provides an overview of the questions and issues to consider at the beginning of the planning process. These issues are all clearly interrelated; decisions in one most certainly affect decisions in others. But questions 1, 2, and 3 have the most relevance here (questions 4 through 8 will be covered in subsequent steps).

The key elements for setting objectives are as follows:

1. What is the purpose of the survey?

   Measuring organizational change

   Measuring employee satisfaction

   Measuring workplace conditions

   Communicating new vision or strategic direction

   Measuring leadership and management effectiveness

2. What are the expected outcomes of the survey?

   Managing change

   Improving employee satisfaction

   Improving performance

   Improving understanding of vision or strategy

   Instilling new leader and manager behaviors

3. Who will be involved in the survey?

   Respondents

   Item designers

   Task forces

   Groups in the organization that will be involved

   Groups in the organization that will not be involved

4. What will be the content of the survey?

5. How and when will the data be collected?

   Paper and pencil

   Voice response unit

   On-line

6. What will the final reports look like?

   Level for cutting the data

   Complexity and detail needed for recipients

7. How will the data be reported out and by whom?

What type of training and support will be needed?

What is the expected timeframe for various stages of roll-out?

8. What steps will be taken as a result of the survey?

Who will take them?

When will they be taken?

How will we measure progress?

Will there be a resurvey (time 2) and if so when?

As we have already discussed, the very first question concerns the basic purpose of the survey itself. Simply put, why do you want to do a survey? Is it to assess the degree of change toward some future state? Are you concerned with employee attitudes, opinions, and morale? Is it an exploratory process designed to identify areas for improvement? Do you want to find out how well the various internal communication systems are working and whether employees understand or believe the messages provided? Is it meant to communicate a new set of values or behaviors that are important to the future success of organization? These are the kinds of questions that need to be answered.

A sample purpose statement provided to employees in a cover letter from senior management in a recent survey effort centered around a corporate initiative as follows:

> The purpose of the enclosed questionnaire is to enable us to measure our progress, at least in the eyes of our people, and to improve our effectiveness towards achieving our goal of improving customer service. Every employee throughout the company is being asked to participate; therefore, for equal representation from all areas, your input is especially valuable.
>
> We are initiating this survey to develop a picture of how employees view the company. In answering these questions, please focus on the company as you experience

it in your day-to-day work life. The results are intended to give a broad measure of how we are doing in key areas of mission accomplishment, leadership and management practices, work group performance, and employee satisfaction and effectiveness. To be the best, we must have a unified vision of where we want to be, and a strategy for how to get there. This is especially true in the difficult area of providing improved service to customers.

Once the purpose and objectives of the survey are clear, the questions about anticipated outcomes and who should be involved in the process should follow naturally. If the survey is intended only to be used as a static measure, for example, regarding progress toward some change effort (for example, to become more customer-focused), then the outcome of the survey process (but not the larger change process) may simply be the presentation of the survey results to those groups involved. However, if the survey is designed to become an integral and perhaps annual part of the overall organization development, organization effectiveness, or related HRD or personnel research function, then the desired outcomes might reflect, for example, significant improvements over time in employee working conditions, attitudes, and morale.

As to who should be involved in the planning and design process, besides the very basic guideline of including some representation from line and staff personnel, the best approach is usually one in which a survey task force is formed that represents a broad cross-section of employees from different levels, functions, and backgrounds. In this way the survey objectives, outcomes, content, and even implementation strategy can be designed with input from a variety of opinions and perspectives.

As with most complex organizational activities, the clarification and objective-setting process can be an easy and quick one, or it can be a very arduous and time-consuming task. In large part, the level of effort required in this area depends on the number of people involved and the degree of similarity in expectations among decision makers. Setting objectives for surveys when done for a single client or a small homogenous group can be achieved with relative speed and ease. If the goals of the survey are limited enough in scope to be well matched to such a small group of planners and implementers, then the effort will likely proceed smoothly. Conversely, the objective-setting process can quickly become unwieldy as the number of constituents and decision makers increases in size and diversity of opinion. When multiple parties are involved who have different, often competing objectives, setting the ground rules may require the assistance of someone with good process consultation (Schein, 1988), group facilitation, and conflict management skills.

It all comes back to the issue of effective contracting. From the realm of organizational consultation (for example, Block, 1981) we know that good contracting at the beginning of any effort, including an organizational survey, can prevent a significant amount of aggravation and disappointment at a later date. In fact, there is no substitute for good contracting with the client, whether that client is external or internal. What we have been talking about all along, that is, setting clear, measurable, and strategic survey objectives, is really part and parcel of establishing a solid survey contract with your client—the survey owner and sponsor. When undertaking a survey initiative, set clear expectations and objectives at the outset. This means actively seeking input from key decision makers about their specific purpose(s) for the conduct of the survey and the desired end state they hope to achieve through its conduct. It also means identifying the specific goals, roles, and processes of all those involved and, most important, the deliverables of the survey itself.

Many perfectly good survey efforts meet with a less than positive reception because they are not what clients wanted or thought they would be getting. Setting clear goals from the start helps eliminate confusion and lack of clarity during the survey process itself and also helps prevent frustration caused by unmet expectations. Therefore, making underlying assumptions about survey objectives explicit and gaining consensus on key issues and stated outcomes is necessary for the ultimate success of any survey, large or small.

Returning to our travel analogy, if each person on the trip has a different set of directions, all of which highlight contradictory routes, how can everyone possibly expect to end up at the same destination at the same time? The best route needs to be mapped out in a participative fashion for all to see.

Obtaining Commitment

In our earlier discussions we alluded to the importance of having a stated set of objectives for the survey effort itself. The support, participation, and commitment from organization members is equally important. A well-designed and integrated survey will undoubtedly result in wasted effort and frustration on the part of its sponsors if neither senior leadership nor the rank and file acknowledges or understands its use. This is why determining which constituents should be involved in the initial goal-setting and design stages is very important and why we already have placed so much emphasis on it. Clearly, one of the easiest ways to build support and commitment among management and employees is to include them in the survey process from the start.

Let us start with senior management. It can be a relatively easy task to involve them strategically when a senior leader is willing to sponsor or at least serve as a figurehead for the survey effort (as in our example), but it can be much more difficult when the process has been initiated solely from lower levels in the organization. Some organizations have relatively autonomous line operations that are capable of supporting a survey effort of their own; however, others can be in the difficult position of having to sell their idea to (that is, get permission from) their corporate superiors. If an HR or OD function is the initiator of a survey effort, there is the likelihood of a negative connotation or attitude backlash on the part of senior management. This backlash often occurs because the senior managers realize that, for their expenditure of a significant amount of money and resources, they are likely to be

- Seen as targets for all the collective woes of the organization because they are responsible for most policy and strategic decisions

- Expected to do something about the results, even if they are extremely negative and not within their control

For these reasons many organizationwide survey efforts are tied to large-scale development and change initiatives (Kraut, 1996a; Church, Margiloff, Coruzzi, 1995; and Kraut and Saari, 1999). There is often an expectation generated among respondents taking the time to complete the questionnaire that something will be done; this expectation can be a real and palpable force to be reckoned with. Senior managers are often the target of employees' frustrations, particularly when job security and salary levels are prominent concerns. In our experience the most successful change-related survey efforts are those that have been used in conjunction with a new or emerging leader, or the introduction of a set of core values or behaviors that are fully supported by the senior ranks.

Survey feedback, for example, was used effectively after the Smith-Kline Beecham merger (Burke and Jackson, 1991) as a way to help monitor how much progress the company was making toward achieving its new senior-management-inspired mission of creating a "Simply Better" culture. The results of the second survey, about two years later, showed significant improvements in areas such as rewarding and celebrating achievements, using people's skills and abilities, and being more customer-driven rather than profit-driven (Bauman, Jackson, and Lawrence, 1997).

Support from senior leadership can provide both the tangible and intangible benefits (for example, credibility, perceived importance, financial support, and decision-making latitude) for reaching the objectives of the survey process. The degree to which senior management support is needed depends to some extent on the purpose of the survey. A general assessment of workspace conditions, for example, may require less active participation. But even the simplest of survey projects can benefit from having the stamp of approval from the top of the hierarchy. When the survey effort is part of a more significant change initiative, however, obtaining this support is imperative. Moreover, most attempts to formalize a survey process to ensure repeated administrations (including planning for a single time to resurvey effort) typically require this level of senior management commitment as well.

Besides senior management, people at the other end of the hierarchy—the employees—need to be actively involved in and committed to the effort as well. For the moment we use the term *employees* in its broadest sense to encompass all types of organizational members, including middle-management ranks. Employees are the backbone of any organization; they represent and enact the social structure and organizational culture on a day-to-day basis. For this reason nothing truly meaningful, whether accurate assessment or fundamental organizational change, can be accomplished without their participation in some manner, even if it is only to clear their desks and physically leave the plant when it is downsized.

Surveys are subject to these same social forces. They involve asking a large number of people a great many questions about personal perceptions, management behaviors, work conditions, or the organization in general. When you are planning to conduct an organizational survey, remember that you are fundamentally making two assumptions about the people you intend to assess: (1) that they will respond to your questionnaire and (2) that their responses will be accurate and valid (that is, reflect their perceptions of the current organizational reality rather than some other agenda or anticipated response set).

As we will discuss in Steps Two through Five, neither of these assumptions should be taken for granted. One way of increasing the validity and utility of the process at the very start, however, is by involving employees at all levels. As we mentioned earlier, one of the best mechanisms for ensuring this type of participation is to use a task force or several task forces designed to shepherd various aspects of the survey process. Groups of employees serving in task forces can provide opportunities for obtaining cross-functional and cross-level representation among different organizational constituents. These groups may need the assistance of a trained facilitator to help them work collaboratively rather than competitively, particularly if the differences in perspective among functions or locations is strong. But the end result can be a much more informed, accurate, and influential survey process that can truly affect the organization and how it functions.

Of course, the extent to which such task forces can be used varies considerably. In some companies, for example, we have seen the task force approach take the form of a group devoted to a specific issue, such as enhancing team spirit or improving managerial leadership. These more active groups often allow the team to develop a real sense of ownership of their project. They tend to be involved in all aspects of the process, ranging from the identification of key issues and survey objectives, through designing individual items and questionnaire formats, to the recommendation and even implementation of very specific development and improvement initiatives subsequent to the data feedback process.

However, we have seen some companies use the task force approach as a form of employee representation. In situations like this, the group may be a "survey team" responsible primarily for asserting the voice of the employee on general issues and concerns regarding the process. Sometimes these groups are also used to test the individual items for wording choice or applicability to the workforce across various levels and departments. The idea here is that even though these individuals do not really help design the overall objectives or content of the survey, they are involved just enough to promote goodwill and a sense of honesty regarding the effort, which, in turn, is intended to communicate a degree of openness and candor to the rest of the organization. Of course, the former, more involved approach to using a task force tends to be more successful than the latter, although they both have their benefits, depending on the situation. Either way, however, employees must be involved at least at some level in the survey process or they will not respond.

Overcoming Resistance and Apathy

Another means of involving employees in the survey process at the beginning, and one that tends to be successful at targeting and working through resistance, is the use of focus groups; that is, when one or more facilitators have an open discussion with a small group of employees from either similar or divergent areas. Focus groups can be an invaluable tool not only for collecting data and building item content but as a means of communicating and breaking down barriers. When undertaken well, focus groups can be one of the most effective ways of generating positive perceptions of the survey process and converting skeptical or cynical factions into allies. The idea is to provide an objective and safe forum where people can feel comfortable expressing their thoughts, opinions, fears, and ideas regarding whatever issues are relevant. We have used focus groups in the past, for example, to explore topics such as positive and negative experiences with prior organizational surveys (regardless of where employees had their exposure), various change initiatives that worked and those that failed, what it takes to be a high performer or to work well in a team in their organization, what types of issues they would like to hear about regarding a survey effort, and so on.

Even when the issues identified are no longer particularly novel, focus groups remain an excellent mechanism for building trust and support for a survey effort before it gets off the ground. Moreover, they can be helpful in overcoming employee cynicism or resistance to a survey effort—two impeding factors that appear to be on the increase in organizations today due, some have argued, to botched prior survey efforts and over-surveying (Kraut and Saari, 1999; Rogelberg,

1998). Finally, focus groups provide an opportunity to communicate to employees the objectives, importance, and level of senior management commitment of the survey, which in some instances can be very important for the success of the effort.

Following is a sample protocol that was used in a series of focus groups designed to explore prior survey experiences and future expectations. The facilitator asked the group to spend ten to fifteen minutes jotting down their answers to the following questions:

Describe your survey nightmares, that is, what bad results could come from the survey and why?

Describe your positive survey expectations or experiences.

What can we do to make the survey meaningful?

What are the main issues facing your organization that you would like to see included on the survey?

What are the positives in your organization?

If you could make up a wish list for the organization, what would be on it?

Maintaining Confidentiality

One simple decision that has significant implications for creating positive or negative energy in a survey effort and that must be made at the very start of a survey effort concerns the confidentiality of the responses obtained. Determining who will have access to the data is of vital concern. If the confidentiality of participants' responses is breached or even suspect in any way, the entire survey process will lose not only its credibility but its validity. In short, the quickest way to ensure low return rates and "faked" data is to fail to provide this level of protection. If participants do not feel 100 percent confident that their individual assessments and opinions will be kept anonymous and confidential, that is, separate from their name or other information that could reveal their identity, they will either refuse to answer the survey or answer it untruthfully. This is not news to many, but it is surprising how often situations arise that call into question the confidentiality of responses.

For example, on a recent survey project we contracted at the start with our client and with employees throughout the organization, through a series of meetings and focus groups, that we would not process unit- or department-level reports for groups of employees with fewer than ten members responding. We had all agreed that groupings of this size for this particular organization would guarantee the confidentiality and therefore the anonymity of individual responses. When the time came to generate the reports, however, our client was under considerable pressure from his superiors to produce reports for groups of fewer than ten individuals and subsequently was applying a similar level of pressure on us to respond. Despite a clear contracting process with this same individual at the beginning of the survey process, and amid a series of public announcements and discussions with employees of a set policy regarding the confidentiality of the data, there was a strong push to abrogate our preexisting agreement. After much discussion we were finally able to convince the client to adhere to the original agreement because it was the right thing to do.

However, it was a difficult struggle. To be fair, the impetus for our client's request to examine the data at a lower level than originally agreed to was to provide small-group leaders with specific, actionable information. The intention was not to point fingers or to use the data for staff reduction decisions, as can often be the case (and which employees fear the most). Nevertheless, releasing this information would have violated our agreement with employees, damaged the perception of senior management, and served to invalidate any future survey efforts in the organization and probably most other types of organization development initiatives as well.

We hope this example highlights the importance of maintaining ethical practices and policies in the conduct of organizational surveys. Whether one is acting as an internal or external practitioner, educate, advise, and inform clients about potential breaches in confidentiality and work with them to do what is best for the organization as well as the individual. We return to this issue again in later steps.

Deciding What Information to Collect

How do you decide what belongs on a survey? What questions should be asked? What types of background or demographic questions should be included? Who should respond to the survey? As one might expect, the answers to all of these questions can be derived from the core objectives and anticipated outcomes of the survey process. Hence we have another reason for making sure that these elements are clearly and firmly established at the beginning of the survey development process. They will not provide a complete blueprint of what content should be included in the instrumentation; however, being clear about these issues does provide a solid guide to follow.

The content design is augmented, as we have already noted, through the use of directed focus groups as well as research conducted on archival data (for example, past surveys, annual reports, newspaper articles, political issues of the past, and consulting reports).

In some organizations, a conceptual model or framework (Burke and Litwin, 1992; Nadler and Tushman, 1992; Weisbord, 1978) is also used to help provide a more broadly based picture of the organization, particularly when the survey is intended to be more diagnostic in nature. In others there may be a simple series of questions or issues that someone has in mind, with firm plans for assessment. Of course, the danger with this latter approach, although common enough, is that without having conducted some degree of research or discussion on the nature of the issue being studied or incorporating some broader organizational model or framework capable of identifying unanticipated relationships, the survey effort runs the risk of being stilted and limited in its interpretive abilities. Once

again, the extent to which this is a problem for the survey practitioner depends in large part on the objectives and scope of the survey effort. Still, it is always better to have more information than
less when designing contents. Because the survey effort itself is often
intended to help define the parameters of the issues in the organization, the use of an existing organizational model capable of providing detailed analysis is highly recommended.

Balancing Priorities

Step Two discusses primarily the specifics of designing survey items
and formats, so it is appropriate here to speak briefly about the inclusion of other types of information. Because a successful survey
effort is one that involves a significant amount of forethought, it
follows that the inclusion of various demographic or background
variables is critical to allowing the data to be used in the manner in
which it was intended. For example, in the financial services organization mentioned earlier, where the head of the diversity council
was intent on using the survey to examine employee perceptions by
various subgroups, it would have been extremely damaging to the
survey effort if we had not ultimately included questions on respondent gender, age, and ethnicity, among others. A balance is always being struck (see Figure 1.3) between asking too many of these
types of identifying items (they could indeed conceivably be used
to single out individual responses) and not including enough of the
items needed to complete the survey objectives.

In some surveys, for example in organizations where employee
trust in the organization or in the confidentiality of the assessment
process is low, this might mean rejecting some items that might provide for interesting analyses and keeping only those that are absolutely necessary. In discussions with the members of the survey team
in a financial services organization, it was decided that although
gender, ethnicity, age, and education would be retained for analysis purposes (bearing in mind the ten-person-per-group response pro-

Figure 1.3. Balancing Assessment Priorities.

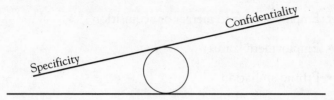

tection mentioned earlier) marital status, child responsibility, and religious affiliation were ruled out as being both too intrusive and too specific in conjunction with the other questions. However, any number of possible items of this nature can be included, as long as the appropriate balance has been struck.

Following is a partial list of these types of variables. Many items may seem overly intrusive to some people; some would certainly be considered illegal to ask of potential job applicants under formal hiring procedures (and in certain countries where requesting such information from employees is prohibited). But a survey is always voluntary in nature, and respondents always have the choice to either leave the item blank, provide a false response, or not respond to the survey at all.

- Age

- Business unit

- Career intentions

- Contact with the customer

- Completion of a past survey

- Department

- Disability

- Gender

- Grade

- Education

- Employer prior to merger or acquisition

- Employment status

- Ethnic affiliation

- Functional group

- Job type

- Length of service with the organization

- Length of service in current job

- Location of primary work site

- Management level

- Nationality

- Number of people supervised

- Payroll category

- Regional location

- Religious affiliation

- Supervisory status

- Training exposure

- Years of experience in a managerial or supervisory position

- Years of experience with your present manager

- Work schedule

At this point, with firm objectives, anticipated outcomes, and the appropriate level of involvement from key constituents in the organization, you are ready to proceed to the next stage of the survey process—the development of the content.

Checklist for Step One

1. Set clear strategic objectives regarding the purpose and uses of the survey.
    *   Determine the purpose and objectives of the survey before you begin—why the survey is being conducted and what will be achieved.
    *   Draw a road map—a guide to show you how to get where you want to go.
    *   Identify a marker at the end that tells you when you have reached your goals.

2. Obtain commitment from senior management and employees.
    *   Gain the support, participation, and commitment from organizational members.
    *   Determine which constituents should be involved in goal-setting and design stages:
        start with senior management
        involve human resources or organization development functions
        involve high potentials and well-respected employees
        set up task forces

3. Identify and overcome negative energy and apathy.
    *   Gather information about survey perceptions:
        conduct focus groups to identify problem areas
        speak with employees about past survey experiences
    *   Communicate plans to deal with issues before surveying.

4. Decide what types of information should be collected.
    *   Include content areas such as leadership perceptions, culture, performance.
    *   Identify background information such as age, gender, and tenure.

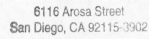

2

Step Two: Developing a World-Class Survey

Ask a stupid question, get a stupid answer.

Unknown

This step deals with the second stage in the survey process—developing the content (the questions) of the survey instrument. Like good contracting, good item development and construction can have a profound and long-lasting impact on the success or failure of any survey effort. All the fancy statistical modeling and the dazzling presentation skills, replete with bells and whistles, in the world cannot mask an obviously flawed survey instrument. If the design is poor, the results and their interpretation are likely to be poor as well. Therefore, mastering the art and science of good, solid, logical survey construction is of paramount importance to any practitioner venturing forth in this arena.

This step concentrates on the design and development of a world-class survey tool. Through examples and descriptions of prior research and experience, the survey practitioner is guided on (1) using teamwork to build quality surveys, (2) gathering, identifying, and working through key issues that need to be assessed, (3) drafting a survey instrument, and (4) testing and refining it for final administration. By the end of this chapter, practitioners should have a better understanding of how to write items that are (1) specific,

(2) clear and concise, (3) free of jargon and other biases, (4) based on sound psychometric theory and research, and (5) appropriate for the respondents to whom they will to be administered.

In addition to the issue of survey design and item writing, which is the main subject of this section, there is a fundamental question regarding instrumentation that must first be addressed in any survey effort: whether the survey team wants to use a standardized or existing tool or create a customized one of their own. We are assuming here that the survey team has chosen to create their own customized tool; however, this is not the only option. In fact, many organizations choose to use an existing instrument that has standardized, highly tested, well-used items that also have useful and relevant norms collected from other companies, industries, or groups. A custom-designed survey tool can include some questions, unmodified, that have been used in other settings for similar comparative analyses. But by its very nature, a freshly designed survey instrument cannot match a standardized product taken off the shelf with respect to the quality or quantity of external normative comparisons. Conversely, standardized tools, because of their applicability to a wide range of settings, are often unlikely to capture in enough depth or assess the specific nature of the information required in many organization survey efforts. Standard survey questionnaires can be very useful for comparison purposes (also known as external benchmarking) and can be cheaper and faster to implement, but they are not well suited to organizational survey efforts initiated in response to some significant and specific set of objectives. Examples are those resulting from a large-scale change effort or a merger or acquisition situation. And because most successful survey efforts do need to have specific goals and objectives to be effective, the utility of a standardized instrument is likely to be questionable in these situations. Even if the survey team decides to choose a standard product, the information contained in this chapter should be useful in evaluating the design quality of the products that are being reviewed for possible use.

Using a Survey Design Team

Developing a survey that is (1) successful in capturing or measuring what it is supposed to, (2) well received, and (3) actionable is not a simple task. To construct a survey that meets these criteria, it is often wise to convene or assemble a survey design team (Rea and Parker, 1992). In some instances this may be the same group as the survey team or task force mentioned in Step One for generating discussion about important issues to be assessed; in others this group may be an entirely different set of employees (for example, experts or experienced practitioners in the fields of survey item design and construction (see Figure 2.1). Because the purpose of this team is to design the core content of the survey instrument, a narrower set of skills than those required for the general project planning and testing phases is required.

The notion of a survey design team may bring to mind the phrase, "There is safety in numbers." However, the purpose here is really more appropriately reflected in the axiom, "Two heads are better than one." This group is not intended to serve as a means for diffusing responsibility. Instead, the design team's basic function is to create clear, easy-to-understand items for inclusion in the assessment instrument. This team is assembled by the principal survey investigator or sponsor for the sole purpose of item development. The survey design team should consist not only of technical and content experts

Figure 2.1. The Survey Design Team.

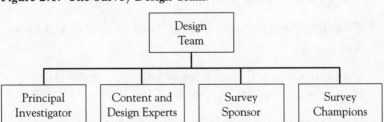

but of key players in the organization—high-potential employees, current and future opinion leaders, and so on. As emphasized in our discussion of the objective-setting process in Step One, a few strategically placed, highly visible, and credible members of management or senior leadership should be involved to help establish the importance of the survey initiative. However, because the design team is clearly more task-oriented than the basic planning group referred to earlier, it is often difficult to obtain any significant level of participation from senior-level individuals at this tactical level. A degree of balance is often needed between involving senior individuals in the planning and goal-setting phase and having their input in the item construction phase. This may, of course, be a somewhat less important issue in organizations where the CEO or the senior management board is the driving force behind the survey effort.

In any case, once a survey design team has been assembled and briefed as to the nature of the survey (for example, contractual arrangements regarding roles and deliverables, survey purpose and objectives, timeline for the roll-out process, key players and supporters, and cost constraints), item development can begin. The item development process should follow the series of five steps outlined next; each is described in greater detail in the next section.

1. *Gather* preliminary information about important issues.

2. *Identify* key issues by summarizing and integrating all available sources of information.

3. *Discuss* your findings with those who gave you input.

4. *Draft* the initial survey document based on your agreed-upon key issues.

5. *Pilot* the survey with your representative group and other organizational members.

Source: List adapted and expanded from Rea and Parker, 1992.

Gathering Preliminary Information

Many clients as well as practitioners have clear ideas about the types of issues and questions that they would like to see included in a survey. However, it is always best to gather information from a variety of sources before beginning any significant item-development work. As discussed in Step One, conducting focus groups with a cross-section of employees is often an excellent source for generating a list of issues, problems, and concerns that could be woven into a survey assessment tool.

Other tools that can be effective include individual interviews with various members of senior management or functional heads, minisurveys or questionnaires with write-in questions distributed to a small, select group of individuals, corporate communications and documents, articles written about the organization in the external media, as well as other types of archival data such as prior surveys, consulting reports, or planning projects previously completed. These latter sources of information can be useful in identifying consistent patterns or trends in the organization's development, but the most useful data are gathered in an open forum where issues, questions, and ideas can be discussed and debated. This is why focus groups are the most commonly used and appreciated technique for collecting this type of preliminary information for the purposes of survey development. Focus groups provide members of the survey design team with the opportunity to discuss in depth and probe possible survey items and issues with a representative sample of participants. Issues inherent in the process itself, such as concerns regarding confidentiality or the purpose and importance of the survey effort, can also be raised and therefore better dealt with in the communication and administration phases.

Identifying Key Issues

Once you have conducted your preliminary data gathering sessions (for example, through focus groups or interviews), it is time to begin the data synthesis process. You will probably begin to see initial patterns emerge in your preliminary data after your third or fourth data gathering session. Unless you already have a standard framework or guide for organizing the information obtained, such as the Burke-Litwin model (Burke and Litwin, 1992) or Nadler and Tushman's (1992) congruence model, these early patterns can be used to provide you with potential categories of issues or main themes for classifying and quantifying the data. Frameworks, whether preexisting or created on the spot, are important because they provide us with a way to view the world in an organized fashion. Through the use of such models it is also possible to identify linkages between issues and concepts, which in turn can be used for future initiatives and action planning (more on this in Steps Five and Six). You will need to have a clear and concise method for categorizing all the comments and perceptions you collect in this initial step of the development process.

For many consultants and survey practitioners the use of a simple 2 × 2 model is often an important diagnostic tool for working with such data. In this way, members of a survey team can present or work with complex data directly and easily. Figure 2.2 shows a sample of how data can be organized and presented using this simple dichotomous approach.

In this example, let us assume that Company XYZ is interested in undertaking a large-scale organizational survey of all employees to determine areas for change within the organization. Focus groups and interviews are then conducted with a cross-section of the organizational membership to identify the areas most in need of change and to assess the perceived difficulty in achieving this change.

The 2 × 2 model in Figure 2.2 provides a simple comparative framework for looking at all the issues raised during the data gathering effort. Based on the results displayed in the model, items in the full employee survey would be best directed at the topics de-scribed in the "Long-Term Goals" and "Quick Gains" sections, as these areas represent content that is of high priority but can also be changed (either in the short or long term). The nature of the mes-sages to be communicated to employees about the expected speed of action that will be taken as a result of the survey effort may tem-per the extent to which items reflecting quick gains are emphasized over those based on the more long-term goals. However, items re-flecting the "Low Priority" section, although useful to include from the standpoint of having issues that can be actioned quickly, are not likely to have much impact because their importance is relatively low. Similarly, the issues noted in the "Not Likely to Change" sec-tion are, for the most part, best ignored in the survey because the assessment of opinions in these areas is only likely to raise expecta-tions that will probably not be met for some time, given their rela-tively low priority and difficult nature. Members of the survey design team need to find some mechanism to identify the key issues that can be changed, as well as those that need to be changed in order to build a survey effort that will have significant and meaningful re-sults for people.

Figure 2.2. Classic 2 × 2 Model: Summary of Interviews and Focus Groups for Company XYZ.

	High *Importance of Organizational Factors* Low	
Hard to Change	**Long-Term Goals**	**Not Likely to Change**
	leadership	bureaucracy
	policies and procedures	organizational structure
	unified culture	salary
	Quick Gains	**Low Priority**
	technical training	speed of corporate
	employee recognition	communication
	flexible hours	more social outings
Easy to Change		

Ease of Change

Discussing Your Findings

When you ask people for their advice, opinions, and ideas, they want to know that you have understood and appreciated what they had to say. From the perspective of survey design, this means you need to present the findings of your data gathering efforts not only to the survey sponsor but, at least in a summary form, to participants who provided you with input from the focus groups and interviews. Often this feedback loop affords an opportunity to verify that the issues you think are important and deserving of item content, based on your synthesis of the results, are the same ones that others want to see reflected in the survey instrument.

A written report that summarizes your key findings is often a good approach to take. The format of this report can be based on a simple categorical approach, similar to the one just described, that serves to prioritize key issues along a set of dimensions (for example, high to low importance, positive versus negative change, high

Exhibit 2.1. Sample Memo to Survey Sponsor.

To: Mai Client
From: The Principal Investigator of the XYZ Survey Team
RE: Key Issues

Dear Mai,

I hope everything is going well. I am enclosing a brief synthesis of the key issues on which to concentrate in our survey identified by the XYZ Survey Team, based on our recent interviews and focus groups conducted in your organization. Please review these findings to see if they coincide with your assessment of the key issues for your organization. We would like to incorporate these into our draft version of the survey.

If you have any questions or comments regarding our findings, please call.

to low degree of changeability), or it can be based on a more structured approach along the lines of the classic OD technique of content coding responses. The data collected in this initial gathering step should be presented in a clear manner that highlights the issues the survey design team have found to be the most important. Exhibit 2.1 shows a sample memo.

Here is a synthesis of some key issues based on a series of employee focus groups, which is a good example of this type of approach.

Focus Group Questions

What are the barriers and hindrances you experience in your work?

What is exciting about your work?

Focus Group Participants

Two hundred Company XYZ employees from all levels, functions, and locations within the organization

Barriers to Work

- Poor work-life balance. (120 responses)

    I'd like more balance between work and personal life.

    I wish I had more time to spend with my family.

    Workload.

    Lack of support for home life.

- Lack of team focus. (98 responses)

    Bureaucratic process, no team emphasis.

    Not a lot of teamwork and coordination.

    Lack of coordination between departments.

Exciting About Work

- I like the people. (133 responses)

    Bright, energetic, creative.

Personal relationships.

Working with people.

- Nature of work. (99 responses)

  It's different every day.

  The work we do is important.

  Nature of the projects; I feel very fortunate.

- Given freedom and autonomy. (22 responses)

  Like running my own program.

  Like to be managed loosely.

Drafting the Initial Survey Document

The next step in the survey design sequence is the drafting of the survey pilot instrument. This is easily the most complicated and labor-intensive phase of survey development. Figure 2.3 provides an overview of the basic steps involved in the process. Almost anyone can formulate a simple question to ask, but not everyone can write a valid and reliable survey item. There is much more to developing the contents of a survey questionnaire than simply writing items, many of which will be covered in more detail below.

It is necessary to the success of the survey effort that the design team, in conjunction with the client, sponsor, or end user of the survey results, spend time at the outset defining some of the more general parameters of the item-writing process before drafting begins. Key questions to consider here include

What is the maximum number of items we want to have in the survey?

Should the questions all use the same scale or a variety of different ones?

Are one or two items enough to cover main topic areas or do there need to be more?

Figure 2.3. The Item Construction Process Map.

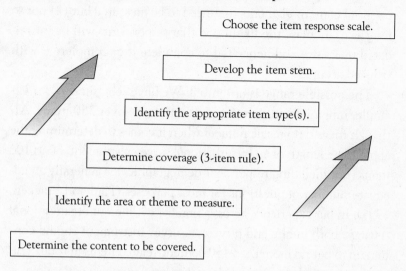

Should the survey be short and densely packed or well spaced and easy to read?

By clarifying and delineating at the start many of these types of parameters for the survey instrument in terms of content and presentation, it will help all parties involved, including the survey design team, achieve greater clarity about the end product they are working to achieve. Much like good contracting, defining the look and feel of the survey early on and with significant specificity can save a great deal of heartache and unmet expectations later in the process. The remainder of this section details the pros and cons of the wide range of options for survey design, layout, item construction, and response formats.

Survey Length

As a former consulting colleague of ours was fond of saying, "Size isn't everything." However, when it comes to survey development, the size or length of the assessment instrument is indeed an important consideration. The objective of the survey design team is to formulate a questionnaire that is (1) long enough to capture all the essential content elements that need to be measured but (2) not so long as to increase the likelihood that respondents will be intimidated by its size and hence fail to complete it or complete it with reduced accuracy.

The possible range is unlimited. We have seen surveys, for example, ranging from only 4 or 5 questions to over 250 items. Although there is no magic number when it comes to determining the appropriate length of an organizational survey instrument, 80 to 100 items (not including respondent demographics) is generally an adequate number of questions for most purposes (Paul and Bracken, 1995). In our experience across a number of different organizational settings, both public and private, a survey instrument should contain up to but no more than 150 content-related items in total. This tends to err slightly on the side of increased numbers of data points while increasing slightly the burden on respondents. However, in practice we have found it to be an effective limit in terms of both the level and quality of data received, as well as psychologically, when working with clients and trying to meet their demands. It is often the case that if given a choice, the survey sponsor would want to include enough questions to thoroughly alienate the entire respondent population; sponsors usually favor collecting every last bit of detail or asking the same question seven different ways.

Despite these general guidelines, when determining the appropriate length of a survey instrument, it is best to consider a number of factors in combination, including

- The goals and objectives of the survey effort
- The background characteristics of the respondent group
- The budget for the assessment project
- The method of survey administration (see Step Four)
- The type and format of the items of interest
- Expected turnaround

Remember that the goal of the survey construction process is to design a tool that is both concise and comprehensive (Edwards, Thomas, Rosenfeld, and Booth-Kewley, 1997). Table 2.1 provides an overview of some of the potential differences between a "shorter" survey effort and a substantially "longer" one for each of the factors listed. Any combination of the factors listed can be considered when designing a survey instrument; those in Table 2.1 provide some general preferences based solely on survey size.

Number of Items Per Content Area

Another issue to consider when designing a survey instrument is the number of items assigned to measure each content or topic area (for example, leadership, communication, and employee satisfaction). A good and often-used rule of thumb with respect to this issue is three to five questions of coverage per concept or theme. The thinking behind this simple formula is that each content area should be asked from several different vantage points to ensure complete coverage.

Here is an example. The items presented in Table 2.2 were designed to measure the degree of teamwork experienced by employees in Company XYZ. As you can see, the questions assess the level of teamwork at the organizational, business unit, and individual

Table 2.1. Potential Differences Between Characteristics in Shorter and Longer Survey Efforts.

80 Items or More

Goals	Group Membership	Budget	Method	Type of Item	Expected Turnaround
In-depth survey	Non-managers	Larger	Paper or computer	Close-ended	Ample time

Fewer than 80 Items

| Quick assessment | Managers | Smaller | Interview or voice response | Open-ended | Little time |

Table 2.2. Sample Items to Assess Teamwork in Company XYZ.

To what extent does the Company XYZ culture foster teamwork?

1	2	3	4	5	DK*
Culture does not foster teamwork.				Culture fosters teamwork.	

To what extent is there an integrated culture among the business units in Company XYZ (that is, a unified approach to accomplishing work)?

1	2	3	4	5	DK
Culture is poorly integrated.				Culture is highly integrated.	

To what extent do work group members cooperate in accomplishing work?

1	2	3	4	5	DK
Work group members work individually, without much interaction or cooperation.				Work group members rely on each other and collaborate to get the job done.	

*DK = Don't Know

work group levels. By including items that access this concept at each of these levels, the data collected will provide the practitioner with a better understanding of the specific nature of teamwork in Company XYZ.

In most surveys, having more than five questions on a specific concept borders on redundancy. Having too many questions on the same topic, unless these represent distinctly different facets of behavior such as the broader area of managerial behavior, runs the risk of unnecessarily increasing response burden as well as potentially irritating respondents. Even if the items are well dispersed throughout the survey instrument, respondents are likely to identify those appearing to assess the same construct. They often point this out to survey practitioners, even when the items are intended to assess more subtle differences in perspective. Shown next is an example of four different items that were intended to measure different facets of motivation but probably represent too much overlap in content:

1. To what extent are employees motivated in Company XYZ?

2. How motivated do you feel in your job?

3. How motivated are you to do your job well?

4. To what extent do managers motivate employees?

Of course, the questions may be too similar in focus, but it is possible that employees will rate these items somewhat differently (a hypothesis that can be tested during the pilot phase of the design process) or that the survey sponsor may want to include all these items, regardless of the amount of overlap, for other reasons. For example, the message communicated in the inclusion of four separate items assessing employee motivation might be important.

Two Types of Survey Items

Survey items, like people, come in many different shapes and sizes. They can be long (wordy) or short (simple). They can be qualitative or quantitative in nature. They can be designed to assess facts or attitudes. They can be measured on nominal, ordinal, or interval-level scales. They can ask how you feel or how other employees feel about a given topic. However, all survey items must fit into two categories; they must be either *open-ended* or *close-ended* questions (Edwards and others, 1997; Fink, 1995; Rogelberg and Waclawski, 2001). Each of these item types has advantages and disadvantages associated with its use.

Open-Ended or Write-In Questions

Open-ended or write-in questions ask survey respondents to provide an answer to a given question in their own words. These types of questions do not have a limited range of responses; their boundaries are defined solely by the respondents themselves and are similar to the essay questions found in many school examinations.

Here are some examples of typical open-ended survey items reflecting different types of content:

1. How long have you been at Company XYZ?
2. How clear are employees about the mission of Company XYZ?
3. To what extent does Company XYZ value its employees?

Question 1 is designed to elicit a simple numerical response; questions 2 and 3 are more general in nature and could result in a variety of responses. There are several significant benefits of open-ended questions:

- They are less sterile or flat than close-ended questions; they can enrich and enlighten one's understanding of the data by adding a more descriptive human element.

- People can answer these types of questions from their own unique perspective instead of being forced into the response options that are driven by the paradigm of the survey practitioner or design team. In this way they allow for more individuality and expansiveness on the part of the respondent.

- They allow people the opportunity to let off steam, thus are an effective avenue for catharsis.

- Last and perhaps most important is that these types of questions allow respondents to answer in their own words (Edwards and others, 1997).

Because of the complexity of analyzing and standardizing the responses obtained from open-ended questions, it is generally considered good industry practice to use them sparingly and in conjunction with a number of close-ended items. In fact, some practitioners recommend that organizational surveys contain easy-to-read, close-ended items wherever possible (Rea and Parker, 1992). We think this recommendation is a bit too strong. In our view, a well-conceived and constructed survey instrument should include a balanced complement of both these basic item types.

Although open-ended questions can and do provide the survey practitioner with rich data, which can lead to a better, more in-depth understanding of respondents' issues and concerns, they do have several serious limitations that should be recognized and factored in when constructing and implementing an organizational survey tool. The main disadvantages of the open-ended format include the following:

- The time required on the part of respondents for completion is considerably longer.

- They are much more time consuming for the practitioner or survey task force to content code and analyze.

- By their unstructured nature they have a tendency to produce redundant or extraneous information.

- They rarely assess the level of intensity of a given issue, feeling, or concern.

Close-Ended Questions

The other basic type of survey question is the close-ended question. Close-ended items, the most popular of formats, by design present a question and a limited number of options from which respondents must make one or more choices. Examples can be found on any true-false or multiple-choice test.

Table 2.3 lists examples of close-ended survey items. It should be apparent to the reader that even though these same questions were asked in the open-ended example, the quality and quantity of

Table 2.3. Sample Close-Ended Questions.

1. How long have you been at Company XYZ?
   01   Less than 1 year
   02   1–5 years
   03   6–10 years
   04   11–15 years
   05   16 years or more

2. How clear are employees about the mission of Company XYZ?

1	2	3	4	5	DK
Not clear		Moderately clear		Very clear	

3. To what extent does Company XYZ value its employees?

1	2	3	4	5	DK
To no extent		To a moderate extent		To a very great extent	

information that can be obtained from the close-ended format is very different. Responses to question 1 would probably be very similar; questions 2 and 3 in this format would produce a very different type of information than might be collected when used in a write-in method.

A number of benefits of close-ended questions make them particularly useful for survey practitioners:

- They are fast and easy for the respondent to answer.

- They provide data that are easy to understand and interpret.

- They ensure uniform responses across respondents in different functions, areas, and even organizations, thus making comparisons simple and efficient.

- They provide the respondent with helpful memory cues to facilitate some sort of response.

- They can remind respondents of ideas or potential options that were unknown or forgotten (Edwards and others, 1997; Rea and Parker, 1992).

Of course, the close-ended format has its disadvantages as well. For example:

- The questions chosen to be included in the survey instrument may not be representative of people's attitudes and opinions regarding a certain content area.

- These types of items compel respondents to express attitudes, even if they truly do not have them.

- The response options provided may not reflect the full range of needs or opinions.

Despite these problems, however, close-ended items are extremely popular in organizational assessment survey efforts.

Types of Close-Ended Questions: Measurement Scales

Three levels of measurement are available to the survey practitioner when working with close-ended items: categorical-nominal, ordinal, and interval (Fink, 1995; Rea and Parker, 1992). Each of these levels provides a different type of data, and each is useful to the survey design team in grouping specific sets of items or variables in a particular way. The various properties of these levels are described next in order of increasing complexity.

Categorical-Nominal Variables

Categorical or nominal variables, the most basic type of close-ended questions, include items such as gender, ethnicity, religion, political party membership, prior exposure to a survey effort, and so on. Questions like these can be broken down into discrete *categories* or groups in order to determine the relative frequency of each response. These categories are often arbitrarily labeled by the survey practitioner in a numerical fashion. However, since the data collected from these types of items do not inherently possess differences in magnitude or size, the assigned numerical values on a questionnaire, for example, would be for identification purposes only. There is no implied difference in valuation. By attaching numerical values to these types of variables, however, survey practitioners are able to take nonnumerical concepts and measure them quantitatively in the form of the frequency of responses selected.

As you can see in the following example, the numerical system assigned to gender is for descriptive purposes only.

What is your gender?

1. Female

2. Male

Although gender is a relatively simple example, a more complex version of this type of item, yet one that provides important information none the less, is displayed in Figure 2.4.

The only real limitation with nominal-level items, although it is significant, is that because the data collected do not really reflect a numerical relationship, the data are somewhat more limited with respect to the types of statistical techniques and analyses that can be used.

Ordinal Variables

Ordinal-level variables have response options that differ in magnitude or size but are not exactly and proportionally different from each other. In effect, these variables are used for ranking different *ranges* or *groupings*. Some of the most common examples of ordinal-level items found on organizational surveys are such factors as educational level, supervisory status, and grade level. In fact, survey instruments tend to have more ordinal measures than any other type (Fink, 1995).

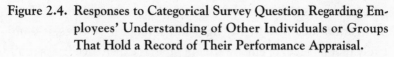

Figure 2.4. Responses to Categorical Survey Question Regarding Employees' Understanding of Other Individuals or Groups That Hold a Record of Their Performance Appraisal.

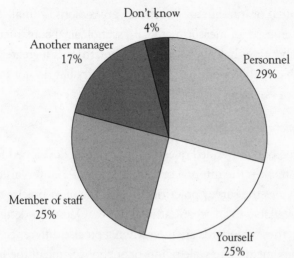

Note: Percentages are based on total number of choices selected and are not forced to be mutually exclusive.

A scale that measures the extent to which a condition is present or absent, for example, is an ordinal-level item. This type of item is used when there are clear differences expected in the relative magnitude of the construct being measured on the survey, but it is not possible to specify whether these differences are absolute. Let us consider the construct of empowerment.

To what extent are you empowered to do your job as you see fit?

1	2	3	4	5	DK
To no extent		To a moderate extent		To a very great extent	

Most people would agree that there are likely to be differences in the extent to which employees feel empowered to do their jobs effectively. Most would also agree that these differences in perceptions of the level of empowerment experienced simply cannot be measured as accurately as individual differences in height, weight, or age. Even in organizations with highly rigid and autocratic cultures, it is unlikely that *no* level of empowerment at all is experienced; it is probably just limited or infrequent. For these very reasons ordinal-level items are often used for measuring social-psychological constructs or phenomena because they allow the survey practitioner a greater degree of specificity than nominal categorical scales but do not make the mistake of assuming precise or absolute differences.

Interval-Numerical Variables

The final type of close-ended question that can be developed for a survey instrument is the interval or numeric item. An interval-level variable provides the survey practitioner with the most precise type of measure available to an organizational survey. Questions designed according to these standards are used when a precise difference can be assessed among discrete scale points or anchors. Some of the most frequently used examples of interval scales are age, tenure, income, height, weight, IQ, and temperature, simply because the range of options can be designed to be equidistant from one another (for example, in five-year blocks).

Length of service in Company XYZ:
   a. 1 to 5 years
   b. 6 to 10 years
   c. 11 to 15 years
   d. 16 to 20 years
   e. 21 to 25 years
   f. 26 to 30 years

Types of Close-Ended Scales: Summary

Ordinal-level items are the most frequently used of the three close-ended measurement scale types in organizational survey instruments. The popularity of these types of scales derives largely from the latitude they provide survey practitioners in developing items. They are also favored because of the limitless possibilities they provide in terms of response scale options. There are a great many options for these types of items. Table 2.4 provides an overview of just a few of the more commonly used response categories on organizational survey instruments.

How Many Response Options?

Each of the scales detailed in Table 2.4 consists of five points, anchors, or response options, but survey scales of this type can range from as few as two points to as many as needed to provide a meaningful degree of discrimination. Some questions might warrant a simple set of options such as agree, disagree, or neutral; others such as the empowerment example are best measured using a more graduated set of options, ranging in magnitude.

In practice, organization assessment survey items usually provide 5-, 7-, or 9-point options (Fink, 1995), particularly when they have been designed to assess more intangible organizational, behavioral, or social-psychological content (for example, the quality of senior leadership, the degree of responsiveness to the external environment, the usefulness of corporate information mechanisms)—the primary concern of most survey efforts. Scales can consist of even-numbered anchors (for example, 4, 6, and 8 points) as well, but these types of items are less common in practice because they do not allow for the possibility of a neutral midpoint, particularly in items with scales that are bipolar in nature (described in more detail in the next section).

Some survey practitioners prefer to use these types of even scales to artificially force respondents to make a positive or negative selection (in items with bipolar scales) or at least in the direction of more or less (in items with a single unipolar extent or magnitude scale) because they feel that it provides more poignant data. Although many practitioners and researchers have examined the effects of scale length in more general contexts, with decidedly mixed conclusions

Table 2.4. Types of Response Options.

	1	2	3	4	5
Endorsement	definitely false	false	don't know	true	definitely true
Frequency	never	almost never	sometimes	very often	always
Intensity	none	very mild	mild	moderate	severe
Influence	no problem	very small problem	small problem	moderate problem	big problem
Comparison	much less than others	somewhat less than others	about the same as others	somewhat more than others	much more than others
Satisfaction	very dissatisfied	dissatisfied	neutral	satisfied	very satisfied
Effectiveness	very ineffective	ineffective	neutral	effective	very effective
Quality	very poor	poor	average	good	very good
Expectancy	much worse than expected	worse than expected	as expected	better than expected	much better than expected
Extent	to no extent	to a small extent	to a moderate extent	to a great extent	to a very great extent
Agreement	strongly disagree	disagree	neutral	agree	strongly agree

Source: Adapted from Edwards and others, 1997, and Fink, 1995.

(for example, Edwards and others, 1997; Schuman and Presser, 1996), we have found in our work that 5-point scales may indeed be the best overall, based on analyses of differential level (mean) and shape (variability) effects among the same instrument using 4-, 5-, and 7-point scales in an organizational setting (Church and Waclawski, 2000). However, this process adds a level of response bias to the process that cannot be removed in subsequent examination and analyses, which could in turn lead to more spurious findings and recommendations. It is always possible, for example, to explore what would happen to the data if the respondents who chose the midpoint were simply removed on an item-by-item basis during the analysis phase. The practitioner should try to remember that although too much information can always be reduced, it can never be expanded. This is one reason an early initial meeting with the survey design team and the survey sponsor to define the working parameters and expectations of the survey instrument is an important first step in the design process.

Unipolar Versus Bipolar Response Options

Besides the total number of response options offered, another issue in survey item construction concerns whether or not the questions will be rated using a unipolar or bipolar scale. Unipolar response scales are those in which the response can range solely in the relative degree of magnitude of the given statement or phenomenon. Examples of these include extent scales (for example, "the extent to which employees feel empowered in their jobs") as well as frequency scales. Any item that ranges from nothing to something represents a type of unipolar assessment. Conversely, a bipolar-response-scaled item provides the survey respondent with two different options that can vary in meaning on either end of the scale. Agree–disagree scales are a good example of this type of scale. Neither option is necessarily better than the other, but unipolar scales provide the respondent with a greater range of subtlety in terms of response options, whereas a bipolar scale limits the degree of options by adding a more specific level of detail to the data.

Two sample scales are provided in the following example that highlight some of the differences between these response options:

My business unit has clear-cut goals.

Unipolar scale	Bipolar scale
1 To no extent	1 Strongly disagree
2 To a little extent	2 Disagree
3 To some extent	3 Neither agree nor disagree/ neutral
4 To a great extent	4 Agree
5 To a very great extent	5 Strongly agree

If the respondent were to agree with this statement, four levels of extent are available on the unipolar scale but only two options on the bipolar scale. If the respondent were to disagree with the statement, there is only one option on the extent scale, and that does not directly assess the level of disagreement. But the two clear choices on the bipolar scale would more accurately reflect an opinion. In the end, the best choice regarding these response scale types is made based on the nature of the content being assessed (for example, does the survey team care about relative presence of the phenomenon in the workplace or whether or not the idea elicits a positive or negative opinion) in the survey instrument and the ease and relevance with which these different approaches fit the questions being asked.

Guidelines for Survey Construction

Having obtained a solid understanding of the differences among the various types of items and response scales that can be used, it is now time to turn to some basic rules of thumb with respect to survey item construction. These generally agreed-on principles apply to all types of items and to all survey efforts. Practitioners and their survey design teams should keep these in mind when developing their instruments (Edwards and others, 1997; Fink, 1995; Jones and Bearley, 1995; Rogelberg and Waclawski, 2001). A brief synopsis of these principles is presented here.

PRINCIPLE 1: Keep the Issues in Mind.

One of the pitfalls or unexpected negative side effects of using a survey development team is the tendency for people to become fixated on their own beliefs or values about the necessity of certain survey items that, in reality, may or may not be appropriate to the assessment effort. Team members often have such a vested interest in pursuing issues that they personally believe to be important that even when confronted with the question of relevancy, they continue to promote their item agenda. If taken too far, a survey instrument can quickly become overly long, unwieldy, and off-target due to such pressures. Although this outcome may not have been the intention of the members of the survey design team when advocating for their issue, it can easily be the end result. To a large extent having a conceptual framework such as the Burke-Litwin model (Burke and Litwin, 1992) surrounding the design and analysis process or a thorough examination of the preliminary data can help the survey practitioner reduce this risk.

Another force that can affect the aim of the group is the intragroup process itself (Schein, 1988). Sometimes a bad group process can quickly undermine even the best strategy or integrated organization development framework, resulting in a survey instrument that has been designed by a committee rather than by a team. Therefore, when the team is engaged in developing survey items, it is often a good idea to have one of the members take responsibility for monitoring the group process and progress (to serve as a process consultant [Schein, 1988]) to help the team stay on course. This means keeping track of what the key issues are for the organization and goals of the survey effort, and making sure that individual members of the development team do not deviate too far from these objectives in pursuit of their own personal agenda.

In the end, what you ask for is what you get. The practitioner must never forget that once the heat of the moment has passed and the data have been collected, there is no turning back to fix a bad item or add one last item that was dropped in favor of something else. Remembering the needs and wants of the survey sponsor and keeping these in mind should be foremost in the thoughts of the survey design team.

PRINCIPLE 2: Be Parsimonious.

This principle is related to the comments made earlier regarding the appropriate number of items needed to measure a given construct or issue. Use enough items to measure what you need on a given topic, but no more. As previously mentioned, one rule of thumb for the total length of the survey instrument is somewhere between eighty and one hundred items (Paul and Bracken, 1995). Many topics may be of interest, but if they are not necessary to the goals and objectives of the survey initiative, the design team needs to seriously consider deleting them or saving them for a future assessment. These days more than ever, time is a precious commodity for people in organizations, and they do not look favorably on people who waste theirs. When a survey is perceived as being too lengthy and time consuming, it can create not only a negative opinion of the survey but of the corporate initiative to which it has been tied, the usefulness of surveys in general, and even the company as a whole. In addition, we have heard many people in organizations say that they are feeling "surveyed to death" these days. Remember that *your* assessment tool is probably not the only one they are being asked to complete. It is good survey practice to take this into account when constructing and administering your instrument.

PRINCIPLE 3: Avoid Double-Barreling.

It is necessary not only to keep the survey relatively short and simple but to make sure that the items themselves are clear and uncomplicated. One of the most common mistakes in item construction is attempting to measure more than one idea at a time—commonly referred to as double-barreling. Most survey practitioners at one time or another have used questions of this nature, even though it is probably the biggest survey no-no in the book. Double-barreled items are usually the result of an effort to reach a design compromise or get the biggest bang for a buck in terms of the total number of concepts measured in the survey. The interpretation of the data collected using this type of item is uncertain at best and may prove relatively useless and unsatisfying. However, in some cases the data gathered from this type of item are not as much of a problem in analysis, particularly when the assessment in question is highly attitudinal in nature from the start. Again, these types of problematic items can often be avoided through group process checks, quality control, and appropriate attention to the pilot testing process. It also helps to have an objective third party proofread your items, particularly with regard to this issue.

Here are examples of commonly used items that seek to measure more than one construct:

To what extent are you satisfied with your salary and benefits?

To what extent do employees support the mission and vision of Company XYZ?

To what extent does your manager earn the trust and respect of employees?

To what extent does your manager coach and mentor people in new assignments?

The concepts presented are similar in each of these sample items (for example, between mission and vision in question 1 or trust and respect in question 3), but they are not the same. Because of politics and personal agendas, however, the use of these types of questions is commonplace. These items should be used sparingly, if at all.

PRINCIPLE 4: Be Clear and Concise.

It is better to be clear and concise with a survey item than long-winded and obtuse—simple enough in concept but difficult to accomplish in practice. Words and phrases that are clear to one person or group are often obscure or out of context to another.

Consider carefully and understand the respondent group or audience that will ultimately be surveyed when developing survey items. Factors such as the target group's educational background, reading level, and whether or not English is a first or second language must be taken into account. The best practice is to develop individual survey items with the lowest common denominator in mind. Making the items clear and simple will ensure greater readability and a more favorable translation into other languages if necessary. Practitioners should avoid the use of esoteric or uncommon words or expressions. In this way you can increase the likelihood that the majority of the survey respondent group will have little or no difficulty in completing the survey. A good way to combat threats to readability and the likelihood of inappropriate language is to test the survey with a diverse group. Outside proofreaders are also recommended.

Similarly, the use of jargon in surveys or questionnaires should be avoided when possible. In particular, jargon that is culturally specific to a nation, an industry, or an ethnicity can be confusing and frustrating to people of different backgrounds. For instance, instead of asking, "To what extent do team members work toward win-win solutions?" one should ask, "To what extent do team members work toward mutually satisfying outcomes?" Likewise, rather than trying to measure the "value-added" of an intervention or approach, it is probably better to measure its "contribution."

Another source of confusion is negatively worded items. An example of this would be, "To what extent are employees demotivated to do their jobs effectively?" We have heard many practitioners and survey sponsors advocate the inclusion of a few of these types of items because they think the change in format will make respondents really think about their answer. However, in our experience these types of questions represent a significant source of confusion and frustration. They are difficult for respondents to rate and are equally difficult to describe when working with the survey feedback. At the very least they must be reverse-scored for analysis purposes, which assumes that the scale in reverse is comparable to the other scales used in the survey in their original form. When these types of items are used only a few times in a survey instrument, they often go unnoticed by respondents who have a certain response in mind, based largely on the understanding of the response scales used throughout the rest of the instrument. Because of this, participants respond in a manner exactly opposite to what they had intended. These items often have to be removed from the final reporting process because they are potentially invalid and difficult to work with.

Unfortunately, it is not always easy to be clear and concise in one's item writing style, nor is it simple to assess the quality of an instrument by oneself. For example, we were in a client meeting discussing our progress on a new survey draft. One of the participants, who was not one of the survey design team members, voiced her concern that there was too much ambiguity in some of the items. After the meeting was over, the survey team reconvened without this person and debriefed the meeting. We were all wondering what had happened. At the time of their initial construction, the items had seemed perfectly clear to us. We had spent so much time and effort working together, participatively and supportively, to craft the items contained in this new draft that we thought we had achieved synergy and a sense of team spirit. Instead we had obviously confused and disappointed this person. After some discussion someone in the group chimed in, "Well, you know what they say. A camel is a horse created by a committee." This brings us back to the idea that sometimes groups working together can fall prey to their own ineffective processes. In the spirit of collaboration and everyone putting in their two cents worth, we created a draft survey instrument that to this outside reader was unclear and muddled. As a result, we had to review the entire questionnaire and its relationship to the project objectives. Then we had to examine the individual items piece by piece to make sure that each of the issues assessed was clearly worded and distinct from one another.

PRINCIPLE 5: Avoid Leading and Biased Questions.

This might seem like common sense, but remember to avoid constructing survey items that are either overly leading or biased toward a certain response by design. Survey items should provide an appropriate range of options, and the wording of the item itself should be made to be as free of value judgments as possible. The inherent interests of the survey sponsor or various key constituent groups are likely to be evident to the respondents at a relatively broad level (for example, a survey on the interest in various benefits options is probably related to an initiative of the human resources function). The less the items show the preferred responses the better.

For example, the question that follows reflects the general assumption that senior leadership is overpaid:

To what extent do you think the senior leadership of your organization is overpaid?

1	2	3	4	5	DK
To a very small extent		To a moderate extent		To a very great extent	

Although this may indeed be the case, by phrasing the question in this manner the respondent is (1) forced to agree with this sentiment to a very small extent at least, even if he or she feels that the statement is not true at all, (2) is reminded of the pay disparity issue, which might negatively affect the remainder of the items to be rated following this one, and (3) is given the subtle message, presumably endorsed by the survey sponsor, that senior leaders are overpaid.

A better item reflecting the same type of content might read as follows:

With respect to pay, senior leadership is

1	2	3	4	5	DK
Very underpaid		Fairly paid		Very overpaid	

PRINCIPLE 6: Ensure Item–Scale Agreement.

The final principle of good survey item design concerns the extent to which an item stem matches the scale options provided. We have paid attention to the type of question, scale options, and specific issues and pitfalls when phrasing new items. However, regardless of the format or content, the item should be internally consistent. This is another relatively simple idea in concept, but in practice it is easy to confuse or obscure the response options by adding too many additional or unrelated scale descriptors. For example, the question below regarding value placed on employees ranges from not being valued or respected to being treated well (whatever that means to the respondent):

To what extent does Company XYZ value its employees?

1	2	3	4	5	DK
To a small extent (employees are not valued or respected)			To a very great extent (employees are treated well)		

These two options neither match each other or the item stem. One of the simplest ways to correct many of these inconsistencies is to ensure that the only words used in the ends of the scale are those taken from the stem of the item itself. Additional outside readers and testing also help a great deal.

Piloting the Survey

The last step in the survey design process consists of piloting (or pretesting) the survey with a real group of respondents. This is the acid test as to whether or not the instrument that has been so painstakingly designed is clear, understandable, and comprehensive with respect to what it purports to measure (Rogelberg and Waclawski, 2001). The piloting process is often one of the first elements to be curtailed when project timing begins to slip and timelines are readjusted, but the pilot is really one of the few legitimate places where problems and issues inherent in the survey tool can be identified and resolved before they cause significant damage to the overall survey effort. It is often the only phase in which people not directly involved in the planning, development, and construction process have an opportunity to provide their relatively unbiased input.

When piloting a survey instrument the respondents should assess the content of the questionnaire itself according to the following three criteria:

1. *Clarity:* Are the instructions and items easy to read and understand?
2. *Relevance:* Are the items meaningful to the participant?
3. *Specificity:* Are the items sufficiently detailed, or are they too general in nature?

It is useful to query participants about these three components of the survey through the use of a pilot survey questionnaire. This survey-within-a-survey asks them to rate the larger instrument on these three basic dimensions. It also allows for other types of information or hypotheses to be gathered and tested as well (for example, assessing differences in content layout and item ordering, using extra numbers of items with the intent of reducing a certain number, determining the average length of time needed to complete the tool). Exhibit 2.2 provides a sample instrument of this type that has been used in an actual pilot survey assessment project.

Exhibit 2.2. Sample Pilot Test Survey Questionnaire.

Purpose of the Questionnaire

You have been chosen as one of 200 employees who are being asked to participate in a pilot test of the enclosed Company XYZ survey. Your participation will help refine this survey for use throughout your organization and is therefore very important.

This questionnaire is designed to give senior leadership in your company feedback from employees on important issues facing your organization today. Over the past few months, a sample of employees has been queried on this matter, both in interviews and focus group meetings. The key themes that have emerged have been translated into this survey, which you are being asked to complete. It should only take 30 to 60 minutes of your time. When completing the survey please consider its usability in terms of the following criteria, as you will be asked to evaluate this survey after you have completed it:

Clarity: Are the instructions and items easy to read?
Relevance: Are the items meaningful to you?
Specificity: Are the items detailed, or are they too general in nature?

Please be frank in responding to this questionnaire. This information will be of little value unless you provide as accurate an evaluation as you can. Your responses will remain completely confidential. Under no circumstances will your ratings be released to others in your organization. The data will be analyzed by an outside contractor.

Instructions: Please answer the following questions
1. How long did it take you to complete the questionnaire? Circle your response.
   a) Less than 30 minutes
   b) Between 30 minutes and 1 hour
   c) Between 1 and 1 and 1/2 hours
   d) Over 1 and 1/2 hours

2. What were your general reactions to the survey? (Please write in the space below.)
   a) Very negative   (continued on the next page)

Exhibit 2.2. Sample Pilot Test Survey Questionnaire. *(continued)*

---

   b) Negative

   c) No reaction (neutral)

   d) Positive

   e) Very positive

3. What were your reactions to the cover letter and instructions (for example, was the intent of the effort clearly communicated)?

4. Please list any items that were difficult to answer and specify reasons using the list below:

   a) Unclear

   b) Not relevant to my work site

   c) Too general in scope—hard to rate

5. Did the response scale (1 = To a very small extent to 5 = To a very great extent) provide you with enough choices in making your ratings?

6. What themes or areas, in your opinion, received either too much or not enough coverage (in terms of items)?

Areas covered too much:

Areas not covered enough:

Areas not covered at all:

7. Are there any other issues, concerns, or suggestions you would like to raise to help improve the survey?

Results from this type of test assessment provide the survey practitioner and the survey design team with invaluable information about the draft document beyond the standard means, standard deviations, ranges, and missing data frequencies associated with a pilot of only the survey tool itself. In combination, this information should be used to guide the survey design team in making the necessary modifications to the style, content, and language of the final instrument. The objective nature of the pretest data (assuming the test was conducted with a group of individuals not associated with the survey project) is also useful in helping survey team members construct an instrument free of their own biases and create a survey that is truly customer-driven. At this stage, the survey team should have a completed assessment tool that has been well tested and is ready for the next phase of the survey process—administration.

Checklist for Step Two

- Convene or assemble a survey design team.

- Involve strategically placed, highly visible, and credible members of management.

- Involve technical and conceptual experts.

- Gather preliminary information about important issues.

- Identify key issues by summarizing and integrating all sources of information.

- Discuss your findings with those who gave you input.

- Draft the initial survey document based on your agreed key issues. Consider the following:

  Survey length
  Number of items per content area
  Number of response options

Unipolar versus bipolar response options
The key issues
Parsimony
Double-barreling
Clarity of wording
Leading and biased questions
Item–scale agreement

- Pilot the survey with your representative group and other organizational members.

3

Step Three: Communicating Objectives

What we've got here is failure to communicate.
Frank R. Pierson and Donn Pearce

Communication is one of the primary means by which people structure themselves into the social systems that we call work. Without the ability to communicate, contemporary organizations as we know them would cease to exist (Katz and Kahn, 1978). Communication is something we do all the time, every day, in our personal and professional lives. We often take this process for granted (both personally in our immediate work setting and systematically within the rest of the organization and beyond). But our ability to communicate allows us to coordinate and collaborate our actions, make important decisions that affect more than one individual at a time, and ultimately function as an organizational entity. Whatever else changes, either in the external environment or internal to the organization (for example, leadership, management, organizational structure, or team-based reward systems), communication will always be the glue that holds different functions, groups, and individuals together.

We all know what can happen when people communicate poorly: messages can be confused, misunderstood, misinterpreted, or even altered in various ways when being transferred from individual to individual or from group to group. Communicating effectively with others, particularly when the messages are complex in nature, is rarely as easy as it is made out to be. Differences in people's perspectives also add to this quagmire of complexity.

For example, we were involved in a large-scale survey of the administrative staff of a large, prestigious, world-renowned academic institution. After several meetings with our client and our client's supervisor, we conducted an initial focus group with fifteen senior HR personnel and staff members from different areas to determine the main issues that were facing the organization. Before the meeting could get under way, however, the topic of discussion turned to the specific intent of the survey effort as detailed in the official cover letter being sent to employees. These participants refused to proceed with a discussion of the issues until they were comfortable with the purpose of the survey and the message that was being given to employees regarding this purpose. These concerns are perfectly understandable and legitimate, but we had been led to believe that this group was already on board with the survey effort and were aware of the project plan and intent. However, all they knew was that a survey was in the works for some undisclosed reason. Needless to say, it produced a significant amount of anxiety that had to be dealt with before the discussion of important issues could begin. When we challenged our client regarding this issue, she responded, "I don't want them to know too much." Had the communication process been more open with these senior-level staff personnel in HR, the focus group would have gone more smoothly and been better received, which in turn could have benefited the survey effort by generating greater commitment and support among this group. Instead, more resentment and suspicion was generated than necessary. And all this was among a group of only fifteen people. Imagine the impact if a survey had been simply dropped on some lower-level employee's desk without any significant information regarding its objectives and intended uses! The effect could have been enough to defeat the assessment process before it even started.

Effective communication is a necessary ingredient for all types of organizations and organizational initiatives, as well as for the success of organizational survey efforts. We have already touched on the importance of effective communication, particularly in the initial phases of the survey development and project planning process, but we have yet to consider the key aspects of communication as it specifically relates to the survey roll-out process to end users—employees. This step discusses some of the key issues that are part of this process.

First, however, a better understanding of the general nature of organizational communication is required. This will be achieved through a brief introduction and overview of the CPR (Content-Processes-Roles) model of organizational communication (Church, 1994b, 1996). Based on an integration of theoretical approaches taken from social psychology, management science, and sociology (for example, systems theory, information processing models, and symbolic interactionism), the CPR model provides a simple yet effective means of both integrating and advancing our understanding of how communication actually works in organizations. It is through this approach to understanding the levels of communication in organizations that effective survey communication efforts can be facilitated.

The CPR Model of Organizational Communication

Many people talk about the *supportive* nature of communication in relation to the success of various organizational initiatives such as an organization assessment survey. However, in practice this important element is often considered only as a background or contextual variable. This is true, despite the fact that the context of "good" communication—usually described as a combination of being open, honest, participative, or direct with others—has been recognized by total quality management (TQM), HRD, and OD practitioners as being one of the cornerstones of the successful implementation of *any* large organizational change initiative (Beckhard and Pritchard, 1992; Burke and Jackson, 1991; Sashkin and Kiser, 1993), including survey efforts (Kraut, 1996a).

Arguably the first step in improving organizational communication efforts is a firm understanding of how this process works in a given organizational setting. The CPR model of communication (Church, 1994b, 1996) is a simple yet effective framework for understanding the basic issues and levels of communication in an organizational system. By using this model, one can gain a better understanding of the three key components of organizational communication and some of the interrelationships that describe its character and function. These consist of

- The *what* that is communicated (content)

- *How* it is communicated (processes)

- *Who* does the communicating (roles)

Organizational communication can be conceptualized and understood using three primary dimensions: content, processes, and roles. Each of these elements has been derived from existing theory and research. Figure 3.1 depicts these three factors and their relationships. The outer circle encompassing the model represents the permeable boundaries of the *primary system of focus*. This reflects the highest level of analysis to which the model is being applied, that is, the entire organization or organizational unit being assessed in the survey effort.

The triangular image of the model depicts the causal relationships among the three dimensions. *Content*, located at the top of the triangle, is the single most important dimension to consider when trying to understand the character and function of communication process in a given organizational system. *Processes* and *Roles* are located at the bottom of the triangle. Without an understanding of the nature of the survey content itself, it is virtually impossible to grasp either the preferred method of transmission (process) throughout the organization or what groups or individuals (roles) are responsible for and involved in making this transfer of information occur. For a

Figure 3.1. The CPR Model of Organizational Communication.

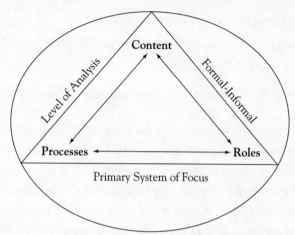

Source: Church, 1994b, p. 31. Used by permission.

given survey effort, it is important first to understand the objectives and goals of the survey process before determining the best means of communicating these to respondents and key stakeholders in the organization.

The two arrows pointing from Content to Processes and Roles in Figure 3.1 reflect this differential level of importance. However, since both processes and roles can also positively or negatively affect the nature of the message being communicated, the arrows also point up from these two dimensions, indicating this reciprocal relationship. The arrows connecting processes to roles reflect their *interdependent* nature.

Taking each of these three aspects of communication separately, the C in the CPR model refers to the actual *content* of the communication exchange, or the *what* that is being communicated. The information we are referring to here will provide answers to the following types of questions:

What are the key messages to be communicated regarding the survey effort?

Why is the survey being conducted?

Who is responsible for the survey effort?

What types of issues are they interested in asking me about?

When can I see some results?

What is the commitment to action based on the data collected?

If the basic content message of the survey is either weak or unclear, that will have a significant impact on the perceived utility and subsequently the outcome of the entire process. This is why, as we stated earlier, the content of the message itself is probably best thought of as the single most important element for approaching any type of organizational communication. Next, the arrows are directed downward, affecting both the process and roles involved.

The second dimension or factor of the CPR model, P, describes the systemic *processes* of organizational communication. Included under this category are the mechanisms, methods, systems, and patterns of interaction by which the actual content is implemented or transferred from one subsystem to another within the organization—that is to say, the *how* of organizational communication. Here the questions to ask regarding a survey initiative include

What are the key direct and indirect methods of communication to employees in this organization?

By what means should the messages about the survey process be communicated?

How do we ensure that we involve everyone who should be involved in the process?

There is both a formal and an informal side to the processes dimension. Examples of formal processes include management information systems, computer networks, bulletin boards, forums, senior management presentations, and company newsletters. The informal transfer mechanisms consist of meetings, social networks and contacts, and formal and informal reporting relationships. The key to choosing the most effective means of communicating to employees regarding survey efforts depends in large part on the nature of the existing processes. However, we discuss some general guidelines regarding survey-related communications later in this section.

This third factor, R, in the CPR model refers to the *roles* and responsibilities of those involved in the communication process. Remember that the role of the conveyor of information plays an important part in determining how information is presented and ultimately received. Here it is possible to identify exactly *who*—an individual, group, or all members of the organization—is accountable for or otherwise involved in the selection, endorsement, establishment, and maintenance of various communication processes vis-à-vis the survey effort. Issues here include

Who should write the cover letter and memos announcing the survey initiative and its intent?

Who should be available (for example, internal HR staff or independent external consultants) for calls and questions regarding the instrument during its administration?

Who should provide the initial and follow-up reporting of results to individual unit heads in the organization?

An important assumption of the CPR model is that in order to understand organizational communication fully you must examine the nature of the actors (or the roles that they inhabit), as well as the processes and the content of the situation. Of course, the focal point for these roles is determined first by the content of the information itself, and only then in relation to methods of its dissemination in the organization.

For example, to understand how a survey effort aimed at conveying information about a company's newly constructed mission and vision should be conducted, first become familiar with all the key messages that need to be communicated to employees regarding this mission and its importance to the organization. Next, the specific vehicles for delivering this message should be in alignment with prior communications regarding the mission and vision. For example, if a corporate news video was produced for the new mission and vision, it is probably appropriate to link the survey announcement with that same channel of distribution. Then the key players, in this case the most senior leaders of the organization, need to be included in the communication plan as well. However, a survey effort designed simply to assess people's opinion regarding the desirability of various possible options for a new personnel benefit program is probably best handled by HR staff in conjunction with senior HR sponsorship and through more direct lines of communication with people.

First Contact with Employees

With a firmer understanding of the basic aspects of organizational communication, we can now move to the process of first contact. As we discussed in Step One, the first action in creating a successful survey effort is to generate clear, well-defined, achievable, and measurable objectives. Once these elements have been put in place, and the content of the survey itself has been identified and delineated in the form of concrete questions, the people who will ultimately be responsible for providing the data must be brought up to speed as well.

This is achieved first through some form of initial communication and then followed up through the administration of the actual survey instrument itself. If the objectives of the effort are unclear to the practitioners or the survey sponsor, they cannot be communicated to others. Rest assured, employees will know if a survey is being pushed on them without a clear purpose. Even in cases where there appears to be a relatively simple assessment plan for those initiating the survey effort, it is likely that other players in the organization will still want more detail regarding intended objectives and desired outcomes. In today's competitive and overworked business environment, time is a precious commodity, and a survey effort had better have a justifiable reason for infringing on people's time. For example, in many discussions with survey planning groups in organizations, the question is often raised as to whether or not employees will be irritated by the additional time required (typically only forty minutes to an hour) to complete a questionnaire. Thus, as we discussed in previous steps, gaining clarity of the content and purpose is crucial for obtaining support from employees.

Assuming that the goals of the effort have been well defined, however, let us start to outline a typical survey communication process. We begin with the initial exposure to the concept of the assessment initiative. People need to be informed that the survey is forthcoming well in advance of receiving the instrument. They need time to reflect on the importance of the survey and its relevance to their day-to-day experience. They also need to be clear about why the survey process has been initiated and *what to expect* from their contribution. If a survey is simply distributed without warning (for example, dropped on people's desks one morning), the initial reaction is likely to be one of suspicion or frustration, as in the examples described earlier, rather than interest and excitement. In the absence of knowledge, the assumption is often that "senior management must be hiding something; otherwise they would have let us know this was coming." Although it is not always possible to predict employees' reactions to the idea of doing a survey, even with a carefully orchestrated communication effort, strong negative responses are particularly likely in organizations where fear and mistrust are rife— a common situation in organizations that have experienced downsizing and related staff-reduction plans. Employees, or others to whom the instrument is to be distributed, should be well informed in advance about the survey process and its intent.

The process for conducting this initial communication can be facilitated in many different ways. Some of these include corporate videos, newsletters, glossy pamphlets, booklets, electronic documents posted on intranets and Web sites, e-mails, letters and memos, town meetings, formal announcements at other gatherings such as "all hands-on" management meetings, and postings on bulletin boards. Each format or method of delivering information to employees has its associated positives and negatives. Table 3.1 provides an overview of the differences among four commonly used modes of communicating survey messages.

The best option for any given organization probably depends on the type and style of communication that is currently in place. For example, in an organization where the company newsletter or news-

Table 3.1. Differences in Communication Methods.

Organizationwide Processes	Individualized Processes	Video or Newsletter	Intranet or Web, Letter, E-mail
group approach	group approach	personal approach	personal approach
standardized	standardized	customizable	customizable
formal	formal	formal	variable formality
flexible amount of detail	flexible amount of detail	requires more detail	requires more detail
high cost	variable cost	moderate cost	low cost
variable reach	variable reach	full reach	variable reach
high political factor	high political factor	moderate political factor	moderate political factor
delayed speed of recovery	variable speed of delivery	delayed speed of delivery	quick delivery
no direct reply	direct reply option	no direct reply	direct reply option
complex effort	variable effort	moderate effort	variable effort

Note: Level of complexity of content and process (for example, video feed, interactivity, degree of personalization, number of different versions of message, degree of electronic connectivity) will affect each method.

paper is a widely read and appreciated vehicle, it might be appropriate to run a full feature article on the upcoming survey effort. In these circumstances, information such as the origins of the initiative, the intended objectives, the intended timeframe (from administration through to the delivery of results and action planning), issues of confidentiality (who will get to see the data and in how much detail), and the content and types of issues need to be assessed. Of course, this means that the timing of this communication may have to be coordinated with the existing publication and production schedules of the in-house newspaper system, unless a special edition is pursued.

Other organizations, both large and small, prefer using a formal letter from the CEO, the head of human resources, or some similarly high-placed senior manager (the champion of the survey effort) to convey the intent of the survey effort. These more formal letters or memos cover the same issues but in a more direct one-to-one exchange with each employee (particularly if mailed to their home address rather than through internal mail at work). Unless the company is very small or very informal, a letter addressed to each employee from the CEO regarding the survey effort can be a powerful form of communication.

Still other companies have used corporatewide e-mail, Web-based and related electronic media announcements, small postcards with a survey or other corporate-initiative-related logos and slogans, or internal television programming as means of conveying their message. Smaller organizations often rely on word of mouth or direct contact with senior individuals on site. How communication is accomplished depends on the nature of the organization and the types of processes and roles that make up its total communication system. For example, although it may seem as though every employee in every organization today has access to e-mail, making it the perfect communication method for survey work (not to mention survey administration—see Chapter Four), the fact is that many companies have yet to embrace the information age. Although the headquarters of most larger firms is likely to be fully "connected," in certain types of industries (for example, many types of retail) intranet connections are limited at the individual location or unit levels (specific stores, branches, and affiliate locations). We came across just this situation recently when working on a census survey based on eighty thousand employees in a well-known and respected national grocery store chain. When questioning corporate HR representatives regarding e-mail communication (and potential on-line survey administration), we learned that, despite interest in this approach, none of the stores were linked at that level except for the inventory and pricing applications being used. Employees did not have their own e-mail accounts, let alone computers; in some cases no personal computers existed at the location. Although there were plans to install machines in the coming years, it would be some time before this process would be ready for full-scale and individualized communications to employees. Thus, a traditional paper-mailing process was used. Moreover, even if a company is fully connected (or e-mail enabled, so to speak) the reality is that many executives and some middle managers still have their administrative assistants print out their e-mails for them to read and respond to in writing! In years to come, as the workforce continues to shift in demographic composition and in skills and electronic communication becomes dominant in our society, this situation will likely change. Everyone will be fully connected. For now, however, it is important to assess the current communication process and match the level of access appropriately.

Communicating the Survey

Once the initial contact regarding the survey effort has been made, employees are left waiting for the final product—the survey itself. Some time is needed between the first message and the survey administration in order to soften the impact and initial resistance to the assessment process, but this delay often leads to increased anxiety and apprehension on the part of employees. They begin to doubt the messages originally provided, particularly in organizations where trust is lacking. Therefore, regardless of the resting state of the organization, it is necessary to have a strong, well-defined second level of communication provided with the survey instrument. Often this takes the form of a cover letter from senior management or an introductory section to the instrument that delineates to the user once again the key messages of the survey. The survey's purpose, item coverage, and, above all else at this stage, the confidentiality of the data to be obtained should be described.

People want and need to know what the survey effort is all about. They do not need to know the details of survey construction or of the vendor selection process or why certain individuals are supporting the survey and others are not. It is extremely important to provide information about the general intentions of the survey effort; however, the quality and level of detail must be tempered to meet the needs of the specific audience. If a full feature story is being produced about the assessment project in the company newspaper or internal corporate Web site, then more detailed information can probably be provided. The cover letter and survey instructions need to be accurate and complete but not overly complex or inscrutable. The idea here is to let respondents know why the survey is in their hands, why it is important to their day-to-day jobs, why they should participate, and what will happen afterward. Too little information fails to provide key messages; too much detail can obscure them. Figure 3.2 gives an overview of this dynamic.

Figure 3.2. Balancing the Right Amount of Information.

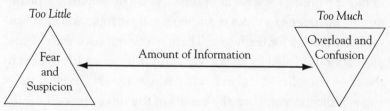

It may seem relatively straightforward to compose a simple cover letter for a survey; however, a number of subtle issues should be addressed in order to ensure that the messages have been communicated clearly and effectively. The decision to include a cover letter from a senior official in the organization can be an important one, particularly if the use of surveys is either new or has a negative history in the organization. Having the effort endorsed by the board of directors, a new CEO, or the head of HR sends a clear signal to respondents that someone important is behind the initiative and has taken the time and effort to encourage people to respond. Your internal client may want to be the one to write and sign the cover letter, but this person may not be the most appropriate figurehead for gathering support for and commitment to the effort. This can become a political issue, as people's private agendas are likely to become involved in some level of the planning effort (as discussed in Step One). Nevertheless the survey effort must receive appropriate sponsorship and credibility from a recognized, senior source in the organization. Exhibit 3.1 provides a sample cover letter from a recent survey effort, written by the CEO of a multinational corporation, that was mailed to the entire management staff (approximately 4,800 individuals).

If we look closely at the letter, it does indeed cover many of the issues and topics discussed. For example, there is a clear reference to existing organizational initiatives and progress already made to date (the word *promise* was capitalized to reflect another corporatewide program). The survey is then positioned as a part of this ongoing process and as a tool for building a better company. Notice there is no hint of negative consequences (for example, downsizing or finger pointing) as a result of the survey. The emphasis is on obtaining management views regarding a specific topic and establishing a benchmark for the future. There is a reference to the external protection provided by an outside consulting firm with respect to the confidentiality of the individual survey results. There is also a vague indication of when the results of the survey process can be

Exhibit 3.1. Sample Survey Cover Letter from a CEO.

Dear Survey Respondent,

In the past two years, we've come a long way toward fulfilling the promise of our organization. Yet, much needs to be done. As a member of Company XYZ management, you share a strong interest in and deserve much of the credit for the success of our continuing efforts in building a better company.

This survey is another tool in those efforts. Its purposes are (1) to obtain your views on "how we are doing" at Company XYZ in such key areas as leadership, teamwork, job satisfaction, overall effectiveness and others, and (2) to establish a data "benchmark" so that we will be able to compare how we are doing over time. In short, I believe this kind of information will allow us to make the continuous improvements so important to our ongoing business.

Be assured that all responses will be summarized by an outside contractor, and individuals will remain completely anonymous. Both results and separate business reports will be available later in the year.

Please complete and return your questionnaire in the enclosed envelope, or as directed by your General Manager. Thank you for your prompt and thoughtful response.

Sincerely,

Ure Leeder
Chief Executive Officer

---

expected and in what forms. This information could just as easily be woven into the introductory pages of a survey (see Exhibit 3.2 for an example of this type of approach), but the impact of having it presented in a stand-alone memo from the CEO was enough to generate significantly better than expected returns (73 percent of all

Exhibit 3.2. Sample Survey Cover Letter from
a Unit or Department Head.

Dear Colleague,

Here is the questionnaire for the 1996/97 staff survey. As with the first survey in 1995, we want to know your views on the future direction of Company XYZ, the way that it is managed, and how you feel about many aspects of your job and working environment.

The questionnaire should take about 50 minutes to complete. I have asked your managers to give you a chance to complete this questionnaire during work time. We want you to be frank and honest about your opinions, and in return we guarantee complete confidentiality. No one in Company XYZ will see your responses, and the way the results are reported will prevent anyone's responses from being identified.

In addition, each member of the management team will be given the results for their own department. This will help them consider what their staff have strong views about and where improvements can be made. This means that your views count for your department and the unit, as well as for Company XYZ as a whole, and you will be able to see the results at each of these levels.

I will act on the 1996/97 staff survey results. Between March and April your manager will discuss the department results with you and decide how each department will deal with the issues raised. The unit management team will then decide what we should be tackling throughout the entire unit. I will then take some of your suggestions to the senior management board. Later, when the companywide results are published, you will hear the board's response and their plans for the whole organization.

Everyone who works at Company XYZ can contribute, directly or indirectly, to making an excellent product. Becoming a better-managed organization is central to this. Please help us make this happen in our business unit and the organization as a whole by filling in the questionnaire. Your views are important, and your help is appreciated.

Thank You,

Linus Q. Managere
Unit Head

management) for this first survey effort in this organization. Given the high degree of uncertainty in the company, due largely to a recent merger, the level of involvement in and commitment to the survey was indeed a positive surprise.

Sometimes the letter accompanying a survey effort can be very effective when it comes from the local-level senior manager, that is, the person with line authority over a business unit. In more decentralized organizations, such as the one from which the sample in Exhibit 3.2 originates, if the individual in that position presents a strong and visible image, the key messages regarding the survey effort can be even more effective coming from this source.

The similarities between this cover letter and the one from the CEO presented in Exhibit 3.1 are obvious, but there are also clear differences. Most notably, because of the more direct nature of this individual's position in the business unit, he or she was able to make much more specific commitments to employees regarding the timing and outcomes of the survey. The letter is clear in its message that this survey is important enough to warrant time spent on its completion by employees during work hours—an issue that is often hotly debated in the planning phase and one that many organizations are not willing to commit to upholding (even if it has been agreed to in policy).

Exhibit 3.3 is yet another example of introductory survey communication—this time a statement of purpose—taken from an instrument used in a large financial organization.

This message to all respondents represents the output of several focus group sessions designed to set the key objectives of the survey, as well as planning meetings with the survey development team and our client. Compared with the letters from the CEO and unit head presented earlier, this sample includes (1) more detail regarding the nature of the item formats and layout and (2) a greater emphasis on the confidentiality of the data and what will happen to raw responses after they have been tallied but (3) is less well crafted with respect to conveying key messages about the survey's intent and likely outcomes.

Exhibit 3.3. Sample Survey Introduction.

This survey is intended to establish a baseline measurement for determining our progress toward our strategic plan. It will also serve as a starting point for making improvements to our business. Your participation in the survey is very important, so please take the time to complete it.

The questions in the survey concern your business unit as well as the entire organization. The questions cover many aspects of the organization and are intended to measure progress in key areas of performance, leadership, customer service, and employee satisfaction.

With the exception of the write-in comments included at the end, please answer all questions on the Response Form provided. The questionnaire form has a total of one hundred questions for you to complete.

Each question is rated on a 5-point scale, with 1 and 5 reflecting the opposite ends of the scale. Please consider the full range between 1 and 5 in making your response. Each statement should be answered according to your own experience and opinion, and should reflect your perception of present overall conditions.

Space is provided at the end of the survey for any comments you may have. These comments will be transcribed and grouped with others according to common themes as a part of the survey results analysis.

An external firm will process these questionnaires. *Your individual responses will not be released to anyone in Company XYZ.* This survey is completely confidential. After scoring, your answer sheet and write-in commentary sheet will be destroyed.

Survey results will be communicated to senior management and then immediately reported to all employees in a special edition of the company's newsletter. Then senior executives and business unit heads will integrate this information into their yearly action plans. You will have the opportunity to discuss the survey results with your manager and business unit head.

When you have completed the questionnaire, seal your Response Form and write-in comments page in the return envelope provided. If you have any questions regarding the completion of the survey, please contact the external firm at (999) 999–9999.

Guidelines for Communicating to Employees

Now that we have covered the two types of preparatory communications related to a survey effort, we shall summarize briefly the specific types of information that need to be covered. Several simple guidelines exist with respect to communicating to employees about a survey effort. Most of these have been alluded to, but they are important enough to reiterate more specifically here:

- Provide an adequate amount of advance notice regarding the survey effort as well as at the time of its administration.

- Provide as much information as possible concerning the survey effort without overloading people with excessive detail.

- Convey the key messages involved clearly and effectively.

- Use multiple methods and processes to reinforce the same messages (for example, a letter from senior management, reminders in the company newsletter, e-mail teasers, internal Web site articles, pop-up messages, or postcard reminders).

- Convey honesty and openness; surveys are a participative, voluntary data gathering process, not a mandated directive.

- Highlight the sponsorship, roles, and various levels of participation in the survey among key organization members.

- Involve the highest and most credible level of formal support available for a given group (for example, the CEO for an entire organization, the unit head for an entire function).

- Make a commitment to action as a result of the survey and to a time it can be expected.

People need to know as much as possible about the survey effort so they can take it seriously and understand its relationship to their everyday work life. Otherwise they will see the whole process as just another boring assessment effort that will have no impact and is therefore not worth participating in. Even worse, they could see it as an unknown and highly feared instrument; in that case, people will alter their responses in attempts to second-guess its true purpose.

Some practitioners do try to hide key information (for example, regarding objectives) either because they think employees will not understand the effort or they have some agenda that they (1) do not want to be made public or (2) do not want to commit to fully unless certain conditions are met. For example, in one survey initiative in which we were involved, we were working closely with our client in HR to develop the survey instrument. In fact, we were very close to putting the finishing touches to it when, seemingly out of the blue, we heard from our client that a member of the CEO's staff wanted to meet with us regarding the survey. We were informed, to our amazement, that this individual had been totally unaware of the survey effort and its intent, and subsequently did not agree with many of the decisions that our client had already made and begun to implement. HR had decided to survey employees without checking first with the rest of senior management, let alone procuring their involvement. Needless to say, this presented us with some significant resistance, and we had to work on relationship management (as well as contract readjustment) before the survey effort could move forward.

Organizations that find it difficult to openly communicate key messages to their employees are often likely to have related issues emerge during the survey implementation and feedback process as well. These are often the same projects, for example, in which issues of confidentiality and mistrust are raised later, after data have been collected. Because it is not always possible to identify these situations before they occur, it is best to get the survey sponsor to publicly identify his or her goals and stance regarding the confidentiality of data. As with the idea of generating measurable objectives, by having the sponsor state his or her position on issues of data confidentiality and use, the organization can later support the integrity of the effort beyond just the practitioner's personal ethics. However, this is often a risky proposition because it amounts to getting the client to agree to make a very public commitment to his or her intended approach. It is also, of course, one of the few ways to ensure honesty and follow-through amid a sea of political pressures and demands that are often issued after the initial presentation of results (more on this issue in Steps Five and Six).

Recognizing Informal Systems

Prior to the next stage of the survey process—the administration—we need to say a few words about the power and potential impact of informal methods of communication during a survey effort. To understand and make good use of the formal means of communication in an organization is important. However, the role of the informal processes must also be recognized; they can have a significant effect on any type of initiative, particularly if they are used extensively as a means of communicating among employees. For example, in a company where fear and distrust of management is strong, messages transmitted by word of mouth can damage the entire survey process, regardless of whether or not those messages are correct.

But is this a problem? How much do employees rely on informal as opposed to formal modes of communicating anyway? The answers to these questions most certainly lie in the specific configuration of the organization in question, but we do have data that speak to this issue. Let us take an example. In a recent survey effort designed to measure corporate culture conducted in a large, publicly funded organization in the United Kingdom, the internal corporate communications group asked us to include a relatively comprehensive section in the survey instrument regarding the extent to which different communication processes or mechanisms provided information to employees. Figure 3.3 shows a display of the results of this question based on responses from approximately 4,500 employees across all levels of management.

Despite the hard work and good intentions of the communication staff, it was apparent that employees in this organization relied most heavily on the grapevine for their information about what was going on in the organization. The next best source for these employees was the external coverage of their organization by the media (not unexpected in this organizational setting, given the nature of their busi-

Figure 3.3. Effectiveness of Various Communication Mechanisms in XYZ.

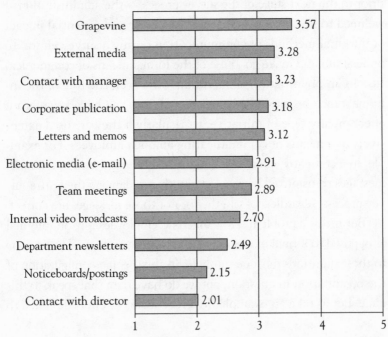

ness and their high degree of visibility to the public), followed by discussions with their immediate manager or supervisor. Corporate publications, letters and memos, and e-mail, all of which were discussed earlier as potential outlets for formal survey-related communications, were only moderately effective (above a 3.0 on the rating scale) and by no means the most frequently relied on source. In this organization the informal methods were just as important, if not more so, as the formal ones for providing information. Not surprisingly, as a result of these findings, changing employees' perceptions of the relevance, timeliness, and importance of corporate communications became one of the initiatives of the communications function.

These types of informal methods of exchange will always exist in organizations. They cannot be removed or diverted. All practitioners can do is (1) try to enhance the perceptions of the formal internal communication process or (2) try to find ways to use the informal mechanisms to one's advantage to reinforce the appropriate messages regarding various development and improvement efforts. Once again, we recommend using several parallel messages regarding a survey effort wherever possible. It is important to remember that the messages communicated during a survey process reflect and reinforce people's perceptions of the quality, importance, relevance, and meaningfulness of the entire intervention or corporate initiative to which it has been linked. Therefore, extreme care is required when preparing and planning for a survey effort.

Checklist for Step Three

1. Remember the CPR model of organizational communication.
   - Determine *what* will be communicated (content).
   - Determine *how* it will be communicated (processes).
   - Determine *who* will do the communicating (roles).

2. Communicate with employees beforehand.
   - Generate clear, well-defined, achievable, and measurable objectives well in advance of the survey.

- Consider the positives and negatives associated with different modes of communication (for example, letters to employees, e-mails, videos, Web notices).
- Follow up with the administration of the survey instrument.

3. Consider the following guidelines for effective communication:
   - Provide an adequate amount of advance notice regarding the survey effort.
   - Give as much information as possible without overloading people with excessive detail.
   - Convey the key messages involved clearly and effectively.
   - Use multiple methods and processes to reinforce the same messages.
   - Convey honesty and openness in approach.
   - Highlight sponsorship and roles among key organizational members.
   - Involve the highest and most credible level of formal support available.
   - Make a commitment to action as a result of the survey and when it can be expected.

4. Consider the impact of informal systems.

4

Step Four: Administering the Survey

I have the consolation to reflect that during the period of my administration not a drop of the blood of a single fellow citizen was shed.

Thomas Jefferson

Prior to the administration process, the task of designing an effective survey has primarily been a cognitive one, full of planning, building interest and commitment, generating items that reflect key issues in the organization, and all the other elements that have been discussed to date. Now comes the legwork—the actual job of producing and distributing (or making available electronically) the assessment tool and gathering the responses for analysis. For some practitioners and in some settings, this is the easy part. Just send out the surveys and wait for them to come back. In other organizations, however, this can be an extremely laborious, tedious, and overly complex task.

But sometimes it can prove to be informative, particularly when the channels of distribution may not be as well known by the HR functions as previously thought. We have seen a surprising number of survey efforts in which, as a result of the administration planning of the survey, the internal staff were unable to identify fully the entire organizational structure. This may seem odd, but in large organizations, particularly those undergoing restructuring, it is common to find isolated units and functions that, after the survey effort is fully under way, are not included in the initial roll-out plan.

In most situations the administration of the survey is not the most important element to the success of the overall initiative; the attention to detail and level of complexity involved can play a crucial role in managing the quality and depth of the data collected, as well as the entire image of the survey effort. The purpose of this step is to explore the issues involved in the survey administration process. Topics discussed include the key elements of survey timing, project planning, the pros and cons of various methods of administration and data collection, what to expect regarding response rates, and how to use feedback from the process in real time to improve the survey effort.

Timing of Administration

One of the first questions asked about survey administration is, When is the best time to survey people? Whenever organizations are embarking on a survey effort, it never seems to be the *right* time. Common reasons or excuses for this include "We've just reorganized," "We're just about to reorganize," "We've just employed a new CEO," "This is our busiest time," and "We are doing budgeting now." The issue here, of course, is one of the anticipated reach of the survey effort (that is, how many employees will receive the survey instrument and have enough time to complete it), and the resulting quantity and quality of the responses that are likely to be obtained.

Timing is always a tough issue, yet there are definite windows of opportunity for each stage in the process, and some times are better and worse than others. July and August, December and January, for example, are typically poor survey months because of holiday schedules. People are not available to complete and return the instrument. Early spring (March or April) and early autumn tend to be more successful times with respect to response rates and levels of receptivity. The only significant exception is accounting or tax firms; autumn is the best time for them.

In general, the optimal amount of time to leave a survey open for responses is somewhere between one and two months. Although some practitioners and organizations are enamored with the possibility of using various electronic methods to ensure rapid (even overnight) administration, the feasibility of such approaches, particularly for large-scale surveys with lengthy and detailed instrumentation, is questionable. Although this type of quick-hit process can easily be done with very focused questionnaires using small, intact units where access is high, it can be highly problematic (both in terms of IT-related resources and expected response rates) to expect enormous numbers of employees to gain access to the same server in a single day or even a single week. Between competing priorities, travel, training, sick time, vacation, and issues of connectivity with remote locations (and even nonremote ones), a more realistic timeframe of a month or even two will result in more people responding. Of course, such an approach is necessary in the case of certain types of on-site administrations, as will be described later. In any case, the addition of extra time affords greater opportunities for follow-up contact and repeated mailings or corrective action to on-line response systems, not to mention time for the inevitable procrastinators and others who are simply not motivated to respond.

For example, let's say a survey is successfully launched in May and early June. In this instance, July and August would be used primarily for the data analysis phase, with an expected presentation roll-out in early September, assuming that a more immediate timeframe is not required for some reason. In any case, the survey administration should be planned so that respondents feel that they have adequate time to complete and return the instrument. Similarly, the amount of time between the closing date for returns and the subsequent presentation of results must also be managed—the smaller this window the better (more on this topic in Steps Five and Six). Always keep in mind, though, the survey objectives and linkages among the data collection effort itself and concurrent initiatives or processes occurring in the organization (for example, annual budgeting, performance appraisals, training and development opportunities, pending changes in management positions, reengineering efforts, formal structural relationships, or the launch of a formal culture change campaign). When the results of a survey effort are intended to be tied to one of these types of existing process, it is important that the data be collected, analyzed, and reported back in time for its effective use. If a survey effort is intended to provide input into the annual performance management system of managers in various business units regarding managerial strengths and areas for improvement, for example, the data can be rendered useless if the survey results are not complete and in recipients' hands in time for the planning process. Timing decisions should be based in part on obtaining the best quantity and quality of responses possible, and administration dates must be made with a clear set of goals and targets in mind.

Working with the Project Plan

A point we have tried to make clear throughout this book is the importance of having well-defined goals and objectives for any type of organizational survey effort. Goals and objectives help lead the practitioner through many of the early stages of survey design and into the analysis and action planning portions of the project. Just as these goals and objectives drive the entire survey process, there is a need for a clear, comprehensive, and reasonable plan for the survey administration phase as well. In this case, however, rather than undertaking a series of more strategic objectives as outlined in Step One, the plan must be specific and detailed with respect to the following key elements:

- When the survey will be launched and when it will be closed
- The method by which the survey instrument is to be completed
- The respondents to whom the instruments are being distributed

- The means by which the instruments are going to be distributed

- The length of time respondents will have to complete and return the instrument

- The timing and types of additional information regarding the survey

The survey administration plan also provides an opportunity to clarify the specific roles and responsibilities of each of the parties involved in the process. This includes everything from who does the printing and survey-packet mailing (or who develops and launches an on-line survey process), to how the response tracking procedure will be conducted, to the number of times the survey sponsor will receive updates. Table 4.1 provides a sample survey administration plan for a 3,500 census paper-based mail survey. This script could, of course, be easily modified for an on-line capture session.

One of the first rules of thumb when preparing a survey administration plan is to realize that you cannot plan for everything. Always expect the unexpected. Slack or extra time should be built into the project timing so that last-minute adjustments can be made. The sample plan in Table 4.1 does not specifically provide additional time, but because the timing is not tied to specific dates, the entire process can be moved if necessary (for example, if the printing process takes longer than expected). Other options might include making the survey-packet printing and preparation steps longer or perhaps including more time for the open administration period. The same issues can be applied to other forms of administration. For example, if survey data are to be collected via an on-line, Web-based application and a new capture process is being developed, it is always a good idea to build in additional time for potential design or software-related problems.

The survey administration plan needs to be relatively specific and clear, but it must always have some maneuverability inherent in its design as well. Someone else must often be involved in the survey approval or communication process at the last minute, or

Table 4.1. Sample Survey Administration Plan.

Task	Provider (Role)	Timing
Survey-packet printing and preparation	Printing vendor	3 weeks
• Print 3,500 survey instruments		
• Insert 3,500 inner return envelopes with address preprinted	Printing vendor	
• Print 3,500 optical scan response-answer sheets	Scanning vendor	
• Acquire 3,500 generic outer mailing envelopes	Stationery supplier	
• Provide employee home mailing address labels	HR staff	
Survey-packet assembly and external mailing		1 week
• Create 3,500 survey packets	Mailing vendor	
• Attach mailing labels	Mailing vendor	
• Frank outer envelopes, sort by postal code, distribute	Mailing vendor	
Internal administration option		1 week
• Assemble 500 additional packets without labels	Mailing vendor	
• Determine additional numbers and channels needed	HR staff	
• Distribute to internal staff as needed	Survey representatives	
Open response period		4 weeks
• Track and receive responses and optically scan to data file	Survey practitioner	
• Monitor response rates (daily)	Survey practitioner	
• Provide updates regarding response rates (weekly)	Survey practitioner	
• Compare incoming data to population data	Survey practitioner and HR staff	
• Conduct general follow-up	HR staff	
• Conduct specific follow-up with nonrespondents	HR staff	

some additional change needs to be made to the instrument, cover letter, Web-page instructions, or some other element. For example, we have seen a number of large-scale survey efforts in which, only days from administration, instruments have suddenly been pulled from production to be reexamined or reworked. Occasionally surveys are halted by some powerful group in the organization that had not been included or represented in the design process. This type of last-minute intervention can be extremely problematic from a production standpoint, as well as potentially damaging to the credibility and subsequent reliability of the survey effort. Consider, for example, a survey where the launch date has already been communicated to employees and then the survey is held for a few extra weeks. These kinds of problems can often be avoided with careful work at the start of the project and if enough time is allotted to the testing and development of instruments. But this is one of the reasons we have stressed the importance of involving the appropriate individuals in the survey design process in Steps One to Three.

Related to this issue is a simple rule of thumb regarding the use of administration dates. Although the initial release date should be well communicated, the closing date for survey returns should be used (printed) sparingly throughout various documents and supporting materials so that if they do indeed change, as is often the case, there is less rework involved. For example, if you go ahead and print four thousand copies of a custom survey return envelope with the closing date on the outside, and the survey is held up for any reason, the closing date will probably need to be shifted back, making the envelopes useless. Although intranet survey applications might be better suited for correcting these types of date and text-based issues, if the Web site or the server on which it resides is not ready at the official start time as communicated, the first round of employees who try to respond on-line will likely be frustrated at the errors and "refused access" messages they receive. Although these types of errors are common in organizations and are not very costly in the scheme of things, in this age of continuous improvement and better, faster, cheaper, it is better to avoid these kinds of wasteful and frustrating occurrences whenever possible.

Sample Versus Census

One of the key decisions in the survey administration process, besides the issue of timing, is the nature of the respondent group. We alluded to this issue in Step One; indeed there should be some consideration of this in the survey plan. But in the administration phase this issue must be resolved because it can affect both the overall size of the survey effort and the best means of distribution. More specifically, in survey work a choice must always be made at some point before roll-out between conducting the survey using some sort of sample of employees or collecting data from the entire organization in a census effort. Both methods can suffer from some problems and biases, as mentioned earlier with respect to instrument design and communication issues; however, there are more specific pros and cons for each of these approaches. Table 4.2 provides a summary of the differences in assumptions and possible outcomes.

Table 4.2. Sample Versus Census: A Comparison.

Sample	Census
• Smaller and easier to administer	• Larger and more complex to administer
• Less costly	• More costly
• Provides representative responses	• Provides complete responses
• Involves only certain employees	• Involves all employees
• Potential for sampling biases	• No sampling biases
• Easier to work with data	• More difficult to work with data
• Data analysis can be more limited	• Provides for greater depth in analyses
• Not appropriate for smaller organizations	• Should be used in smaller organizations

For the most part, the decision regarding a sample or census comes down to issues of cost and the complexity of the administration process. Sample surveys are easier and cheaper to conduct. In an organization where there is a shortage of time, money, and staff, for example, a sample survey is often the only option; they are particularly useful when used between larger census administrations, for example, as an interim assessment of improvement in a given area. Where the survey effort is fully supported by senior management and is part of the fabric of a much larger organization development and change initiative, a full-scale, all-employee census is probably preferred. If one of the objectives of the survey process is to communicate some new set of corporate values or behaviors to employees, pursuing the census option is necessary as well. In such situations, the use of a sampling process is likely to result in (1) the dilution of the messages being communicated, (2) a decrease in employee commitment and perceived value of the survey effort, (3) concerns regarding who was and was not included in the sample identified, and (4) why (Paul and Bracken, 1995). Some practitioners have gone so far as to advocate against the use of sampling (for example, Breisch, 1996), but this is often not practical from either a time or financial standpoint, particularly in large organizations (ten thousand employees or more).

For these same reasons, sample surveys are popular in industry today. If the sampling process is done correctly, the data provided can be just as valid and reliable as those provided by a census. Conversely, a bad sampling process can introduce such significant biases as to at least skew the data in some specific direction, and at worst render the survey data totally useless. Thus, if a sample is warranted or required, the survey practitioner must have a firm understanding of sampling theory and all that is involved.

This information is beyond the scope of this book, so we refer the interested reader to the following sources on sampling issues and construction: Frankel, 1983; Rea and Parker, 1997; Schuman and Kalton, 1985; Sudman, 1983. However, the primary concern in sampling is one of representation, that is, does the sample used adequately reflect the demographic, functional, and even dispositional makeup of the total population of interest? As the interested reader will see, a number of methods and approaches for generating samples indeed meet this criteria.

Except for the potential for additional bias and the fact that fewer people are involved in the assessment process, the only other significant limitation of a sample survey is an inability to provide more detailed cuts and analyses of the data, based on the full range of demographic variables. A sample survey can provide an equally accurate snapshot of the total organization, and perhaps even some of its larger functions or regions; but even with a 90 percent response rate, the sample will begin to fall short in representing smaller groups as the number of data points is decreased. A full census is limited in this regard only by the response rate. Because all employees were included, the potential is there to analyze the data and look for trends at the absolute lowest level (assuming that the confidentiality of responses remains protected—an issue we discuss in Steps Five and Six as well).

Methods of Administration and Data Collection

Another decision to be made in the survey administration process is the primary method or type of administration desired. There are a host of different options, depending on the needs and objectives of the survey effort. Moreover, new forms and approaches to data collection continue to parallel advances in information technology, which can make choosing a method somewhat confusing. Fortunately, these choices are not mutually exclusive; practitioners often employ more than one at a time (as in our example in Table 4.1). This range of administration methods can be described as varying along two primary dimensions: (1) the means of administration and (2) the means of data collection.

Regarding the method of administration, there are two options for the practitioner: (1) distribute the instrument individually to respondents to complete on their own, or (2) have them respond collectively in some form of orchestrated groups sessions. Individual methods are by far more popular in practice than collective assessments but, as with all choices in the survey process, each method has its strengths and weaknesses. Table 4.3 provides an overview of the basic differences in these two approaches.

Table 4.3. Methods of Survey Administration.

Individual	Collective
For example, individual survey questionnaires distributed to employees' e-mail accounts, or paper versions mailed to employees' home addresses with return postage paid envelopes preprinted with an external collection source	For example, on-site survey "capture sessions" offered multiple times a day in different locations and across several weeks with independent proctors and either secure data collection receptacles, such as locked drop bags in a central location, or multiple stations for on-line survey completion (for example, intranet, disk, or Web-based) tools
• Greater privacy for respondent	• Less privacy for respondent
• Autonomy as to when and where to respond	• Fixed choices as to when and where to respond
• Individual choice to respond or not	• Individual can be required to attend session
• Response rates more affected by idiosyncrasies	• Response rates less affected by idiosyncrasies
• Response less susceptible to intentional biases	• Responses more susceptible to intentional biases
• Fewer staff required to administer	• Staff-intensive and costly to administer
• Responses returned via mail or e-mail over time	• Responses collected immediately
• Highest level of confidentiality when used with outside source to collect data	• Potential for reduced levels of perceived confidentiality when collected on-site

A review of Table 4.3 should make it evident why individual methods are preferred over collective ones. On-site survey administration tends to be a more expensive, complex, and time-consuming process than individual methods. The on-site, group-based survey sessions can have the benefit of (1) enhancing response rates by requiring individuals to attend during working hours and (2) sending a good message regarding the level of commitment from management to the survey effort. But these positives can also backfire. For example, with an on-site administration method there is still no way to ensure that respondents feel secure about the confidentiality of their responses; they are being watched while they respond, which means there is more potential for bias and for response effects. In addition, despite the positive corporate survey messages about taking time during business hours to complete the survey, individual managers do not always agree with this policy (their people are missing work, after all) and can sometimes sabotage the message completely. Individual methods, regardless of the method of data collection, place a greater degree of trust in the respondent to complete and return the instrument. This can lead to lower-than-desirable response rates in organizations where the importance of the survey effort has not been clearly communicated or established.

If an on-site plan is required, the logistics of the administration process must be clear and well defined to ensure an adequate level of response options for employees. Table 4.4 provides a sample schedule for this type of on-site survey administration.

Note that in Table 4.4 the list of survey sessions was designed to provide optimal exposure at the same locations across different days and times. Even in this relatively simple example, the number of permutations is significant. In addition to these variables, another consideration here was the administrator or survey proctor, who was assigned to work at each of the settings. This individual needed to be appropriately prepared. For example, if a bank of data-entry terminals are to be used for an intranet-based collection method, the survey proctor should be well equipped to answer technical ques-

Table 4.4. Sample On-Site Survey Administration Plan.

Location	Date	Time	Administrator
First Ave.	10-June	9:00–10:00 A.M.	1
Second Ave.	10-June	11:30–12:30 P.M.	2
Third Ave.	10-June	2:00–3:00 P.M.	3
Second Ave.	11-June	9:00–10:00 A.M.	1
Third Ave.	11-June	11:30–12:30 P.M.	2
First Ave.	11-June	2:00–3:00 P.M.	3
Third Ave.	12-June	9:00–10:00 A.M.	1
First Ave.	12-June	11:30–12:30 P.M.	2
Second Ave.	12-June	2:00–3:00 P.M.	3

tions from respondents regarding the workings of the software, as well as the content of the survey instrument. Moreover, this person's personality and appearance can have an impact on the nature and quality of the data collected, so varying the person across settings is also a consideration. That way, the survey data can be examined for effects or biases that may be attributable to the individual's instructions or mannerisms. Of course, one way to minimize the impact of individual differences is to have a clear and consistent script for the on-site survey administrator. Exhibit 4.1 provides a sample script of this type, used with a paper-based survey effort.

The script in the exhibit covers many of the key issues required of the survey communication process that we discussed in Step Three, including the purpose and objectives of the survey, some background and context regarding the larger change effort of which it is a part, the specific format of the items and response forms included, how the confidentiality of the data is to be handled, and who will have access to the individual responses. When the survey instrument is to be administered on-site, it is often better to deal with these issues directly through the proctor than to use a more formal letter, as would be the case in an individual method.

Exhibit 4.1. Survey Administration Script.

[Total time for introduction: 15 minutes]

Hello, my name is [Sir Vey Proctor] and I am here to talk you through the 1998 XYZ employee opinion survey process.

[Or, for ABC Consulting representatives:]
I am a representative from ABC Consulting Inc., an independent organization consulting firm in New York. We at ABC have developed the 1998 employee opinion survey you are about to complete.

[All read as follows:]

Staff at ABC have been working with XYZ on a variety of projects over the past year. We have been involved in a merger and acquisition, and the development of this new employee survey. ABC has considerable experience with conducting large-scale organizational surveys with many different types and sizes of organizations.

I am here specifically to help ensure that: (1) the survey process will be properly explained and consistently administered across the various departments and branches of the organization, (2) that there is an impartial person to answer questions and concerns you may have, and (3) to collect the data immediately after you have completed the forms and return them directly to ABC for processing.

This is all part of a process to ensure the accuracy and confidentiality of the responses obtained. I cannot stress enough to you that your individual responses will not be revealed to anyone outside ABC. This survey is completely confidential. After it is scored, your response form and write-in commentary sheet will be destroyed. Your responses will only be included in aggregate reports with other XYZ employees—never in isolation.

Let's now turn to the purpose of the survey itself. Why is the company conducting a culture survey at this time, and why are your responses important? A great deal of change has taken place in the organization over the last two years, including the merger and acquisitions, the new systems that have been put in place, structural changes, and so on, and this can be unsettling and difficult to manage at times. Now that things have settled a bit and employees have been working together in new functions and

Exhibit 4.1. Survey Administration Script. *(continued)*

relationships for a while, senior management is very interested in knowing how you feel about the organization. Thus, this survey has a large number of items covering many different aspects of XYZ, including the pressures you face from your competitors, your awareness of the mission of the organization, perceptions of senior and business unit leadership, how you feel about the computer systems, training, and pay, the strengths and weaknesses of your managers, the helpfulness of the formal organizational structure, and your level of motivation and the overall performance of the organization.

There is a strong commitment from the top of XYZ to use the results to help people in their jobs and help the bank become a better place to work. To ensure the validity of our process going forward, it is important that we get a strong initial baseline response. That means that our goal is to get *everyone* to participate. You are a very important part of the organization; your perceptions and observations are crucial to helping us understand what is good and what could be improved within the organization today. Thus, your participation is very important. Although it is not required that you respond, this time is yours. We strongly encourage you to take the time in the next hour to complete the survey.

Can we get started? *[If people do not wish to complete a survey, they can leave at this point.]*

With the exception of the Write-In Comments form included at the end, please answer all questions on the Response Form provided. On the Response Form, darken in, with a soft lead pencil, the circle representing your choice among the alternatives. The questionnaire form has a total of 125 questions for you to complete. Please do not write on the questionnaire booklets. Record all of your answers on the blue bubble form provided.

[Distribute a booklet, a bubble answer sheet, and a Write-In Comments form to each person.]

Each question is rated on a 5-point scale, with 1 and 5 reflecting the opposite ends of the scale. The sixth choice "DK" (don't know) is only to

(continued on the next page)

Exhibit 4.1. Survey Administration Script. *(continued)*

be used if you feel you are unable to answer a particular item. Please consider the full range between 1 and 5 in making your response. Each statement should be answered according to your own experience and opinion,
and should reflect your perception of present overall conditions.

The second part of the answer sheet is the Write-In Comments sheet for
any additional comments you may have—issues we didn't get to in the
survey or you would like to expand on. As with the other results, these
comments will be kept confidential by having them transcribed and
grouped with others according to common themes as a part of the survey
results analysis. Your comments will not be linked to you personally in
any way.

If you have any questions regarding the survey please let me know and I
will come over and talk to you individually. If you have any questions in
the future, please call ABC at [telephone number].

Besides the method of administration, the remaining key decision for survey administration concerns the type or method of data
collection. Even when you have a well-defined and valid survey
questionnaire in hand, there is still the issue of how to give it to
people and by what means you intend to gather their responses. As
with most aspects of the organizational survey process, once again
there are a number of options, most of which can and often are used
in conjunction with one another to meet various needs in the administration process. Some of these methods include

- Paper-and-pencil responses (for example, circling or
  checking an item on the survey document)

- Optical scan forms on which the appropriate bubble
  corresponding to an item in a survey booklet is dark-
  ened with pen or pencil

- Voice response technology, which allows people to call in to a central computer and enter their responses using the number pad on their telephones

- Fax-back survey methods, which use OCR (optical character recognition) technology to scan text responses as they are faxed back to the receiving machines

- On-line survey response forms using either intranet or Web-based applications

- E-mail response formats, which rely on simple reply functions as well as more complicated downloadable, executable files (for example, macros and templates for Lotus Notes, Microsoft Excel, or Microsoft Word) that send results to a central server when finished

- Individual disk-based methods, which are used and then returned in their entirety for central processing

Table 4.5 provides a listing of these data collection types and the pros and cons associated with their respective use.

In terms of utilization of these various approaches, the current state of data collection in organizational surveys can best be characterized as a mixed bag of single and multiple approaches. Although some methods, such as e-mail and on-line applications, appear to be on the rise, others appear to have a less bright future. For example, the use of disk-based surveys seems to have already passed its peak and appears to be somewhat antiquated. Aside from the problems associated with running different operating systems (not to mention different versions of the same one) and with defective media, the real question is, Who uses disks anymore? Why not simply use e-mail or the Web? These are good questions and appear to be driving those who are considering disk-based assessments, at least for survey applications, to use alternative electronic formats.

(continued on page 134)

Table 4.5. Methods of Survey Data Collection.

	Positives	Negatives
1. Paper and pen or pencil response	• Most intuitive survey approach to data collection • Allows great flexibility regarding types of items and scales • Participants work right on the survey document • Moderate level of confidentiality (concerns regarding handwriting can be an issue) • Easy to change at last minute • Can be completed anywhere, at any time, in any order	• Costly to print in large booklets • Costly to administer via mail • Response burden can be high in long documents • Data processing is costly, complex, time consuming, and more prone to errors due to hand entry or scanning process • May require good writing skills • Appears "low tech"
2. Optical scan form response	• All data contained on single page or multipage booklet • Easily faxed, low cost to mail • Ease and speed of data processing • Low-cost data entry • Extremely low error rate • High level of confidentiality when individual completes on own time and mails themselves • Can be completed anywhere, at any time, and in any order	• Response burden higher when using opscan form • Reduced flexibility in working with multiple types of items and scales on same form • Costly to change at last minute • Printing time can take weeks • Test-like appearance
3. Voice or telephone response	• Data collection and processing is immediate	• Often requires that hard copy of survey be administered electroni-

Table 4.5. Methods of Survey Data Collection. *(continued)*

	Positives	Negatives
3. Voice or telephone response *(continued)*	• Enhanced error correction at entry if screening methods employed • Greater flexibility in use of context-sensitive items and responses (branching) options for follow-up questions • May be perceived as more interactive by respondents	cally or via mail anyway to ease response burden • Reduced flexibility regarding length— fifty items maximum recommended • Open-ended comments must be voice recorded • Confidentiality may be suspect • Costly to change at last minute • Potential for multiple responses from single individual unless tracked • Requires significant time for initial setup • Complex to administer in multiple countries due to phone-line quality and access
4. On-line intranet or Internet-based Web site response	• Data collection and processing is fast and immediate • Enhanced error correction at entry if screening methods employed • Easy to administer on network and users can login via laptops or desktops whenever they like • Can be easy to change at last minute • Variety of interactive formats and programming techniques available	• Response requires a computer or terminal • Requires computer literacy (and familiarity) on part of respondents • Requires network access and connectivity • Confidentiality highly suspect due to nature of ID systems often used • Potential for multiple responses from single individual unless tracked • Can require significant time for initial setup and

(continued on the next page)

Table 4.5. Methods of Survey Data Collection. *(continued)*

	Positives	Negatives
4. On-line intranet or Internet-based Web site response *(continued)*	• Perception of being cutting-edge and in alignment with e-business mentality	debugging, even with existing "engines" • System errors/server problems/network traffic/limited bandwidth can crash entire process and frustrate respondents • Less sophisticated systems can be problematic (for example, cutting write-in text off at too few characters; not allowing user to save a partially completed survey to finish later, or alter prior response, or submit a form if incomplete)
5. Disk response	• Participants work right on their own disk or laptop • Moderate level of confidentiality • Enhanced error correction at entry if screening methods are employed • Variety of interactive formats and programming techniques available	• Response requires a computer • Requires computer literacy (and familiarity) on part of respondents • Costly to produce disks and administer them through the mail • Greater levels of complexity and time in data processing due to disk reading and copying process • Requires significant time for initial setup • Costly to change at last minute • System incompatibilities and software bugs can be frustrating to end users

Table 4.5. Methods of Survey Data Collection. *(continued)*

	Positives	Negatives
6. E-mail response	• Data collection and processing is fast and immediate upon return or reply • Enhanced error correction at entry if templates or executables used (not in simple reply method) • Easy to generate and send simple e-mails and relatively easy to create templates • Easy to administer on network, and users can respond off-line on laptops or desktops whenever they like • Can be easy to change at last minute • Can be perceived as more personal and informal	• Response requires a computer or terminal • Requires computer literacy (and familiarity) on part of respondents • Requires network access and connectivity • Confidentiality highly suspect due to nature of e-mail signatures • Potential for multiple responses from single individual unless tracked • Server problems and network traffic can frustrate respondents when trying to submit results—may not try more than once • Templates and executables may require facility with origin programs
7. Fax-back response	• Data collection and processing is immediate upon return or reply fax • Easy to administer multiple faxes to employees • Easy to reply and fax back • Text or responses are automatically scanned	• Response requires access to a fax machine • Office faxes are often shared, making distribution more questionable • Faxes can be illegible on either end • Quality of reply scanning may be poor, making data questionable or requiring significant cleaning efforts • Amount of data that can be collected is limited to simple fax-page format

Similarly, despite the fact that some organizations are still pursuing telephone-based methods with vigor (see Kuhnert and McCauley, 1996; Kraut, 1999; Kraut, Oltrogge, and Block, 1998), based on limitations inherent in the method itself (for example, access to phone lines internationally, limited number of items, need for paper copy for respondents) it seems as though this method is less likely to be dominant in the future for organizational surveys. This is probably a good decision because there may well be differences in the quality and quantity of data received via automated phone surveys as opposed to other methods. More specifically, some practitioners (for example, Kraut, 1999; Kraut, Oltrogge, and Block, 1998) have reported positive response bias findings between 9 and 28 percentage points for phone over traditional paper-and-pencil approaches. In addition, other studies (see Booth-Kewley, Rosenfeld, and Edwards, 1993) have pointed to a host of potential effects inherent in telephone methods, including differing levels of candor. Our experience with the use of this method has produced some interesting and divergent findings as well.

More specifically, we were involved in a comparative study of survey methods conducted during a large-scale organizational survey effort in a multinational pharmaceutical organization. Having conducted a prior survey using only optical scan technology, the primary client in charge of administering the survey (an OD specialist) wanted to implement and strongly encourage an internally designed and managed voice response option, as well as a more standard paper-and-pencil method for the resurvey process. The reasons for using a dual data collection methodology were that (1) the internally designed voice response option would cost less than traditional methods, and (2) dual methods would reach as many employees as possible. Not all employees had equal access to good phones (and definitely not to computer systems), but they could all receive mail, even if it arrived on camel back, as some batches did. After some initial discussions relating to the information provided, the survey administration plan involved multiple translations of the survey document and subsequent mailing of hard copies of the survey to a stratified random sample of nineteen thousand employees (representative of the total fifty-four thousand employees in the company). Thus, in addition to the mail-out, a toll-free voice response unit was established and widely promoted in each country (fifty-six in all), even across different regions, to handle incoming calls from employees with a response protocol to screen inaccurate data. Because all employees included in the sample received their copies of the survey instrument by mail, they were all given the choice of completing the survey on the document and returning it or calling in their responses using the voice response units.

In the end, despite some significant problems with last-minute changes to the protocol and issues inherent in setting up toll-free lines in different countries, the process was indeed launched using both methods. After a two-month response window, the survey effort closed with 70 percent total rate of return, which is quite good, particularly in a large-scale global organization of this nature. Interestingly (and to the client's total surprise), among the approximately thirteen thousand responses, 65 percent of employees chose to return the completed paper-and-pencil survey; only 35 percent availed themselves of the voice response technology. A deeper examination of the data revealed that this was because many countries simply did not have adequate or reliable phone access in the first place. When we looked at those countries in which both response methods were viable options, we found some striking differences in preferences. Employees in France, Japan, and the United States had much stronger preference for voice response over paper (90, 57, and 71 percent, respectively), whereas employees in Germany, Italy, and the United Kingdom clearly preferred responding via paper (90, 81, and 62 percent, respectively).

Thus, given the underuse of voice response technology overall, the anticipated cost saving associated with this method was not fully realized. Moreover, besides some of the difficulties already mentioned with the initial setup of this system, data gathering errors were introduced in the form of repeated responses due to a programming glitch. Finally, additional subsequent analyses of the full data collected from these two methods suggested that the employees using the voice response option were in fact slightly but significantly more *negative* in their perceptions (based on the ratings provided) than those responding via the paper-and-pencil survey. Moreover, this trend was mirrored across about 60 percent of the survey questions themselves, including ratings of leadership, customer service, and innovation.

Although the results and research just described are by no means conclusive, they do suggest some significant issues inherent in voice response methods. Preference and ease of use are issues, as is the bias inherent in the data collected. Thus, for the survey practitioner, if the client insists on using phone-based methods for data collection, our best advice is to use this approach as widely as possible. Don't allow multiple methods in this situation—the data simply do not appear to be that comparable. Conversely, it might be best to persuade the client to use another approach entirely. Despite this advice for the practitioner, however, telephone applications are likely to remain an important data collection method in other types of survey efforts such as political polling and marketing (Babbie, 1973; Lehmann, 1989), when sample characteristics and branching responses are the most critical factors.

Another survey response method that never really took off is the fax-back approach. The idea behind this approach is to have a software program generate a series of automated fax survey documents, which are distributed to multiple office locations. Once completed, the faxes are sent back to a central receiving machine, which scans the incoming responses using OCR technology (Kuhnert and McCauley, 1996; Macey, 1996). Although the fax machine is certainly as ubiquitous and irreplaceable as morning coffee in the office, it is far from being completely reliable as a survey delivery mechanism. As many offices share faxes, relying on the assumption that each individual in an organization (or each member of a highly customized sample for that matter) will receive the fax specifically directed to his or her attention is questionable at best. Just think about how many times a fax you were supposed to receive never got to your desk or ended up on someone else's desk—or even in the garbage! This situation, of course, makes the results from a fax-back approach suspect, not to mention the methodological limitations in the scanning technology and number of items that can be included on a single piece of paper. Moreover, research has indicated that, even though fax-back methods may be faster, response rates were actually higher using more traditional paper-and-pencil surveys via regular mail anyway (Tse, Ching, Ding, Fong, and Yeung, 1994).

Paper Versus Electronic Methods: A Comparison

Now we come to what is quickly becoming *the* central debate in the administration process between survey practitioners and their clients: Should we go paper or electronic? This debate is largely due to the competing factors of familiarity of the paper-and-pencil or scan technology and the inherent "sexiness" of using newer electronic methods, even when neither approach might be best suited for that situation. Although these approaches are broken out in more detail in Table 4.5 for comparison purposes, they are similar enough in characteristics and current utilization levels that we can have a single discussion about paper versus electronic methods.

Let's face it, paper methods are easy to use, require no computer literacy, can be completed almost anywhere (at home in bed, on a plane, during a meeting, at lunch), and in almost any order imaginable (from front to back, back to front, and so on). They are also quite familiar, at least to people in the United States, as well as in some other cultures, who have been exposed to "bubble forms" (Exhibit 4.2) for years in the form of SAT and ACT (achievement) tests. Although some complain of their "test-like" appearance (Macey, 1996), others find it comforting in a data-processing sort of way.

Further, paper forms are easily mailed and faxed to various locations. Responses are highly individual in nature (you reply directly on them and can return them in a separate envelope) and are easily

Exhibit 4.2. Sample Optical Scan Form.

1. ①②③④⑤	21. ①②③④⑤	41. ①②③④⑤
2. ①②③④⑤	22. ①②③④⑤	42. ①②③④⑤
3. ①②③④⑤	23. ①②③④⑤	43. ①②③④⑤
4. ①②③④⑤	24. ①②③④⑤	44. ①②③④⑤
5. ①②③④⑤	25. ①②③④⑤	45. ①②③④⑤
6. ①②③④⑤	26. ①②③④⑤	46. ①②③④⑤
7. ①②③④⑤	27. ①②③④⑤	47. ①②③④⑤
8. ①②③④⑤	28. ①②③④⑤	48. ①②③④⑤
9. ①②③④⑤	29. ①②③④⑤	49. ①②③④⑤
10. ①②③④⑤	30. ①②③④⑤	50. ①②③④⑤
11. ①②③④⑤	31. ①②③④⑤	51. ①②③④⑤
12. ①②③④⑤	32. ①②③④⑤	52. ①②③④⑤
13. ①②③④⑤	33. ①②③④⑤	53. ①②③④⑤
14. ①②③④⑤	34. ①②③④⑤	54. ①②③④⑤
15. ①②③④⑤	35. ①②③④⑤	55. ①②③④⑤
16. ①②③④⑤	36. ①②③④⑤	56. ①②③④⑤
17. ①②③④⑤	37. ①②③④⑤	57. ①②③④⑤
18. ①②③④⑤	38. ①②③④⑤	58. ①②③④⑤
19. ①②③④⑤	39. ①②③④⑤	59. ①②③④⑤
20. ①②③④⑤	40. ①②③④⑤	60. ①②③④⑤

checked for errors during scanning and processing. Why aren't they the ideal method for survey responses?

Aside from the cultural buzz for everything with "e-" in front of it, the fact is that while the total number of individuals on-line in the world today is still relatively small (Waclawski, 2000), it is growing exponentially every year. E-mail has become the preferred mode of communication at work, particularly with new organizational forms, structures, and telecommuting programs; many feel that the Internet holds the future to our entire world economy. For some, this makes the use of electronic data collection methods seem like an inevitable and unstoppable force; many organizations are already there. At IBM, for example, on-line or e-business administration methods are used for nearly all survey and multisource assessment processes (Waclawski, 2000).

The fact is that in today's business environment the electronic methods (primarily on-line and e-mail-based applications) do indeed represent the more cutting-edge approach (Kraut and Saari, 1999; Kuhnert and McCauley, 1996), particularly for organizations engaged in the e-business arena (Waclawski, 2000). Therefore, they are much more exciting and enticing to many practitioners and their clients. Although organizations continue to rely on paper and optical scan technologies, more and more we are finding that survey clients and sponsors are requesting (or at least exploring) these electronic methods. This even includes those senior-level executives in Fortune 50 corporations who are as yet incapable of using their own e-mail.

Unfortunately, the complexities associated with the successful implementation of electronic survey administration methods vary considerably by application and by vendor. Aside from technical issues such as software design and provision of needed bandwidth for the number of responses to be obtained, significant factors that prevent the full-scale use of these methods include employee perception of confidentially and security, systems acumen and ease of implementation, and cultural familiarity with computers (and different types of rating formats) in general.

For example, despite the boom in e-commerce sales using secure credit card information on-line, the occasional breach in security has caused many to question the sanctity of the data being exchanged over the Internet (assuming they ever believed in it). Similarly, and perhaps partly because of this misperception, many employees feel that the personal information and survey responses they might send to a database via an intranet or e-mail system are also insecure and can be traced or seen by others (perhaps even their supervisor). In essence, the very attributes that make electronic data methods so useful—widespread access and speed of response—make these individuals uncomfortable and uneasy about divulging their true attitudes and opinions about the state of the organization, its management, and their own personal levels of satisfaction.

Of course it doesn't help to know that someone somewhere (even if it is just a computer programmer at some external survey consulting firm) can trace the location of the original response. This is simply not the case with paper-based survey returns. Most e-mail programs typically leave a trace from the respondent (unless it has been processed first through some sort of anonymizing processor), and the source of the data point can always be determined by the receiver. Moreover, placing entry-level controls and screens using ID or other uniquely identifying codes on these systems does not always help. The typical reaction to such codes is one of heightened concern that it might be linked somewhere in a secret database to their name and Social Security number. Moreover, the use of anonymous intranet methods (as well as those based on voice response that do not have checks to identify users) makes it easier for people to abuse the systems by responding multiple times to the survey effort. Thus, under an "open log-in response" scenario, a disgruntled employee could potentially load the Web page and provide his or her ratings many times without ever being identified as the same individual. Although this same individual could fill out more than one copy of a survey questionnaire or optical scan form by hand, these situations are less likely to occur with more traditional methods because (1) each individual receives only one copy of the instrument in any given form and must therefore actively request more copies rather than simply calling or logging on a second time, and (2) the time and effort required to complete the questionnaire using these types of systems is often enough to prevent their use a second time.

Of course, system abuse is neither the only concern nor the only decision point in the choice of methodology employed. Cost and flexibility of response format are also factors, and this is where electronic formats tend to shine (assuming the appropriate technology and connectivity are in place). Although the cost of using optical scan technology is relatively low with regard to postage and data entry (as compared with key punching or mailing disk versions of a survey, for example), these forms can make it difficult to accommodate a variety of scale types and lengths, even if custom designed and printed. For example, if ten thousand forms have already been printed based on a 5-item-scale format, if the client or a key member such as the CEO in the organization decides at the last minute to go with a 6- or 7-point option, it is impossible to use the existing forms. Similarly, if the survey form is initially designed to accommodate sixty items in total, and ten more late additions are provided by some important constituent group (for example, Union representatives) at the last minute, the existing forms can be rendered useless. In contrast, both on-line forms and e-mail-based survey applications in particular are far more easily altered at the last minute than any form of paper product. Although a carefully designed and planned survey instrument, as described in Chapter Two, should not suffer from these types of changes just prior to survey administration, similar situations do indeed occur; these can be costly and time consuming with paper-based methods.

In short, the method debate still rages. Some practitioners prefer paper; others implement on-line surveys only. Clearly, both methods have their strengths and weaknesses. Moreover, despite the issues raised, research in the field has suggested little in the way of differences among the data collected from on-line intranet applications and optical scan approaches (Church and Waclawski, 2000; Stanton, 1998; Yost and Homer, 1998). Thus, determining the best method (or combination of collection methods) for administering a survey depends more on the goodness of fit of a paper versus electronic approach for that specific culture, infrastructure, and context than any hard-and-fast evidence.

We ran up against one of these issues in a request for an on-line survey implementation a few years ago. This survey effort was conducted in a technological organization; after previously agreeing on, planning for, and designing a custom paper survey based on optical scan response technology, the client decided at the last minute (in consultation with another key internal constituent group) that it would be more progressive and appropriate for the organization to use on-line response methodology instead. Their intranet servers would be the primary means of collecting the survey data. The client intended to provide all employees with a hard copy of the survey (which did not reduce the printing or distribution cost at all) and have them link to an intranet site to input their responses on-line. When he approached his own IT people about designing such a process, he found out that it would take at least an additional five weeks to design and make such a system ready; there was not an on-line response process in place that could be easily adapted. And this estimate reflected an already finalized survey instrument. Because timing was not a major concern in this project, the survey administration was held until the new system was ready. Clearly, unless practitioners have a fully functioning on-line system already in hand or purchase a shell or template (also sometimes referred to as an existing survey response engine) from some external source, there are likely to be significant issues with respect to software development and implementation in this type of approach. Although the dual processes were successful in the end, a problematic server setup in the initial run of the intranet site resulted in the need to extend the deadline for the survey considerably. When all was said and done, however, the results did indicate a slightly greater utilization for the on-line (58 percent) response than the optical scan (42 percent) form. They also revealed almost identical sets of mean scores across the methods (optical scan results were slightly more positive).

On-line survey efforts have come a long way in a few short years, however, and this organization was no exception. The follow-up survey conducted two years after the first, which again used both paper and on-line administration methods, was designed and implemented far more quickly and easily. Once again, however, despite the technological nature of this firm there were server- and software-related problems such as frequent crashes, occasional access problems, issues with truncated write-in responses, and the absence of a save-in-progress function. Despite these complexities, results were once again relatively evenly split between on-line intranet responses (55 percent) and optical scan (45 percent). Clearly, even in a technology-driven firm, some people simply prefer one method over the other.

By this point it should be obvious that there is no definitive answer to the question of which form of the two most popular approaches to survey administration—paper or electronic—is *inherently* better. All we can do is look to continued practice and research for more answers. Nonetheless, despite the growth and popularity in the last several years of the various electronic approaches, paper-based methods (both paper-and-pencil and optical scan) currently remain the most common, even among the leading-edge survey practice, the Mayflower Group (Kraut and Saari, 1999). The expectation, however, is that everyone will be fully *enabled* to use various electronic methods in no time.

Response Rates

In the pharmaceutical survey effort described earlier, the final response rate obtained was approximately 70 percent of the sample, which we said was good for a survey of this type. The response rate, of course, is calculated by taking the number of completed *usable survey responses* divided by the total number of survey instruments distributed (minus any that were undeliverable due to bad addresses or individuals no longer working in the organization). A response rate can range, theoretically, from 0 to 100 percent, but in practice a response rate of somewhere between 30 and 85 percent can be expected. Some large corporations with well-established internal survey efforts regularly report response rates of 80 percent or better (Kraut, 1996b). IBM is an example of a company where the corporate-sponsored opinion survey has been operating consistently for years. However, our experience with newly developed or revamped survey efforts across a variety of organizational settings has suggested considerably lower response rates (see Table 4.6 for a sampling of these).

Most survey professionals agree (Babbie, 1973; Edwards and others, 1997; Rea and Parker, 1992) that a response rate of 50 percent or better is adequate for analysis purposes, particularly when using an individual method of administration. Similarly, response rates above 65 or 70 percent are considered good by most standards. The incremental value of a response rate of an additional 10 percentage points higher is far less than the relative degree of concern for a survey response with 10 percentage points below 50 percent. In fact, anything below 50 percent, particularly if a sample instead of a census was employed, is suspect regarding the appropriate levels of representation of employees (Kraut, 1996b). Survey response rates lower than 50 percent, however, can be common in organizations due to such issues as a resistive organizational culture, cynicism and apathy from oversurveying, or poor or inappropriate administration methods, project planning, survey construction, communication, survey leadership, and survey sponsorship.

The use of monetary incentives included with the initial administration has been shown in a meta-analyses across many studies (for example, Church, 1993) to have a positive impact on response rates in mail surveys. However, survey efforts in organizational settings do not usually have the financial resources required to follow this recommendation.

When a response rate does fall below 50 percent, one approach that can be used to examine the validity and representativeness of the data is to conduct a direct comparison of the demographic in the sample or total population surveyed versus those obtained in the survey. If the patterns of respondents are similar with respect to such variables as grade, age, gender, ethnicity, tenure in the organization, and so on, evidence suggests (at least to some extent) that the responses may not be overly skewed to one group or another (for example, Burke, Coruzzi, and Church, 1996). This practice is equally

Table 4.6. Survey Response Rates Across Various Organizational Settings.

Industry Type	Context of Survey	Target Population	Response Rate
Chemicals	Culture diagnosis and change	Employee sample	78%
Communications	Change in strategic direction	Employee sample	53%
Educational Institution A	Organizational diagnosis	Nonacademic census	36%
Educational Institution B	Organizational diagnosis	Academic sample	45%
Financial Services A (T-1)	Change in strategic direction	Employee census	41%
Financial Services A (T-2)	Track improvement and provide for follow-up	Employee census	37%
Financial Services B (T-1)	Cultural impact and integration of multiple mergers and acquisitions	Employee census	79%
Financial Services B (T-2)	Track improvement and provide for follow-up	Employee sample	99%
Government Agency	Culture diagnosis and change	Employee sample	70%
Government IT	Organizational diagnosis	Employee census	58%
Government R&D (T-1)	Change in culture and structure	Employee census	46%
Government R&D (T-2)	Track improvement and provide for follow-up	Employee census	48%

(continued on the next page)

**Table 4.6. Survey Response Rates Across Various
Organizational Settings.** *(continued)*

Industry Type	Context of Survey	Target Population	Response Rate
Media Programming	Diagnosis of effectiveness of appraisal processes	Employee census	25%
Pharmaceuticals A (T-1)	Change in leadership and direction following merger	Management census	73%
Pharmaceuticals A (T-2)	Track improvement and provide for follow-up	Employee sample	70%
Pharmaceuticals B	Organizational diagnosis and change in strategic direction	Employee census	57%
Religious Organization	Organizational diagnosis	Leadership sample	50%
Retail Food Chain	Change in leadership and direction	Employee census	28%

well suited, indeed recommended, for surveys with greater than 50 percent response rates as well.

Learning While Doing

The final point regarding the survey administration process is a simple one, but it is important nonetheless. Much as we would like to think of survey efforts as discrete projects with a beginning and an end, particularly from the point of view of having a launch date and a closing date for returns, a survey is more appropriately thought of as a continuous process. Indeed, it should be a repeated process as well if the primary goal is to assess organization change and improvement over time. As we stated earlier, it is advisable during an organizational survey effort to be prepared for various contingencies, setbacks, and last-minute changes and to have an administrative design that is as adaptable and flexible as possible.

Checklist for Step Four

1. Consider the implications of timing. Remember that the goal here is to obtain the best quantity and quality of responses with a clear set of objectives. These are key timing factors to consider:
   - What will be the impact on other organizational initiatives?
   - Are people already over-surveyed?
   - How will a survey be received, positively or negatively?

2. Determine a project plan.
   - The timing of the survey launch and closing
   - The method by which the survey instrument is to be completed
   - The respondents to whom the instruments are being distributed
   - The means by which the instruments will be distributed
   - The length of time respondents will have to complete and return the instrument
   - The timing and types of additional information regarding the survey

3. Decide whom to survey (sample versus census).
   - Key considerations here are cost and the complexity of the administration process.
   - Samples are easier, cheaper, and useful between larger census administrations.
   - A census is better for large communication, organization development, and change initiatives.

4. Determine methods of administration and data collection.
   - Consider the impact of method on response rates, employee access, and speed of data processing, complexity of system design, and level of resources required.
   - Use multiple methods (for example, paper and on-line intranet or Web-based systems) if appropriate.

5

Step Five: Interpreting Results

*Look to the essence of a thing, whether it be a point of
doctrine, of practice, or of interpretation.*

Marcus Aurelius Antoninus

The prospect of statistically analyzing data obtained from thousands of responses collected during a survey can be daunting for many people, at least at first. Most people are simply not used to working with so much raw information. Once the initial shock of the size and complexity of the dataset has been absorbed, however, the budding practitioner will find that the analysis and interpretation phase is really a process of creating and communicating a compelling story regarding the current state of the organization (or whatever the survey topic).

This step is concerned with discovering what is going on and why. In addition to detailing the stages involved in the analysis process, this chapter covers some broader issues related to survey interpretation, such as how to balance client expectations with realities (and limitations) inherent in the data, the use of norms and benchmarking data, and how to use write-in comments to enrich the interpretation—the compelling story that is the sum total of the data analysis process.

Before exploring any dataset, remember the basic goal of your efforts during this phase: information reduction. Whereas the concentration during both the survey development and the administration stages has been on collecting more rather than less information, now it is time to compress the volumes of opinions, attitudes, and perceptions into a single coherent picture for the client or for your own organization. When you begin to interpret survey results, you are engaging in a process of data synthesis; the intended outcome is an accurate and meaningful distillation of a few main themes, trends, and issues, as they are reflected in the larger set of responses (see Figure 5.1).

The Role of Statistics

Survey interpretation often involves the effective use of advanced statistical techniques such as multiple regression, item response

Figure 5.1. The Distillation Process.

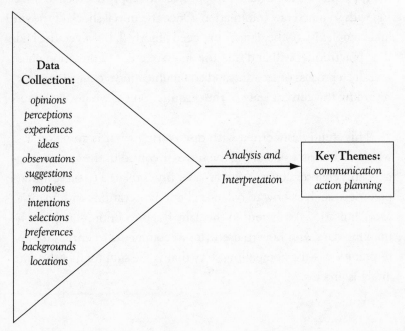

analysis, analysis of variance, factor analysis, reliability analysis, and even structural equation modeling. But these sophisticated tools are not *required* to produce an interesting and compelling set of findings. Like other types of tools, statistics are only helpful to people who know how to use them and understand their strengths and weaknesses. Sometimes the uninformed use of statistics can go a long way to getting the survey practitioner into trouble. For example, someone knows just enough to ask the right questions but not enough to fully understand the complexities inherent in the answers. We have been involved in a number of survey analysis efforts (sometimes being called in just for this portion of the effort). One client's recurring plea was, "Tell me which findings are statistically significant." This is a valid query. However, statistical significance is affected by four primary factors:

1. The relative strength of the observed effect (the difference between mean scores for a given pair of questions or between averages across a series of items for two different regions or functions)

2. The amount of variance obtained in the measures (the degree of similarity or disparity among individual responses to the same questions)

3. The total size of the dataset (one hundred employees versus ten thousand employees)

4. The degree of precision or confidence required to state that a result is indeed statistically significant (for example, 90 percent confident, 95 percent confident, 99 percent confident)

Therefore the question does not always result in a completely straightforward answer, which in turn, often confuses the client even more. To demonstrate this point, see Table 5.1, which is part of a letter provided in response to this very issue that we sent to one of our clients during a large staff survey effort.

Table 5.1. Response to Question on Statistical Significance.

In response to your request regarding significant differences among 1993 and 1994 survey data, as well as within a single report (directorate vs. department, item vs. item, and so forth), I have conducted a number of test analyses in order to provide you with the following rules of thumb. Please keep in mind that the information listed below is only a set of general recommendations for determining important and meaningful differences. Thus, in some cases, not all significant differences may be meaningful to consider (particularly if the sample sizes are very large), and not all nonsignificant differences may be unimportant.

Although the degree of variability among the different items does vary considerably, given the number of comparisons and the use of a similar scale (1–5) throughout most of the items, the primary consideration in determining a statistically significant difference among the survey results is the sample size (or number of respondents).

Sample Sizes for Each Comparison Group	Approximate Difference in Means Needed to Reach Statistical Significance
500 and above	.2
300–500	.3
150–300	.4
50–150	.5
20–50	.6

These problems with the use of statistics can be compounded further when individuals with limited skill in this area attempt to use some type of statistical computer package to provide statistical results without fully understanding the important assumptions and parameters involved in their use. These programs always produce any number of pages of output, particularly when using more recent versions of popular (and advanced) statistical analysis programs that are fully menu-driven and have interactive help screens regarding analysis commands.

Moreover, the inappropriate application of a specific technique is not the only problem with these easy-to-use programs. While working with another consulting firm on the analysis of a recent survey effort, for example, one of the more junior (and non-statistically trained) consultants who had access to the full dataset of more than twenty thousand cases managed to perform, via drop-down menus, a series of simple recodes and select-if statements to answer a specific question. Unfortunately, he forgot that these data screens had been put in place when he started to reanalyze the data for another request, and there was no program audit trail to follow. The result was an entirely spurious set of findings that required significant senior-consultant-level intervention and correction at a later date.

Thus good advice in cases like this is to use only programs and procedures with which one is very familiar. If more advanced analyses are desired or required, the survey practitioners should find someone with experience in survey analysis to assist in the process. And if experience has shown us anything, we strongly recommend keeping a formal programming audit trail (or using a program code file instead of those deceptively easy drop-down menus) of every step taken in a survey analysis process from transformations to labels to recodes to option used on statistical procedures. This way the results can always be recreated by the survey practitioner or other interested parties months, even years later when returning to the dataset.

Keep in mind, however, that the knowledge and use of advanced research methods and data manipulation tools alone do not guarantee a useful or actionable interpretation process. As with most other things in life, survey analysis and interpretation requires a combination of both skill and experience in working with this type of information. Many people in organizations who have advanced, research-related degrees but limited survey experience would probably be willing to run complex analyses if asked. In many cases these same individuals will likely discover that it is much more difficult to create a complete and compelling story based on survey results than it is to simply run their favorite statistical procedures using a computer. This is one reason that some external organizational consultants and some internal practitioners specialize in the conduct and interpretation of organizational survey efforts.

The Importance of Timing

Regardless of the level of expertise and statistical knowledge being brought to bear in this process, it is an unfortunate reality of most survey efforts, at least in our experience and that of others (for example, Kraut, 1996b), that the analysis and interpretation stage is allotted the *shortest* amount of time in the total project plan. It might be desirable to have a two- or three-month period in which to conduct a comprehensive set of analyses and fully examine the data using all possible options, but this is not usually an option. Most survey participants want to see the results as soon as possible, and this results in pressure on the survey analysis team. Managers and employees seem to understand that it can take several months to develop the appropriate questions for use in the survey instrument itself; however, once they have completed their survey and dropped it in the mail, the desire to see the results is almost immediate and tends to peak in just a few weeks (see Figure 5.2). Because people often complete their surveys at different times during an extended administration period, it can easily be a month between receipt of the first and the last survey response forms. By the close of the administration process, those people responding early are already eager to see the results and have been waiting several weeks. Moreover, in some organizations with advanced electronic survey collection and reporting processes, results are expected within a few days or even overnight. Whatever the timeframe and process used, the energy created by participation in a survey effort can indeed be a positive force for organization development and change (for example, Nadler, 1977), but it can also become a barrier when the feeling turns to one of either distrust or apathy regarding the outcome of the assessment process.

Figure 5.2. Relationship Between Response Timing and Level of Interest in the Results.

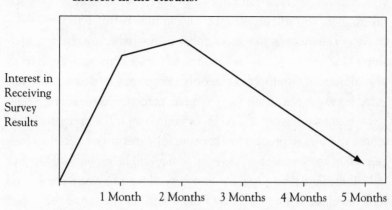

Interest in
Receiving
Survey
Results

1 Month   2 Months   3 Months   4 Months   5 Months

Time After Response

These effects translate to a need for the survey team to be able to work hard and fast during the analysis and interpretation stage. The time from final data collection to the first presentation of an overall report describing significant findings and trends to the survey sponsor or senior management is typically about two to three weeks from the close of the survey effort (in order to capitalize on as many returns as possible). Although automated on-line intranet or Web-based survey systems that allow almost immediate reporting can certainly shorten the report roll-out timeframe (particularly in the form of straightforward reports to individual units and managers), significant time and effort will still be required for the survey team to conduct a comprehensive set of analyses and recommendations for presentation to the senior management of the organization. Although some executives might simply want to pore over the item means and frequencies, if no compelling story is offered (based on a well-grounded and comprehensive analysis of the results), the impact of the survey effort is likely to be seriously limited. Unfortunately, developing that compelling story does take time, making effective time management a critical skill during this stage. Of course, this timing can be further compounded by the need for content summaries of write-in comments if these are collected (as described later in this chapter). Whatever the approach taken, there will still probably be a lag in time between the initial delivery of the findings to various constituents (whether senior leadership or individual managers) and the full-scale communication to all organizational employees. The only exceptions to this rule are targeted survey applications (for example, perceptions regarding a relatively small work group, function, or limited topic) or in organizations where the survey process has become fully institutionalized and accepted. In the latter case, however, it may still be problematic to provide immediate results to some members without having a unified and fully developed interpretation of the results for the top of the house. In short, timing is everything. Keeping the timeframe between close of administration and final reporting as short as feasibly and ethically possible is an important factor in achieving success. Moreover, the shorter the time between when management sees the results and when the rest of the organization sees them is critical to building support and belief in the process, as well as its results.

In some instances the complexities of timing can be further compounded, particularly when senior managers are not pleased with the results obtained and have not readied themselves to accept criticism and acknowledge problems. In such cases, there is often a tendency to withhold the communication of the results to employees until after the message has been reworked and polished so that it better suits their particular objectives. Some level of hesitation and apprehension should be expected when delivering the first set of survey findings to the sponsor or senior management. However, if the data are held too long, the results can become meaningless to employees, which damages both the extent to which the findings will be taken seriously and the participation in future survey efforts. Rapid turnaround in the analysis and interpretation stage is required.

Because this is the only stage in the entire survey process that is almost completely in the hands of the practitioner and survey team, it should be done with an eye toward balancing speed and accuracy.

Often this means preparing much of the groundwork for analysis before the closing date for the survey passes by doing the following:

- Making sure the data entry system is fully operational and has been tested for all types of contingencies (assuming that an active entry system like voice response or on-line entry is not being used, in which case the entry system has presumably already been made fully functioning)

- Installing and testing all data analysis software

- Writing and testing initial analysis code using sample data (or preliminary data if possible or available)

- Obtaining results from previous surveys or related comparison data for benchmarking purposes

- Managing the clients' expectations and anxiety regarding issues with the collected data (for example, ensuring confidentiality of individual responses, tallying the number of calls and queries into the process, providing updates on daily and weekly response rates, and preparing clients for unexpected issues or problems that may arise in the data)

- Preparing a comprehensive and thoughtful data analysis plan (for example, becoming familiar with a theoretical or conceptual model regarding potential relationships among variables or large sets of items, specifying additional relationships or trends to explore, targeting initial and final review dates for various elements of the analysis process, assigning roles and responsibilities for various tasks)

- Developing a framework or outline of the final survey report. This is often based on the model used in the

data collection process and will help the analyst and
the client prepare mentally and psychologically for the
final product

Having prepared the groundwork, the heart of the analysis process is now at hand. The remainder of this step provides an overview of the six main stages involved in the data analysis and interpretation process. Figure 5.3 provides a graphic representation of these stages in the form of an inverted triangle. Note that as one moves through each of the steps, the level of effort, time, and complexity tends to increase. For the most part, this is because each stage requires greater levels of statistical processing and analysis capabilities. The process of analyzing write-in comments, however, is the most time consuming, primarily because of the nature of working with individual responses (often voluminous in nature), as opposed to simple numerics. A detailed discussion of the statistical procedures related to survey analysis is not included here, but pointers as to the utility of certain techniques and procedures, as well as references for more information, are provided during discussion of the various stages.

Figure 5.3. Six Stages of Survey Analysis.

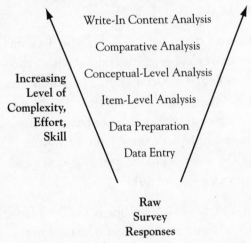

Data Entry

The first stage for any sort of analysis or interpretation process requires that the survey responses be entered into a database. Regardless of the administration method used, the individual responses must be converted from their natural state, whether it be optical scan forms, e-mail responses, pen-and-paper survey questionnaires, fax-back scans, voice response data storage systems, or on-line intranet or Web-based response systems, and converted into some raw stream of numbers and text characters that can be read, manipulated, and analyzed by some type of sophisticated computer software package. Remember, however, that data entry can take time, particularly if the data are in pen and paper form and must be keyed. A variety of professional data entry services are available, but this method can be slower than other options, for example, various electronic data collection methods such as e-mail and on-line approaches (review Step Four); therefore, extra time may be needed to compile information this way. The process of transcribing write-in comments, for example, can be extremely time consuming and complex when multiple languages are involved. Although some applications do work with text (including scanned text from fax-backs and optical scan forms, as well as those entered directly into on-line databases), the quality of the interpretative summaries generated have yet to match good, old-fashioned human analysis.

In comparison, data entry using optical scan forms depends largely on the speed and quality of the scanning machine itself. With the latest and greatest Opscan model from vendors such as National Computer Systems (NCS), data can be scanned easily, quickly, and with a high degree of accuracy. Although various electronic systems and other automated (for example, voice response) data capture methods have gained considerable popularity in recent years and may well one day eclipse paper approaches, the optical scan method still remains the dominant mode for the majority of survey efforts. As discussed in Chapter Four, this is due in large part to a combination of factors, including familiarity, ease, independence, and universality of response approach (it can be completed almost anywhere), perceptions of increased confidentiality, and accuracy. In any case, in order to maximize the time available for analysis, there is always a need for speed of entry as well.

There are undoubtedly a few practitioners lurking in the field who still prefer using hand calculations for the entire analysis process, but the advantages in both speed and applications of personal computers make the process of working with survey data relatively simple, at least in theory. The extent to which this conversion process proves difficult varies with both the method of collection and the sophistication of the technical staff. For example, although the technical people professed the speed and utility of an on-line, Web-based response system in one survey effort in which we were involved, when it came time to convert the data to numerical form for use in a database, it took them two weeks to download the information in a usable form. However, there is usually a way to extract the information in a manner that will be compatible with a variety of software packages.

A detailed discussion of the mechanics of these operations is beyond the scope of this chapter. Suffice it to say that most systems can read and write one of two common options: (1) American Standard Code for Information Interchange (also known as ASCII, pronounced "askey") text files, where each response is represented by a continuous stream of numbers followed by a fixed return, or (2) comma-delimited files (also known as CSV files), which are text files wherein each variable or question is separated by a comma in a long string of text. More sophisticated options include writing specific formats that are directly compatible with various popular database programs. Ensure that the individual managing the database system has a thorough understanding of the nature of the datastream being produced for analysis. The most important information for this process is as follows:

- *The exact order or sequence in which responses to questions are listed,* including any demographic or background variables (for example, years in the organization, age, location code, gender, department, or responses to survey questions should be included. In many cases the order of variables reflects the order in which the questions appear on the survey, but certain applications may require that items be listed in a variety of different sequences, such as when different sets of custom items are used for various functions or departments or when the order has been varied for formatting or research reasons.

- *The number of records or lines of data per individual.* Each line of data is followed by a hard return. In some cases and with some computer systems and applications, however, the number of columns needed to keep an entire set of responses on one line may exceed the number available. In these situations, multiple lines may be needed for each person's response.

- *The type of record format used to write the cases.* There are two options here. The first is called a fixed format in which the data contain exactly the same number of spaces for each variable or question, regardless of whether a response was obtained. With this type of datastream, it is easy to check that everything is in order with the raw scores because they always end on the same last column (and have the same number of lines per response).

The second option is called a variable format; the responses literally vary in length, or the number of spaces used is based on the pattern of responses obtained. Thus, if an individual answers only two questions on a survey of one hundred items, only two spaces would be used in his or her datastream. This type of formatting system is particularly useful when responses to questions might vary in length, for example, in a name, occupational title, or description. Note that in these types of files, some other indicator is required to

separate responses to individual questions. Typical options are to include a comma (as in the CSV file described earlier), a tab, or even a
letter such as X or Z.

This information may seem simplistic; it is necessary nonetheless. If there are errors or miscommunications in the setup information, it is almost certain that the analyses conducted will be
entirely spurious and meaningless.

Three types of software categories and a host of products within
each category are currently available to the practitioner with respect
to the type of program that can be used for data analysis and interpretation. Table 5.2 provides an overview of their strengths and weaknesses, along with some sample applications for each type.

The differences among these products were once considerable.
However, in recent years the number and level of basic functions
has begun to make them almost interchangeable for relatively simple and straightforward types of analyses. Features improve with
each new version. Almost all of these programs, for example, have
the capability to produce excellent, high-quality reports and graphics in their most recent versions.

The choice of a program for use in this stage is dependent on a
combination of (1) the range of functions and types of analyses available in the program, (2) the nature and complexity of the specific
questions and investigations of interest, and (3) the familiarity, experience, and skill level of the individual or survey team tasked with
this process. The decision to use one or more of these programs should
have been made before the data were entered.

Data Preparation

Some people think that once raw survey data have been entered
into a database system they are automatically ready for analysis; in
actuality, an important step must be taken to prepare the data for
subsequent exploration. That stage is called data preparation (clean-
ing) because it represents the process of identifying and removing,

Table 5.2. Computer Software Options for Analysis.

Software Category	Positives	Negatives	Sample Product Options
Statistical	Provides the latest and most advanced statistical techniques	Difficult and complex to use with limited experience	Statistical Package for the Social Sciences (SPSS)
	Highly complex and flexible programming language	Will produce results, even if it is not appropriate to do so	Statistical Analysis System (SAS)
	Capable of working with extremely large files and numerous variables	More than is needed for basic analyses	BMDP, LISREL
Database	Provides relational and multiple linkages among variables	Difficult and complex to use with limited experience	dBASE, Microsoft Access
	Highly complex and flexible programming language	Often limited to only basic level of analysis for specific set of conditions	Paradox Foxpro
	Works well with a variety of file formats and structures	More than is needed for basic analyses	
Spreadsheet	Provides basic and easily understood functions for simple analyses	Very limited analysis	Lotus 1-2-3 Microsoft Excel,
	Moderately complex and flexible in options	Some restraints regarding number of variables and cases per worksheet	Quattro Pro
	Moderately complex and flexible in options		
	Likely to have the widest range and flexibility regarding graphics and charts		

or at least correcting, the various types of problematic responses that often occur in any data collection process, including those collected electronically. No survey is immune. Many people who are only tangentially associated with survey efforts (including some of our clients) are aware that this process occurs. Nonetheless the raw data should be as clean and free of errors as possible before moving forward to the analysis and interpretation process. Researchers and practitioners often find themselves in difficult situations midway through an analysis, or occasionally even later in the communication and roll-out process, only to find that blanks (also known as nonresponses or missing cases) were being treated as real values in a set of computational averages. For example, many programs use a "9" to represent blank responses. When blanks are included, the mean scores for various items are artificially increased or skewed. Since these types of problems can affect the outcome of various analyses and therefore the nature of the survey story itself, the data must be examined and prepared thoroughly before proceeding with the next stage in the process. The survey items that are identified during the analysis phase as being the highest or most important to the organization should be due to actual perceptions or ratings made by respondents rather than because some chose *not* to answer the question and therefore skewed the results.

Several types of common problems or issues must be identified in the data preparation process. The main ones are listed next:

- Missing, incomplete, or partially completed responses

    Blank optical scan form or questionnaire

    First five questions answered; the rest left blank

    Duplicate responses from same individual

- Problematic or intentional response patterns

    All middle scores (for example, all 3s)

    All extreme scores (for example, all 1s or 5s)

    Design scores (for example, scores that make a graphic or range in clear sequences)

Responses to entire opscan form when the appropriate number is far fewer

Redundant or repeating scores
(for example, 1, 2, 3, 4, 5, 1, 2, 3, 4, 5, 1, 2, 3, 4, 5)

- Incorrect use of scales

Indicating a noninteger response on a scale with integer options (for example, 2.5)

Selecting more than one response when only one is requested

Negatively worded items

Inconsistencies in responses to similar items

- Damaged forms, computer malfunctions

Optical scan forms that are torn, faxed, or otherwise made unreadable to machines

Crashed disks, database systems that drop cases, glitches in writing cases

Each of these problems is discussed in greater detail later in this section, along with some suggested solutions. Although the identification of and ultimate solution to some concerns are relatively easy and straightforward, others are more subtle and may require considerable attention as well as some important decision making on the part of the survey practitioner or team. However, the problems that occur during this process are those due to individual respondents (for example, not following directions) and not the instrument itself (for example, badly constructed or unreliable items), or the method of administration (for example, software bugs or server accessibility problems). In the former the solution usually lies with the individual datastream itself; in the latter, the solution is more systemic; it concerns modification of all responses for a given item or section.

Missing, Incomplete, or Partially Completed Responses

The first and most easily identifiable type of data problem that must be corrected is that of missing, incomplete, or only partially completed responses to a survey instrument. It is an unfortunate fact that employees often return survey forms that have not been completed; sometimes only a few items carry responses. This can also occur with on-line intranet, e-mail, and even voice-response based-systems, depending on how they are configured and whether or not individuals quit, exit, or otherwise become detached in mid-response. Because blank returns can be accidentally counted toward the total response rates, or worse, included in various computational and analysis work as described in the earlier example, it is best to identify and remove them from the dataset. These types of forms or datastreams are easily seen in either hard copy form or on a database system. Once identified, if they are found to be completely blank they should be discarded or removed from the database. These forms can and should, of course, be counted as a blank return in the overall response rate but not as a usable form. Partially completed responses should be retained and used for analysis purposes unless the number of completed items is less than 10 percent of the total set of questions provided (for example, less than ten completed out of a total of one hundred items on a survey). Less than 10 percent complete suggests a significant problem with that respondent and raises questions about the validity of those data. Of course, this means ensuring (through programming) that various electronic data-entry systems allow for incomplete responses. Some on-line surveys we have seen, for example, will not let users submit their responses to the server or central database until the entire form is complete. Although useful from an item-completion perspective, respondents can see this approach as frustrating and overly rigid, particularly if no means for saving answers part-way and returning to the form later have been provided.

Duplicate Responses from the Same Individual

Another potential problem in survey work is duplicate responses, particularly when multiple forms of response options are provided such as a pen-and-paper survey, voice response option, or a Web-based reply. Some administration systems have built-in safeguards to prevent this problem from occurring (for example, providing individually coded questionnaires, key codes, or response forms per each employee and not allowing unidentifiable responses to be used). But these are less common because some respondents may think the confidentiality of responses would be compromised. Unless one of these types of systems is used, however, the dataset should be examined for duplicate responses, as these can artificially alter the mean score and response rate obtained. It is quite possible (and has happened in one dataset we have seen), for example, that one disgruntled employee might try to have his responses entered into the system ten or more times. This is particularly relevant if his manager is being rated on a section of the survey. A few duplications of this nature probably do not overly affect the survey findings, but they can be unfairly damaging to the specific manager or department receiving feedback.

In practice, duplicate or multiple responses are relatively rare. Clients often ask that this issue be examined, but usually only a small number appear to be duplicates. We have only seen significant cases of multiple responses in three or four organizations out of many surveyed. The likelihood of receiving exactly the same set of responses is low in surveys with a large number of items. In fact, exactly the same pattern of responses (whether they are duplicates or not) is uncommon in large surveys. Finding such duplications in any dataset depends on (1) the number of questions asked and (2) the number of responses obtained. More items on a questionnaire means a reduced probability of finding exact matches that are not duplications, but larger databases tend to offset this, with greater probabilities of duplications. Based on probability theory, with sixty items or more and at least ten demographics, exact matches that are *not* duplications are highly unlikely, regardless of the size of the dataset.

Identifying duplicate responses can be a difficult task, particularly in a large dataset with many items and many responses. The most efficient way to test for this problem is to use a sophisticated computer program to (1) sort the entire dataset in order of every variable, including the demographic responses, and then (2) using a "lag function" test for an exact matching pattern of responses between each datastream and the next. When such a program is not available, the only other method is to sort the data using a basic word processing program and examine for duplicates by hand, which is not recommended. When an exact duplication is confirmed, however, and item number and sample size are large enough for this occurrence to be unlikely given probability theory, the multiple responses should be deleted. Keep in mind, however, that one does not want to ever discard data with the same pattern of responses if they are in fact from different individuals, so careful examination of this issue is required.

Problematic or Intentional Response Patterns

Another problem in survey work that is more common is related to intentional response problems. Examples include such patterns as providing all middle or extreme scores on a survey (for example, all 3s, 1s, or 5s on a 5-point scale) or drawing patterns on a response form instead of responding. The latter is only possible with an optical scan form; the former occurs in all types of survey administration methods and is probably the most pervasive response problem short of return rates. Hostility, fear, apathy, and anxiety are typically the causes of such problems. Because these data represent totally meaningless results at best or totally biased ones (positively or negatively) at worst, they need to be identified and removed before analyses and conclusions can be drawn with confidence.

In theory, the process of identification is simply a case of checking individual ratings for patterns that do not reflect opinions but some other type of response set. In practice, though, it is often difficult to spot these problems. It is simple to notice responses with all the same scale option but often much harder to find those with graphic patterns or ascending and descending patterns without looking through the individual questionnaires, optical scan forms, or data strings; this can be time consuming. Therefore, many of these problems do get past the practitioner. With any luck, their impact in larger datasets is minimal.

Once identified, the datastream should be removed. The problem, of course, is that the problematic pattern is often not as clear-cut as all responses using the same scale point. Instead, where the pattern may be questionable (for example, mostly 3s or 1s or 5s, but not all), the decision is less clear and is likely to depend on (1) total number of responses received and (2) similar types of ratings from others.

Incorrect Use of Scales

A related issue but one that is less likely to reflect an intentional attempt at influencing the results is that of using the scales provided incorrectly. Regardless of how many points are provided on a scale (3, 5, 7, even 9) some respondents will decide to select a point not included as an option, such as 4.5 instead of a 4 or a 5. This problem is worse with even than with odd scales (see Step Two for more detail on the difference between these options); however, the problem is persistent, regardless of the type of item. The other manifestation of the incorrect use of scales is when people choose more than one response option such as both 4 and 5 or both yes and no in response to a question. These responses are likely to occur more often in pen-and-paper, optical scan, and even simple e-mail replies than in voice response, disk-based, or on-line systems; those response choices are typically monitored and screened by a computer.

If such a problem is present, the best option in both instances is to use an average (or the midpoint chosen as in the first example) of the total set of responses so that the data can be retained for analysis. Many data systems do not allow noninteger responses; the record formatting may result in a missing entry for these responses, thereby making this option unavailable. In such situations, the practitioner can try to merge these data points into the database at a later date or, more commonly, ensure that they are entered into the system as blanks. It is not always desirable to discard data that appear to be legitimate; however, a scale was provided to accurately capture the perceptions of the respondent. If everyone failed to respond appropriately, the item itself would be suspect and likely discarded completely. But with only a few midpoint responses, it is better to assume that the respondent could not appropriately make a discrimination on the existing scale, and their responses for those questions should be dropped (but not for that entire respondent). If the responses for a given item are truly categorical in nature (for example, "What is your primary work location?" or yes-or-no questions such as, "Do you have a personal computer at your desk?") the data must be discarded if they do not fit the response options provided.

Negatively Worded Items

Another type of data problem concerns negatively worded questions. Some survey professionals consider these to be useful for testing respondents' awareness and keeping them on their toes; other practitioners, such as ourselves, consider these items more problematic than beneficial (see Step Two). The issue here is that people often (1) fail to read the items carefully enough and therefore respond incorrectly or (2) do not understand the negative wording. Presumably, the latter concern has been corrected during a thorough pilot testing process, but sometimes bad items do slip through. In any case, always check negatively worded items to ensure that individuals responded appropriately and accurately.

Often the best way to check data is by comparing a mean score for the negatively worded item with a positively worded one with a similar content or theme. If the item did not produce ratings that parallel those of other items from the same individual or other types of abnormalities are inherent in the response set, it probably should be dropped from analysis. If a negatively worded item is to be used for analysis purposes, responses should be recoded so that they match the direction of the other ratings in the survey. For example, if 1 was positive and 5 negative for a particular item, but most others on the survey had 5 as positive and 1 as negative, then the first item should be reverse-scored. This way, the means will be more consistent. The only caution here is that this recoding process should be carefully noted in reports and communications using this item.

Inconsistencies in Responses to Similar Items

The final problem inherent in individual responses is response inconsistency. This problem is both difficult to identify and even more difficult to correct but should be mentioned nonetheless. Often a result of inattention or negativity toward the survey effort, two items with the same general content can receive divergent ratings. Conversely, a negatively worded item might not reflect the opposite of a positively worded one with a similar content focus, as described earlier (see Table 5.3 for an example). These problems are often difficult to identify on an individual level without complex programming using a statistical or database computer program (reliability is a method for testing the general tendency across the entire dataset). However, they often remain in the database despite the interests of the practitioner.

Damaged Forms and Computer Malfunctions

The problems of damaged forms and computer malfunctions are common occurrences that often need to be dealt with during data preparation. With optical scan systems, for example, forms can become easily damaged and otherwise unreadable when torn, faxed, or marked with pen instead of pencil (for those systems that read only pencil). Similarly, the reliability of optical character recognition

Table 5.3. Consistency in Responses

	Positive and Negative Questions	Responses
Consistent responses	a. To what extent is your manager effective at communicating with others?	5
	b. To what extent does your manager have difficulty communicating with others?	1
Inconsistent responses	a. To what extent is your manager effective at communicating with others?	5
	b. To what extent does your manager have difficulty communicating with others?	5

(OCR) used in many fax-back approaches is such that a significant portion of forms will come through with blank or incorrectly scanned information and text, which will require attention. These responses have to be either "re-bubbled" or entered into the data system by hand. In either case, there is a significant loss in both speed and accuracy for those responses. Similarly, frequent backups of active data collection methods such as voice response units or on-line Web systems are highly recommended because no hard copy of the scores is being obtained. A simple glitch in the computer's procedure could cause a permanent loss to the database.

Item-Level Analysis

Now that the data have been successfully cleaned and prepared, the real part of the analysis and interpretation process can begin. As with most complex processes, several levels of analysis are involved in examining survey data (see Figure 5.3). The first, most intuitive, and least statistically complex approach to data exploration is the item-level analysis. As the name suggests, at its most basic this is simply the process of examining the frequencies and descriptive statistics (for example, means, standard deviations, ranges, and percentage of nonresponses or "don't knows") for each item on the survey across all responses obtained. Table 5.4 provides an overview of the information that can be obtained from each of these simple calculations. Because this type of information can easily be generated using almost any type of computer program, including spreadsheets, statistical packages, or databases, it is common among practitioners without advanced degrees or experience in research procedures for entire analyses to be conducted using only these core methods. Even if more advanced analyses are intended, the data should first be examined from this perspective.

There are two objectives or intended outcomes for this type of procedure. First, because the average responses to each of the survey questions are the primary source for all subsequent analyses and

Table 5.4. Descriptive Statistics and the Information Provided.

Descriptive Statistic	Information
Frequency	The relative number (and percentage) of people responding to each scale option for a given item. Most useful for demographic and categorical questions.
Mean	The average response obtained for a given item across all respondents. Most useful for Likert-scale items (for example, extent present, satisfaction, agree–disagree). Often used to identify the top 5 or 10 highest-rated items (most positive), as well as the lowest-rated (5 or 10) items (most negative).
Standard deviation	The degree to which ratings of a given item ranged across all respondents. Very useful in determining if item "worked" or not across different sets of respondents. Also useful in determining the degree to which responses followed a normal distribution or were significantly skewed toward one end or another of the scale. Good indicator of whether or not the item will be helpful in more advanced analyses to determine complex relationships as well.
Range	The degree to which respondents rated the item using the full scale (all points provided) versus choosing middle-range scores. Lack of full use of scale in large samples may suggest a problem with a particular item.
Percent nonresponse, not applicable, or don't know	The relative number of people who did not or could not provide a response to a given item. Can be very useful as a data point itself (for example, percentage "don't know" about how the formal performance appraisal process works), as well as important in identifying items that may be problematic or not well understood by respondents. Often items with high percentages on nonresponse are indicated as such on a formal report, and then dropped from more complex analyses.

interpretation, items that did not work effectively or at all should be identified. Similar to the data preparation stage described earlier, the idea here is to identify any problematic items so that they can be corrected, put aside for the time being, or, in extreme situations, removed from the database. These are items that, for one reason or another, received significantly fewer responses in the form of "don't knows" or blanks than most others on the survey. However, these types of questions may still be useful and should be reported somewhere in the final presentation. When 15 percent or more of the responses were blank, however, these should be interpreted with some caution or flagged for more detailed examination. Similarly, if responses to negatively worded items appear to be in opposition to the general trend on positive questions with similar content, there may be a question as to their validity as well. Advanced statistics such as reliability analysis (whether the items move together with each other in patterns) and item response theory analysis (whether the items reach appropriate thresholds that suggest good response characteristics) are available, but the quickest and easiest tests are made using simpler measures.

Frequencies are often the most useful here. In Table 5.5, for example, it is clear that although the full range of the scale was used

Table 5.5. Identifying Response Patterns.

	1	2	3	4	5	DK
Q1. To what extent are promotions and assignments based on fair and objective assessment of people's skills?	3.2%	7.5%	37.5%	23.3%	8.0%	20.5%
Q2. To what extent do you feel adequately compensated for the work that you do?	25.1%	19.1%	32.0%	17.1%	6.6%	0.1%

on question 1, 20.5 percent of respondents did not feel they could answer the question regarding the fairness of promotions. Compare this with the responses obtained for question 2 regarding the perceived adequacy of the compensation plan. In this case, the nonresponse information on question 1 is actually usable and useful data since this suggests other possibilities.

Of course, in the results for this one item (question 1) alone, two entirely different interpretations can be made, which in turn have very different recommendations for action associated with them. It could be, for example, that many respondents are simply unaware of the organizational processes and criteria used for promotion because they are not well communicated either by the HR function or by their manager. It is also possible that this finding reflects a set of negative attitudes or experiences toward the formal promotion system.

Or to make matters more complex, perhaps the 20.5 percent are all originating from only one or two departments or functions and are not a general trend across all respondents. This is a good example of the complexities inherent in the survey interpretation process, showing it to be an art as well as a science. There are never definitive answers to be obtained from survey responses; these require face-to-face conversations with employees via interviews or focus groups (see Step Two). However, one of the best ways for a practitioner to determine which of these interpretations is more likely to be accurate is through examination of other, related items with similar content, the use of advanced statistics to determine complex relationships among groups of items, or through an analysis of the write-in comments, if these were collected.

The second objective in item-level analysis is to determine the highest- and lowest-rated items and to begin to look for emerging patterns or themes in the data. This involves a simple sorting and examining of all the relevant items on the survey from high to low. Some practitioners prefer to base their analysis work on categorical schemes such as "percent favorable" (the percent responding to the top two scale points on a 5-point scale such as 4 and 5), but the most complete method that uses all the data obtained is to use the aver-age rating for each item. Once all the items have been sorted from highest to lowest, it is a relatively simple task to examine the top ten or twenty and the corresponding lowest ten or twenty items for (1) specific item ratings and (2) any general patterns that might be evident. Table 5.6 provides a sample listing of this type of analysis.

Keep in mind that this process is a relative one, that is, it as-sumes that the highest- and lowest-rated scores obtained are indeed positive and negative findings, respectively. Although this is a work-able assumption most of the time, it is not always true. For exam-ple, if the five highest-rated items on a survey using a 5-point scale are all less than 3.10, the survey team would be hard pressed to claim that these responses are *positive aspects of the organization* be-cause the mean scores are so close to the midpoint of the scale. Rather, the interpretation would probably have to be that employ-ees in the organization are generally unhappy or dissatisfied (or per-haps simply tough raters) and that these areas received the highest ratings relative to other questions. Conversely, if the lowest ratings received, using the same 5-point scale, are all above 3.10, this sug-

Table 5.6. Sample Item Sorting by Mean Score Obtained.

Item text	Mean	Ranking
1. To what extent does your manager stand up for what he or she believes?	4.21	1
2. To what extent does your manager take public responsibility for mistakes?	3.23	2
3. To what extent does your manager contribute actively and openly to the work of the team?	3.02	3
4. To what extent does your manager operate truth-fully when delivering good or bad news	2.07	4
5. To what extent does your manager deal with problems objectively and fairly?	1.99	5
6. To what extent does your manager take appropriate action about poor performance from staff?	1.65	6

gests that employees are somewhat pleased overall and that the problem areas are probably not important issues for most people. Once again, although such patterns are uncommon, most large surveys using a 5-point scale do yield mean results with some items above a 4 and some below a 2, making interpretation difficult.

There is one caveat to this approach. If survey questions are to be examined in this manner, it is imperative that two conditions be met: (1) all negatively worded items must be recoded to match the scales of the positively worded ones, and (2) all items ranked together must use the same scales or, at the very least, scales with similar points to them.

Only compare items in this manner with like characteristics. There is no point, for example, in ranking means for items on a 7-point scale along with those using a 3-point scale. That does not make sense because the 3-point items will always yield lower means. Similarly, if a series of items has been rated using a unipolar extent scale, such as "the extent to which this behavior is practiced," it is probably not appropriate to rank these along with items rated using a bipolar agree–disagree scale, even if the number of points used in both scales is the same. In cases like these with significantly different scale lengths, points, or related issues (for example, ranked items or categorical responses), these questions should be examined independently of each other.

Besides the sorting process itself, a few rules of thumb are helpful when evaluating item-level mean scores in a survey. First, don't expect the average of the entire survey to be the midpoint of the scale provided. Just because you use a 5-point scale does not mean that the average should be about a 3, or should be a 5 with a 9-point scale. Most practitioners concentrate on the highest and lowest items, but if a midpoint cut-off value is needed, the best method for determining one is to compute an overall average rating across all survey items, assuming similar scales. This value is then used to calibrate the midpoint and assess the degree to which various items are generally positive or negative.

For the data presented in Table 5.6, for example, the total mean is 2.70. This indicates that any items falling below this can be considered anywhere from mildly to significantly negatively rated. Conversely, those above this rating are generally positive to very positive as far as the survey results themselves are concerned.

This calibration process will provide the most accurate method for assessing positive and negative values. A rule of thumb based on survey experience is that all items that receive mean ratings above a 4 on a 5-point scale or above a 6 on a 7-point scale are generally positive and strong findings. Similarly, most items with mean scores below a 2.0 or even a 2.5 at the low end, regardless of the scale, tend to represent significant problem areas. Whether or not any or all of these items become the focal points for the overall interpretation depends on other factors, including the extent to which more complex conceptual models, frameworks, or analysis are used to explore relationships. Once again, the idea is to craft a compelling story that captures the essence of the survey data and yet will motivate the client to action.

Conceptual-Level Analysis

Once the survey practitioner or survey team has a thorough understanding of the descriptive statistics and item-level means, the next stage in the data interpretation process is a conceptual-level analysis. Although this stage does not have to be overly complex nor does it require a working knowledge of advanced statistics, this is where the most advanced procedures and theoretical models are applied to provide a more complete and rich understanding of the relationships inherent in the survey data collected. This is what survey practitioners live for and where their expertise is best used. The goal is to use some type of overarching framework, model, theory, values, principles, or even a set of observed relationships among variables, that best fits or describes what is going on in the results. The task is to generate four or five main areas or themes out of the entire survey dataset that can be used to explain or characterize the results and drive action planning. This is not always an easy or a simple task, but if done correctly it can make the survey results literally come alive for the client and the organization as a whole.

Two basic approaches to conducting a conceptual level analysis are (1) to use an existing model and (2) build one empirically from the data itself. These approaches are described next.

Using an Existing Model

Probably the most common application of a conceptual analysis is to apply an existing framework to the interpretation and perhaps even the analysis plan for the data. Often this same model may have been used to guide the item development and construction process with respect to content areas (see Step Two). In any case the idea is to provide an overarching means of connecting different ideas and aspects of organizational life together in a comprehensive whole. It is for this reason, then, that in many instances the guiding framework is provided by a well-developed, theoretically sound, and widely used organizational model such as the Burke-Litwin model of organizational change and performance (Burke and Litwin, 1992), the Nadler-Tushman congruence model (Nadler and Tushman, 1992), or the Linkage Research model (Wiley, 1996), which has been used successfully at Sears (Rucci, Kirn, and Quinn, 1998). Readers interested in learning more about either of these two models or other approaches to diagnostic work in organization development and change efforts should see Howard (1994) for a good summary. However, it matters less which perspective is chosen, as long as it provides enough latitude in its categories, descriptions, or proposed relationships among variables to be relevant to the issues at hand.

For this reason many survey efforts are designed and interpreted, not around a theoretical model but with regard to some set of important values, principles, or concepts that are specific to the organization itself. Once again, as we have mentioned several times before in earlier chapters, it is important to link the survey objectives, content, and interpretation to relevant, important, and visible elements of the organization such as the mission statement, strategic initiatives, leadership principles, core competencies, or components of a new vision statement. This is one of the means by which survey results are given significance and therefore make an impact.

Such was the case at SmithKline Beecham (Burke and Jackson, 1991), for example, where an organizational survey effort was used during the initial stages of the merger to (1) assess main issues that needed to be dealt with during the coming years in the management of the merger process and (2) simultaneously communicate the new, desired culture and leadership practices deemed important for the future success of the organization. The Burke-Litwin model was used as a driving force behind the design and interpretation of the survey tool (Burke and Jackson, 1991), but in the end the results were reframed and communicated to employees using the new five core values and nine leadership principles. The use of more than one model or framework is not always easy to reconcile when examining the raw data and creating a story. However, it is often done when working with different professional groups and practitioners because most external survey consultants already have their own models well in hand.

When working with any type of preexisting model or framework, the standard and most basic approach is to use the primary variables, factors, or content areas provided in the model (for example, senior leadership, information systems, culture, motivation, reward systems) to classify and subsequently create averages or summary scores for each area. Questions reflecting various aspects of communication such as clarity, speed, and consistency of messages received might be placed in a category reflecting corporate communication systems. This way the information contained in the multitude of individual items can be condensed into a series of eight to twelve main categories that are all theoretically and conceptually similar in content. Figure 5.4 provides a sample of this type of conceptual analysis based on a comparison of summary scores.

Figure 5.4. Sample Conceptual-Level Analysis Using Summary Scores.

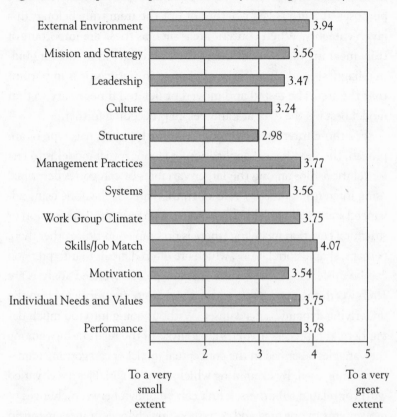

This type of conceptual approach (generating averages) is well within the means of a basic computer program. However, the added benefit of more advanced packages and statistics here is that each item in the category selected can be empirically tested using procedures such as reliability analysis, confirmatory factor analysis, multiple regressions, and even structural equation modeling. Regardless of whether the item was categorized at the design and construction stage before the survey was administered or after the data have all been collected and examined at the individual item level, these types of statistical procedures can help place individual items within main categories. Of course, if the conceptual analysis does not go beyond the categorization scheme, and the content averages such as those listed in Figure 5.4 are not used for personnel-related decision-making purposes, it matters less whether or not the item truly belongs in a given category. When content areas such as these are important or truly meaningful, as in our use of the Burke-Litwin model for guiding diagnosis and organizational change initiatives, it is important that the items be tested and moved or deleted if necessary so that model best fits the data at hand before proceeding further.

For those interested in going even further with this type of approach, the next logical application of a conceptual model is to test for relationships among the larger variables or categories described using inferential statistics. Although this can only be done using advanced statistical modeling techniques such as multiple regression or structural equation modeling (there is no simple substitute other than, perhaps, simple correlations, which are often difficult to interpret and can be misleading), the results of this type of advanced analysis are often worth the extra effort and can yield important insights into the underlying dynamics of a dataset. Without going into too much detail here, this process involves an analysis of the relationships among the variables described in the conceptual model or categorizing framework being used. By examining which types of variables are covaried with (or related to) others, a link can be drawn between changes or movements in one area and corresponding changes or movements in another. For those interested in more information regarding multivariate statistics in general, see Pedhauzer (1982) and Tabachnick and Fidell (1989). More specific information regarding the use of these methods in survey analysis can be found in Babbie (1973), Berk (1983), Schumacker and Lomax (1996), and Stolzenberg and Land (1982). For some applied examples of this approach to using surveys, see Burke, Coruzzi, and Church, 1996; Waclawski, 1996a; or Wiley, 1996.

Figure 5.5 provides an example of what the outcome of this type of more inferential approach might look like when using the same framework as in Figure 5.4.

Based on an examination of these results (and with some knowledge of the organization being surveyed), it is apparent that perfor-

Figure 5.5. Sample Conceptual-Level Analysis Using Advanced Modeling Techniques.

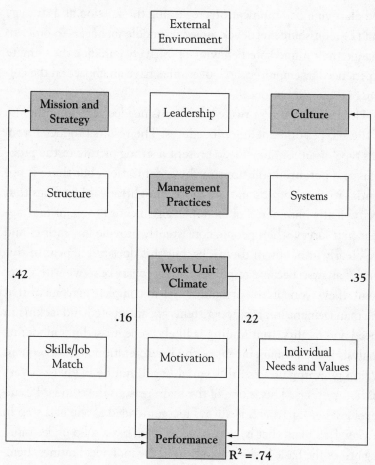

Source: Burke, Coruzzi, and Church, p. 55. In A. I. Kraut (ed.), *Organizational Surveys: Tools for Assessment and Change.* Copyright © 1996 by Jossey-Bass, Inc. Reprinted by permission of Jossey-Bass, Inc., a subsidiary of John Wiley & Sons, Inc.

mance in this financial services organization was being driven primarily by a combination of employees' understanding and awareness of the newly articulated mission and strategy, the rigidity inherent in the existing culture, the degree to which the day-to-day climate was generally positive or negative regarding the change effort, and the behaviors exhibited by middle management in support of the change effort. Based on these findings and the strength of the relationships observed, some of the initiatives proposed included (1) enhancing and clarifying communications regarding the mission and strategy and (2) multisource feedback aimed at middle managers in order to change their immediate behaviors, positively enhance the climate experienced by employees and, over time, have an impact on the culture of the organization.

However, a word or two of caution is needed regarding the use of these types of modeling procedures. The results produced from this type of survey analysis do present a strong picture of the problems and potential solutions in the organization, but there is potential to cloud or obscure the more straightforward findings that are typically obtained. For example, significant problems may appear in a survey when people consistently provide low ratings and are clearly unhappy in their jobs, but this does not appear in this type of analysis because responses do not covary or move with other items. If everyone in the organization is in complete agreement that the management information systems are antiquated and lacking in speed and facility, that finding is likely to be missed if a modeling analysis is the primary means of the interpretation and subsequent action planning process; this variable will not be likely to covary with any others. This is one of the main reasons the standard item-level analysis approach is always recommended as the first step in any analysis plan, that is, so the survey team has a solid understanding first of the basic highs and lows from the individual ratings themselves before moving on to more complex exploration.

Creating a New Model

Besides the use of existing models or frameworks, the other main option for a conceptual-level survey analysis, albeit less often employed, is to generate a new model based on the relationships inherent in the dataset at hand. The survey responses themselves are examined using a number of different sophisticated statistical techniques (for example, factor analyses and structural equation modeling) in order to create a conceptual framework or set of interrelated categories that best describe the data obtained. Although some practitioners, particularly the more traditional researchers, would argue that this approach is fundamentally flawed due to its tautological nature (arguing instead for a theoretically derived framework), in some situations the approach can be very useful. Occasionally, for example, the data, as analyzed according to an existing framework, may not make enough of a compelling story to motivate people to action. In other situations, it may be that certain individuals would rather use the data (rather than a formal model) as the motivating factor. In fact, for organizations with senior leaders who refuse to accept the notion that any preexisting model or theory can represent the issues in their organization, creating a new framework is often one of the few safe alternatives to chaos and ultimate rejection of the survey results.

There are other situations when creating a new model may be useful in conjunction with an analysis plan driven by an existing conceptual model or framework. Let us say you have conducted a survey with a series of items representing each of the twelve boxes or variables corresponding to the Burke-Litwin model. Now, in looking at the results, you realize that although you have a clearly defined conceptual set of items in the management practices category (ratings of specific behaviors of middle managers by their subordinates), over twenty-five different behaviors make up this content area, making a general interpretation of management practices difficult. You could conduct a basic item-level analysis by simply sorting the items in this section from most to least practiced. However, a more empirical approach would be to use a "principle components" factor analysis procedure to isolate four or five groupings of items that covary together statistically. In this application, the content of the items drives what the categories or factors are called. These factors could then be used to create management practices summary scores that are likely to make further interpretation and feedback more useful to others who work with these results. For most people, it is much easier to grasp only a few concepts, such as communication style, rewarding and recognizing others, personifying leadership, managing the task, and empowering others than it is to work through a list of twenty-five items and associated responses. And remember, these data are for only one section out of possibly twelve on the survey, so it is important that it be examined and presented in a way that people can understand and ultimately use for positive change.

Comparative Analysis

An entirely different technique that is applicable and commonly used in large-scale survey work is comparative analysis. Simply put, comparative analysis is directed primarily at understanding a set of results from a survey effort in comparison to some other similar type of information collected either at the same time, or a different time, or even in a different organization. The information and subsequently the interpretations and recommendations obtained from these types of investigations are considerably divergent in focus from the types described in the analysis options earlier. Rather than specifying general relationships or patterns in the data as in the conceptual analysis, they are more likely to point to significant differences in perceptions among specific groups (for example, U.S. employees versus U.K. employees in a multinational corporation), across extended timeframes (for example, time 1 versus time 2) or across different organizations and industries (for example, the external benchmarking of best practices). These three examples represent quite well the three general types of comparative analysis that can be performed on survey data. Each is described in more detail next.

Comparisons by Type

The first and most intuitive form of comparative analysis is one that examines differences in survey ratings (using either items, conceptual variables and summary scores, or even a total average survey response) by various groups, functions, areas, experiences, demographic information, or other categorizing variables that differentiate among types of people. For want of a better term, we have labeled these *comparisons by type*. The primary statistics used in these cases tend to be analyses of variance (ANOVA) because they focus on group differences. The most common comparative analyses of this type are done by background characteristics such as tenure, education, gender, or ethnicity to look for significant trends in responses. Other useful options might include questions that assess the respondent's participation or experience with a particular event such as a performance appraisal, various training courses, or even a prior survey effort. Table 5.7 provides some sample variables of this type and the corresponding types of interesting questions that might be answered with such an analysis.

A word of caution is needed here. Although the results obtained from these types of analysis can provide important information for

Table 5.7. Comparative Analyses Using Demographic Variables.

Variable	Question or Information of Interest
Location	Are there major differences among respondents from different regions or countries?
Age	Do younger employees feel differently about the company or their jobs than older ones?
Tenure	Do employees who have been with the company longer have more positive or negative attitudes?
Ethnicity	Do different groups experience the same level of treatment from managers?
Training	Do employees who have taken various training classes rate their knowledge of their jobs higher or have higher morale?
Gender	Do males and females differ in their perceptions of the fairness of reward and recognition policies?
Level	Do senior managers have different perceptions about the strengths and weaknesses of the organization than do middle managers or shop-floor service providers?

interpretation and action planning purposes, the survey practitioner should not go too far with these comparative tests. In most cases there are likely to be far more variables available for comparative investigations than are practical, given the need for a timely and concise analysis and interpretation of the results. Remember that the purpose of analyzing data in the first place is to condense the information collected into main trends and relationships, not to expand the amount of information provided. However, some practitioners have a tendency to err on the side of information overload by providing numerous iterations of variables cut by demographics and other categories to the point that the core messages in the data are lost to the client or survey sponsor. Although this type of detail is extremely important in the action planning stages (more on how this is generated and used in Steps Six and Seven), it can be cumbersome and ineffectual to provide too much information of this type too early in the process. In most cases, the only comparative results that should be retained and explored in detail at the analysis level are those that truly *reflect main issues* that need to be recognized and considered at the survey sponsor (typically corporate) level. In a merger of two organizations, for example, differences between employees from the two former organizations might be of extreme importance and relevance, particularly if there are significant and powerful differences in perceptions. It probably makes less sense to include this type of information, however, in an interpretation when few differences are evident or the issue is less relevant. Results such as these can be, and often are, added as an appendix to a formal report later in the process.

Comparisons Over Time

The second type of comparative analysis is achieved using additional data external to the current survey effort, that is, *comparisons over time*. Often the burning question here is, Have perceptions improved since last year? Most organizations with an institutionalized survey process, for example IBM or others in the Mayflower Group (John-

son, 1996) or the IT Survey Group, generate time-based comparative analyses as part of the standard analysis procedure to look for
trends in employees' attitudes and perceptions. With these types of
survey systems, senior management, HR, or the OD group can easily
see whether the changes made between assessments yielded a positive or negative effect on employees' ratings. This is one reason organizations undergoing significant change efforts in their mission,
vision, values, or structure implement an organizational survey effort
to measure the impact and success of the change process over time
(for example, Burke, Coruzzi, and Church, 1996; Waclawski, 1996b).

Figure 5.6 provides a good example of how one of these analyses might be used to explore changes in main content-related areas
during the introduction and internalization of new empowerment-
related management practices.

For this example let us assume that these new practices were intended to have a significant impact on the extent to which employ-

Figure 5.6. Sample Comparative Analysis Using Ratings Over Time.

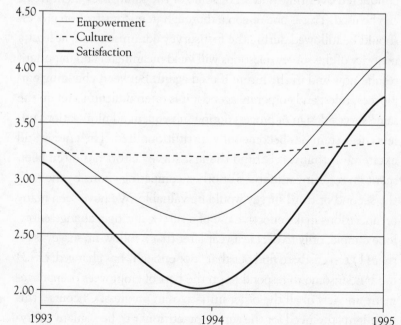

ees felt empowered in their jobs, as well as the extent to which the organizational culture was supportive of innovation in the workplace. In examining the data, it is clear from this analysis, even though only three conceptual variables are being used, that (1) perceptions of empowerment and employee satisfaction seem to be highly related, and (2) although these were negative when the new practices were first introduced (1994), employees appear to be feeling much more positive about both aspects in 1995, at which time the new concepts have taken hold. In comparison, it is interesting that the culture of the organization does not seem to have been affected one way or the other during this change process. Ratings in this area were surprisingly stable over the course of two years. Because significant changes in organizational culture often take more than a year or two, however, this lack of effect is not particularly surprising.

If it is not already apparent, the negative aspect to this approach is the availability of comparative data from prior assessments. This type of analysis is only available when more than one survey has been conducted over time and all or some of the same assessment items can be used. This is one reason a thorough item-construction process should be followed during the first survey administration; at least a majority of the survey questions will yield meaningful and important results now and in the future if used again. Between changing employees, roles, and corporate agenda, it is often difficult to retain the same survey design or process during subsequent administrations unless the system has become fully institutionalized. The energy and excitement that was behind the first survey effort has often been spent on resulting initiatives or other, competing efforts by the time the second or third survey would be valuable. We have seen many organizations make effective use of a survey during a change effort, for example, only to decide a year later that a follow-up survey is either (1) too costly to find out that "not enough" has changed, or (2) too burdensome to respond to on the part of employees or management, in view of all the other initiatives in progress. Of course, this highlights the need for the survey practitioner to be vigilant in trying to instill the importance of repeated assessments for tracking change up-front, at the initial contracting stages. Doing so after the fact can be challenging.

External Comparisons

The third and final type of comparative analysis for survey results concerns the use of *external comparisons* or information, also known as benchmarking data, to provide a reference point for the ratings obtained. As we discussed in the Introduction, benchmarking is a process of comparing the results obtained from an internal survey with a predetermined external measure or benchmark to determine the relative standing of the organization's functions and operations. These external benchmarks include the organization's top competitors or perhaps the best competitors in the same industry. Sometimes companies in entirely different industries but with similar types of processes or issues facing them are used for comparison purposes. Regardless of the nature of the benchmarking database, the purpose of this type of analysis is to determine how well the current organization is doing in various areas relative to other firms that have collected the same or very similar information. At its most specific form, benchmarking has been used for documenting specific processes and procedures for enhancing service and product quality (for example, Camp, 1995; Spendolini, 1992). In other situations, such as survey assessment efforts, the focus tends to be more on a comparison of issues like satisfaction with compensation, benefits options offered by competitors, the level of training and education required for various jobs, and the extent to which managers engage in specific types of behaviors (for example, Johnson, 1996). In fact, benchmarking has become so popular that some survey practitioners and survey-based consulting firms have promoted the use of their benchmarking dataset rather than allow for a custom-designed survey as their primary competitive advantage. For some, a high degree of external comparability more than makes up for a lack of specificity and adaptability in the choice of content or questions.

Some degree of external benchmarking is probably useful most of the time at a general level, particularly given the increasing tendency for organizations to span national boundaries and compete in different markets; however, some practitioners, ourselves included, are concerned with an apparent overemphasis on this type of analysis. By itself, benchmarking organizational assessment survey data is likely to tell the analysis team very little and provides for a rather weak set of interpretative statements. It may add some flavor and background to the results obtained, but it cannot and probably should not be used as the core set of analyses for any large-scale organizational survey effort. What is going on in one's own organization should be far more important and meaningful than how the data compare favorably or unfavorably with other companies at a more general level. We have seen far too many clients, for example, debate the merits of an external comparison or discredit some low survey rating obtained in their own company, such as a mean rating on a 5-point scale of 1.96 for employee morale, because it was equally low or lower in other organizations included in the benchmark. From our perspective, if an organization has taken the time and money to conduct a survey properly, it should use the data gathered from that process and the relative strengths and weaknesses as described earlier in this step as the basis for its analyses, interpretations, recommendations, and action plans.

One final point is needed regarding the use of benchmarking. As we stated in the Introduction, people often think of the word *benchmarking* in terms of external indicators; however, internal survey ratings can be used as benchmarks too. Practitioners often refer to the results of an initial survey effort, for example, as being the benchmark or baseline for the future. Data from high-performing work teams, departments, functions, divisions, business units, or entire countries can be used as internal benchmarks as well. Of course, in the nomenclature used in this step, these would probably be classified as *comparisons by type* or *comparisons by time*, but the idea across all three applications is the same: to compare one set of results to another to look for strengths and weaknesses and enhance the over-all survey analysis picture.

Content Analysis of Write-In Comments

The last stage in the survey analysis process concerns an entirely different type of data altogether—the written comments provided to various short-answer or open-ended questions such as, What is exciting about your job? or What makes you come to work each day? As discussed in Step Two, large-scale surveys often include one or more of these qualitative questions, in conjunction with a series of quantitative ratings, in order to provide greater depth and clar-ity during the analysis process. Unlike the myriad of available sta-tistical options when working with raw numerical responses, the analysis of write-in comments is relatively simple and direct.

The process most frequently employed here is called *content anal-ysis*, which basically means taking the individual, idiosyncratic com-ments and opinions and converting them into a number of main categories or themes for interpretation purposes. If this procedure sounds familiar, it is because this is exactly the same process that is used by many OD, I-O, and HRD professionals to analyze responses from focus groups, interviews, and other types of qualitative data collection. We have already introduced the use of this technique in Step Two with respect to generating survey item content and pro-viding feedback based on information gathering during meetings with organizational members.

Content analysis is a relatively straightforward process and re-quires no special skill other than the ability to conceptualize and sort responses based on a number of categories or themes. Here are some sample write-in comments taken from several different large-scale survey efforts in response to the question, What are the blocks, hin-drances, barriers that prevent you from doing your work effectively?

Change is happening so fast and there is too much of it. So many managers are inexperienced in their new roles when I need information.

Cronyism and sexism dictate advancement far more than do ability and performance. This is still a white, male-dominated institution.

It's quite appalling that this organization still condones a high-handed and humiliating managerial style—cronyism, unfortunately, is not always kind toward people of color.

The bureaucraticness. I'm filling out this survey under lights that blew out over three weeks ago and though reported have still not been fixed.

Lack of any forward planning; no business plan seems to last more than six months. No investment is planned until equipment is worn out or sudden events require it, for example, new safety legislation.

Customer service should be more proactive and less reactive; this company seems to manage with a fire drill mentality.

Departments that do not like or trust one another mainly due to upbringing, education, or class.

Comments and criticism are discouraged in this company and are often held against people who make them. We have a long way to go, and a few "feel good" meetings and employee surveys are not going to mean as much as positive and honest action.

Management is blatant about favoritism, not allowing for others to learn or advance to the same level of growth or promotion.

A very sad lack of management that we can respect. We are appalled at the way we are treated as staff and at the seeming lack of understanding of our feelings of helplessness as we see the erosion of our standards and ways of treating each other.

Staff attitude of "If you don't want the job, there are many others who do."

Morale went out of the window months ago, and yet we are issued a mission statement that probably cost quite a bit of money and would be just as appropriately written on the side of an ice-cream truck.

Frequent management U-turns about our role and responsibilities. Lack of understanding by managers of what we actually have to do to carry out our jobs effectively.

Due to cuts, closures, and reorganizations I no longer have an experienced or accessible senior manager I can turn to.

During the merger senior management lied to employees and were not concerned about our jobs. They did not help those of us who lost our jobs and had to find other employment. They were only concerned about themselves and were not the least bit sensitive toward the rest of us.

The most frustrating thing is our lack of reliable equipment. Our PCs are always giving us problems, the printers are always breaking, we are spending unnecessary hours making up work we lost because of bad equipment. Please give us good equipment so we can do our jobs more efficiently and be happier coming to work!

Changes are made overnight without advising us and without any training provided, yet we are expected to bumble along without a glitch. When our departments were merged no effort was made to bring people together and make us all feel comfortable.

Marriage leave taken away; no Christmas bonus; benefits are terrible, job security a major problem. Always worried about losing my job—can't sleep at night!

I have an enormous additional workload with reduced support. Experience, expertise, and goodwill count for nothing anymore.

The only negative aspect of the content analysis process is that it often requires a significant amount of time and effort to transcribe or input the comments into a computer form for manipulation (cutting and pasting, tabulating, sorting, and so forth), particularly with optical scan or pen-and-paper methods. Some data collection systems can record the information directly in electronic form (for example, on-line Web sites, e-mail response methods, or voice response units), but these methods often have other difficulties associated with their use, including reduced levels of formal written comments, text length and format limits, respondent unease regarding confidentiality, and occasional problems in transferring the data obtained through these methods to other computer programs. Moreover, although sophisticated text-based content coding software applications exist in the marketplace, the output from these programs is still inferior to the output of a "live" analysis approach. In any case, regardless of the method of administration used, the analysis of quantitative data is laborious and time consuming. The richness of the information obtained, however, often more than makes up for the extra effort involved, which is one reason these types of questions are so popular in survey efforts.

Before we get to describing the specific process by which to conduct a content analysis, we want to underscore two decisions regarding the use of write-ins, since the outcomes of these decisions have important implications for how the data are analyzed and subsequently interpreted.

First and foremost is the question of whether to use a sample or a census of the comments obtained. Should the content analysis be based on all of the individual write-ins obtained, or should it be completed using only a random or perhaps stratified random sample? One's initial reaction might be to use all of the data available; however, given the tight time constraints involved in the survey analysis process and the voluminous amount of information gathered with such methods (sometimes several pages of text per individual, particularly if there are multiple questions or large numbers of respondents to the survey), more often than not the decision is to use a representative sample of the comments. This is not a problem because (1) an appropriate sample set of comments is likely to be rich enough to provide meaningful and insightful information, and (2) the entire set of responses can always be coded later, after the results have been communicated at the first or second level. Thus, the general rule of thumb here is a 20 percent sample of the total responses. In other words for a survey with two thousand returns, you would use four hundred write-ins for the content analysis. The only concern besides size when choosing a sample is the extent to which various business units, functions, or countries are adequately represented. In some situations, for example, it might be desirable to ensure that responses from different locations are appropriately represented, particularly if there may be differences evident in other areas.

The second decision in the content analysis process is whether or not the results obtained will be fully integrated with the other, more quantitative analyses produced. If integration of these different sources of information is key to the final interpretation and presentation, which is highly recommended but not always possible, the content coding categories of themes used should match as closely as possible the framework or variables used for the conceptual and comparative analyses results. The write-ins should be classified and selected in such a way as to provide additional support and elucidation regarding the key issues and themes identified in the numerical responses. However, in situations where the write-in questions were asked regarding specific topics, there is not adequate time to integrate the findings into a comprehensive whole, or certain individuals are wary of using write-ins because of their qualitative nature, then the content coding categories should reflect the actual themes inherent in the comments themselves, whatever they may be. For example, in the first situation the comments might be coded according to the twelve boxes in the Burke-Litwin model (for example, leadership, culture, mission, motivation, and systems), whereas in the second case the themes might be more specific such as job security, upgrade technology, increase staff levels, reduce paperwork, or get better managers. The choice here is usually based on a combination of time, resources, types of questions asked, as well as the expectations of the client regarding results.

With these decisions made, the following stages describe the content analysis process itself as it is usually performed:

- Identify the total comment pool available for analysis (sample or census).

- Examine the responses for general tone, potential content themes (assuming main classification categories have not already been identified from a conceptual model or prior analyses), and good representative sample quotes for use in reporting (depending on level of quantitative and qualitative data integration needed).

- Classify all write-in responses from the pool into content categories or themes. It is not considered good practice to classify the same comment into different categories concurrently because it gets listed and counted twice this way. However, it is acceptable to break up a given individual's comments into separate parts or points and classify these in different themes accordingly.

- Refine and adjust the content themes (modification of categories or addition of subcategories—which can be difficult at the software application level) as needed.

- Tabulate the number of responses per category or theme into frequencies once coding is complete so that the relative importance of each issue can be determined.

Table 5.8. Sample Content Analysis Results.

What is exciting about your job? What makes you come to work each day?

	Number of Responses	Percentage of Total
Successfully helping customers	110	31
Challenging work	76	21
Teamwork among colleagues	60	17
Variety and diversity of work	43	12
Opportunity to contribute	25	7
Nothing but the pay check	24	7
Developing new skills	16	5
Total	354	

Table 5.8 provides an example of what the result of this entire process might look like, based on a sample of 354 responses in a larger survey effort.

Checklist for Step Five

1. Determine the role of statistics.
   - Use those in which you are skilled, and use an expert for those in which you are not.
   - Carefully consider using tests of significance.
2. Remember that timing is very important.
   - Prepare the following in advance (analysis and interpretation are usually allotted the *shortest* amount of time of all seven steps):
     1. Make sure that the data entry system is fully operational and has been tested.
     2. Install and test all data analysis software.
     3. Write and test initial analysis code using sample data.

    4. Obtain results from previous surveys for benchmark-
ing purposes.

    5. Manage the clients' expectations and anxiety regard-
ing issues with the data collected.

    6. Prepare a comprehensive and thoughtful data analysis
plan.

    7. Develop a framework or outline of the final survey
report.

3. Remember the six stages for analysis and interpretation:

- *Data entry.* Formally enter results into some sort of
database.
- *Data preparation.* Check for the following: missing,
incomplete, or partially completed responses; duplicate
responses from same individual; problematic or intentional response patterns; incorrect use of scales; negatively worded items; inconsistencies in responses to
similar items; damaged forms; computer or software
malfunctions.
- *Item-level analysis.*
- *Conceptual-level analysis.*
- *Comparative analysis.*
- *Content analysis of write-in comments.*

6

Step Six: Delivering the Findings

It shall be a vexation only to understand the report.

Isaiah

I magine the following scene. You are at work one day, and you are called in to a meeting that your manager feels will be useful and informative to you. So you put aside whatever "mission critical" work you are engaged in and head off for the meeting. Realizing that the meeting is just about to start, you gingerly walk down the hall, open the large oak door, and enter the cavernous board room. The myriad of armchairs are arranged in a crescent shape around a deep-mahogany-colored table. You take a seat on the left-hand side of the table near the front.

During the next five minutes or so, several people (some you know, some from a consulting firm) shuffle into the room and take their seats as well. A professional-looking individual enters the room, goes to the front of the table, pulls out a large report, and starts speaking in a language you have never heard before. You do not know what this person is saying. After the first few minutes of the presentation, you begin to vacillate between feeling bored and uninterested in what is being presented because you cannot under-stand it anyway, and experiencing anxiety every time the others in the room nod their heads in understanding and astonishment at the speaker's comments. You then ask yourself, What does this have to do with me and my job anyway? Why am I wasting my time here when I could be doing something important? And why are these consultants getting paid big bucks for this nonsense?

This is an exaggerated version of what can and often does happen during the presentation of a complex or extended set of survey results when the delivery process has not been well managed. People in the audience can easily get confused, overloaded, or lost in their own issues and anxieties, resulting in your message not being heard at all. Keep in mind that the fundamental purpose of any survey report is to provide a clear, accurate, and appropriately detailed picture of the organization that will allow others to plan for action. In other words, although complex conceptual models, interpretations, and causal relationships are useful additions to a survey report and well worth pursuing, they should not be considered the *definitive* word or the *end result* of a survey feedback effort. Rather, these analyses and interpretations should help the end user understand and make use of the larger dataset collected. It is probably not possible to ensure that all aspects of a presentation of survey findings will be crystal clear and easily understood by everyone on the receiving end, but an effective survey presentation and accompanying report can have a significant impact on the perceived success or failure of the assessment effort, regardless of the nature of the actual results obtained. The purpose of this step, then, is to discuss the issues, options, and applications of presenting and delivering to a variety of audiences the survey results and findings obtained.

However, we would point out that despite our use of the term *delivery* in connection with survey feedback, it is often good practice (particularly at higher levels of management) to approach a results-oriented presentation from a more facilitative than expert perspective, that is, as a working session wherein the results are presented to a group of end users and then a diagnosis and series of recommendations are created jointly through discussion and debate of the issues raised. This more action-research-related approach is often

useful for building enhanced levels of commitment and support behind whatever action plans may result from a survey effort. This
method of delivering feedback, however, also means that the survey
results themselves need to be highly accessible and easily understood.

Understanding the Roll-Out Process

Perhaps the first and most important element to understand when beginning work on the first survey report or presentation is the roll-out
process, that is, the method and sequence by which the results are to
be presented to all those involved, and the role and expectations regarding this initial set of findings. This, of course, takes us back to
many of the issues discussed in the first few steps on the subject of survey planning and objectives. What were the primary objectives of the
survey? Who will be receiving exactly which results and under what
timeframe? How is the information to be used? Because the delivery
of each survey report itself is in some ways the *second half of the analysis process,* the answers to all these questions have a significant impact on the nature of the first and all subsequent reports generated.

In organizations where a survey effort has been initiated in response to some large-scale change effort or new strategic directive,
the results are usually intended to be used at several different levels,
starting with a global picture of the main trends and themes to senior management. This is often followed by more specific regional,
directorate, departmental, or functional reports for various layers of
middle and front-line management. In addition, a pared-down version of the results describing the overall findings, along with commentary or a discussion of intended responses from senior leadership,
is often issued to all employees via a corporate newsletter, special
publication, video, or other means within a short period as well.
Table 6.1 provides an overview of the components and issues of a
roll-out plan of this nature.

This same type of roll-out process is often followed by institutionalized survey systems as well, particularly when they are intended

Table 6.1. Sample Survey Roll-Out Plan.

Target Group	Timeframe from Close of Administration	Objectives and Issues Involved
Survey sponsor	1–2 weeks	Present initial findings, including raw data, trends, conceptual variables, key relationships; adjust highlights and areas for emphasis before moving to more formal presentation
Executive committee	3–4 weeks	Formal presentation of key findings, themes, and interpretations; focus on conveying information in a short period of time (15 minutes to 1 hour)
Senior management	4–6 weeks	Formal presentation to all of upper management (for example, top 200 executives) group to convey key messages and gain commitment to and support of changes that may result; focus on revised version of main issues and interpretations presented to Executive Committee; timing (1 hour versus 1 day) and format (large group all at once versus small groups at different times) used for delivery may vary considerably
Middle management	4–8 weeks	Specific reports of findings based on individual actionable units, departments or functions, or managers; results must be provided with attention to existing timeframes to be used for planning and objective-setting purposes; may or may not contain extensive interpretation or customized conceptual modeling, or other types of advanced analysis for their particular set of responses

Table 6.1. Sample Survey Roll-Out Plan. *(continued)*

Target Group	Timeframe from Close of Administration	Objectives and Issues Involved
All employees	4–16 weeks	General messages regarding survey objectives and highlights of findings; some organizations provide all item-level responses at this stage, whereas others prefer to provide summary-level data only; senior-level commentary or response to results is recommended but not always available; timing can affect acceptance and credibility of results presented (that is, the sooner the better)

to be used for performance management and objective-setting processes. Typically, top-level reports regarding the state of the organization for senior leadership, specific actionable reports for managers to use in their planning process, and a comprehensive message for employees are provided during the roll-out process. In a large-scale organizational survey of this type, it is possible to provide not only reports for every department based on average ratings by its members but one that compares how several different departments rate one another in a variety of areas such as cooperation, integration, communication, and internal service quality. Figure 6.1 illustrates this cascading approach to survey feedback delivery.

In comparison other types of survey efforts may be more limited to a top-level report only by design (for example, by including very limited demographic questions in the instrument). In these situations, unlike in the top-down approach, it is probably best to be as comprehensive as possible regarding the results and interpretation presented to end users. These assessment applications are typically aimed at gathering information relating to a specific topic (for example, effectiveness of communication systems, use of performance

Figure 6.1. Cascading Survey Feedback Delivery Process.

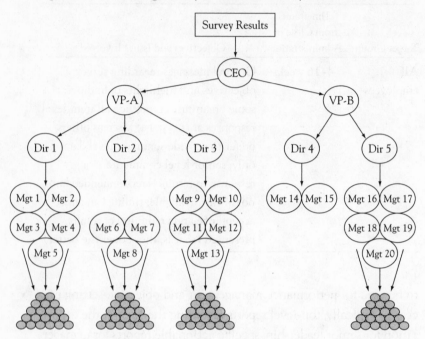

appraisal systems, general morale and satisfaction) for consideration by some action-oriented group or task force.

The final point here concerns the issue of timing. As we stated in Step Five, most people's interest in seeing the results of the survey start to rise from the moment they complete and return their questionnaire until after about two months, when it begins to decline sharply. As with the data analysis stage, timing is very important during the report preparation and delivery stage. What can be considered an acceptable timeframe varies from one organization and its particular culture to another and from one individual to another, based on such variables as relevance and importance at the time of the survey and perceived ability for change on the part of management. However, the level of interest, commitment, and value associated with the survey results obtained does tend to follow this pattern most of the time. Although some organizations have closed the delivery gap to a matter of days, this is not typical and can be problematic in settings where messages will require cascading (for example, in conjunction with a diagnostic effort where senior management's response to the major issues raised is likely to be incorporated into the report in some manner). In our experience, a few weeks lead time is an appropriate and acceptable window for the majority of survey situations.

Regardless of what we feel is appropriate, it is important that the practitioner or survey team involved take enough time in the analysis and reporting stages to provide a clear set of messages in an accessible medium for the intended audiences. Whatever the time required for the report delivery and roll-out process, this information should be clearly communicated to all potential end users (including employees) so that people know when they can expect to receive some feedback. As we emphasized in Step Three, communication is very important during this portion of the process as well.

Preparing the Survey Report

The objectives, timing, and audience of a survey report have a significant impact on the format and contents of the materials ultimately generated. But a number of standard elements are part and parcel of almost any type of survey report; these are listed next and described in detail in the sections to follow.

1. Cover page
2. Executive summary
3. Introduction to the study
4. Review of preliminary research
5. Method of research
6. Survey results
7. Conclusions and recommendations
8. Appendix

Source: List adapted and expanded from Rea and Parker, 1992.

Although this next section is based on the assumption that a paper or an overhead-based (for example, PowerPoint or Excel) survey report will be provided, most of the concepts inherent in good reporting apply equally well to on-line or Web-based documents. Our bias, however, is to provide individuals with hard copies of some form. Based on our experience, we believe that people need to touch, feel, respond to, and make notes on their survey results in order to personalize them and take ownership of the findings.

Cover Page

The first and probably most obvious element of any survey report is the cover page. It does not have to be overly complicated, but it does have to convey the key information necessary to differentiate it from the myriad of other reports, studies, handbooks, manuals, and other assorted papers that are typically generated by and for organizations. Even if the information contained within is highly intuitive, a report without a cover is often seen as just another pile of paper waiting to be thrown out. Unlike the old adage, a book *is* often judged by its cover and, therefore, the way this report looks and feels is important. If time and budget allow, it is often useful to consult someone with expertise in designing cover graphics to help you put together a look that is both easy to read and user friendly. In terms of content, the minimum items to include here are

- A title that is both clear and succinct and that identifies the subject or content area of the study

- The names, affiliations, and complete contact information for each of the principal authors

- The date and status of the report delivered, that is, the initial draft, revised report, final version for the management committee, or senior management, and so on

Executive Summary

The next element, which is the first content-related section of the report, is the executive summary. The purpose of this section is to provide a short and concise summary of the main findings, themes, relationships, and issues identified in the data analysis and inter-pretation phase. Often somewhere between three to six pages in length, this section is designed to convey the most important mes-sages to the reader in a quick and easily digestible manner. It should be thorough enough so those who have time to read only the sum-mary will still be relatively well informed about the main findings. Even if the report will not be presented to executives, this con-densed version of the findings is useful to have available to anyone picking up the report. Thus, as might be expected, this section is one of the most challenging and time-consuming elements of a re-port to prepare, particularly if done well. To this end, the executive summary is usually based on an item-level analysis such as the high-est and lowest questions, with some elements of conceptual or trend analyses woven in. Sometimes this is done solely through the use of explanatory text, as in the following example:

> Employees were less positive about the organization's communication of strategic plans, plans for growth, and success, and how their organization differs from others with the same services.
>
> Also, employees expressed concerns about the orga-nization's interest in employees in terms of their welfare and people's attitudes toward their work. Employees do not experience open communication in the workplace. Specifically, they do not feel comfortable expressing their thoughts and opinions openly and do not see knowledge being transferred throughout the organization in a timely manner.

Figure 6.2. Sample Executive Summary.

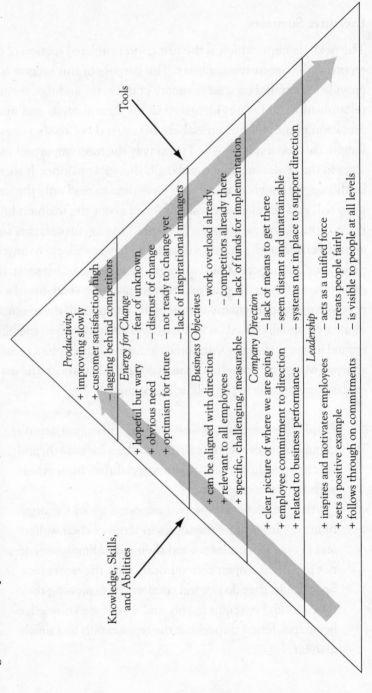

Tools

Knowledge, Skills, and Abilities

Productivity
+ improving slowly
+ customer satisfaction high
− lagging behind competitors

Energy for Change
+ hopeful but wary   − fear of unknown
+ obvious need   − distrust of change
+ optimism for future   − not ready to change yet
                         − lack of inspirational managers

Business Objectives
+ can be aligned with direction   − work overload already
+ relevant to all employees   − competitors already there
+ specific, challenging, measurable − lack of funds for implementation

Company Direction
+ clear picture of where we are going   − lack of means to get there
+ employee commitment to direction   − seem distant and unattainable
+ related to business performance   − systems not in place to support direction

Leadership
+ inspires and motivates employees   − acts as a unified force
+ sets a positive example   − treats people fairly
+ follows through on commitments   − is visible to people at all levels

Regarding leadership, employees expressed little trust in senior management. They do not see senior management as inspirational or in touch with employees at their level.

Finally, organizational members gave the lowest ratings on items concerning restructuring and reorganization. Employees do not think that the rationale behind structural changes and reorganization has been effectively communicated (lowest-rated item 2.9). They also do not believe that structural changes have been effectively managed.

In other cases a graphic or model might be used to help summarize the issues (see Figure 6.2 for an example of the latter). The executive summary usually ends with an overview of the details to follow in the rest of the report. In some instances, when the audience might be in need of a bit more direction, it may be appropriate to include some additional interpretive elements and possible recommendations as well. As we noted earlier, however, this type of highly directive information is less likely to encourage active participation and internalization on the part of the recipient, resulting in a potentially weakened impact of the results.

Introduction to the Study

The third main section in a survey report is the formal introduction to the study. This is where the relevant and important background information is presented. It should be written with the assumption that this section is the true entry point to the rest of the document (in case the executive summary is removed). To this end, topics to be described here include

- Who participated in the study (for example, the characteristics of the survey respondents, including the rate of return, some detail regarding background information,

whether the survey was a census or a sample
[see Figure 6.3])

- Why the survey was conducted (provide the problem
  statement or issues that led to the use of a survey,
  as well as the specific survey objectives)

- When the survey was conducted (the total length
  of time made available for responses, including the
  open and close dates; be sure to note the use of initial
  communications and follow-up reminders during
  administration)

- How the survey was conducted (give some detail on
  the method(s) of administration chosen and why)

Note that this section is not meant to provide a complete listing of all the details of the survey process. This will be done later in
the report. Rather, enough specific information should be provided
in a relatively short series of pages so that the validity and credibility of the assessment process, and therefore the findings obtained,
are readily demonstrated to the reader.

Figure 6.3. Survey Response Rate Information.

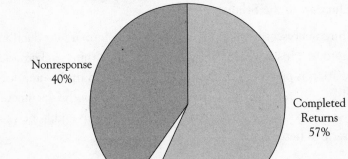

Review of Preliminary Research

With the introduction complete, it is now appropriate to provide significantly more detail regarding the level of preliminary work that was conducted and used to design and develop the current instrument (and conceptual model if appropriate). Because this section is often used more as a reference tool than a main source of information regarding the survey results per se, it should contain as much detail as is available and relevant. Elements that would be relevant here include

- Supporting information available on the nature of the specific problems facing the organization that prompted the survey effort

- Relevant background information relating to other organizational change efforts, strategic initiatives, restructuring, financial performance, and cultural issues

- Summaries of prior surveys, research studies conducted, consulting projects, or other types of written reports related to this initiative

- An overview of the methodology and results highlights of any focus groups, interviews, or related preliminary data collection

- Information on any pilot surveys conducted, test cases, and associated refinement efforts used to finalize the instrument

- Source information and descriptions of any key articles, books, guides, or other external references used; the nature of the role of any related professional expertise or other types of outside sources consulted

- Information regarding main areas of consensus and conflict regarding key issues and decisions made

Method of Research

The purpose of this section is to move the discussion forward by describing the survey administration process and subsequent analysis plan in significant detail. Once again, because this section is more likely to be used to answer specific questions than to provide results, it should be as complete and informative as possible. Mirroring what was covered briefly in the introduction to the study, information provided here should include a detailed outline of the administration methods:

- Who was involved in the design of the instrument and what their roles were

- Who administered the instrument (internal staff, external consultants)

- How employees received the instrument (describe all methods if more than one was used)

- When and what types of presurvey communication efforts were used

- When and what types of follow-up measures were employed

- Who was involved in crafting the communications

- How the sample was selected and verified as being appropriate and accurate

- How names and contact information for the sample or census were identified and adjusted when necessary

- How returns were tracked and processed

Also relevant is an overview and definition for each of the statistics and approaches used during the data analysis and interpretation stage. Of course, if any write-in questions are to be reported, this section would also include an overview of the process by which the comments were content analyzed (and integrated into the findings or analyzed separately) as well.

Detailed Survey Results

After all the background, supporting documentation, and details on administration, it is time to present the detailed survey findings to the end user. As one might expect, this section is the longest in any survey feedback report. It usually contains the following elements:

- Summary scores for all grouping variables used (based on the organization's core values, management competencies, strategic objectives, or some set of key conceptual variables based on an organizational model, framework, or the results of a complex statistical analysis)

- Means or percentages for each item included in the survey (including the specific wording of each item is highly recommended)

- Comparison values or delta (change) scores if relevant (for example, between a prior survey and the present one, or between the larger organizational norm and the current one for some business unit, region, function, or department)

- Content analysis of focus group findings (including themes, frequencies, and sample quotes for each)

- A subsection containing the complete responses to all descriptive or background items

Approaches to how the information is presented in this section may vary considerably, given the myriad of graphic and reporting software available today (some practitioners prefer using frequency tables or presenting data displaying percentages of favorable responses as described in Step Five), but the basic idea is to provide all the information in a comprehensive but user-friendly manner. This means displaying the data using a combination of formats such as tables, bar charts, pie charts, line graphs, 2 × 2 matrices, and even model-related graphics.

Our preference with regard to reporting detailed survey results of this nature is to provide mean scores in the form of bar charts, grouped by specific content areas. Aside from the bar itself, these charts will always contain at least (1) the end points of the rating scale used, (2) the specific wording of the question and its item number on the instrument, and (3) a numerical form of the mean score. Other options include a comparison point (such as the prior year's score, or the norm for the larger organization when using lower-level reports, or perhaps even an external benchmark score if particularly relevant and meaningful), as well as some indication of the total range of responses obtained (for example, using a line or providing a percentile score, or listing the highest and lowest scores for a given area). Figures 6.4 through 6.6 provide sample charts depicting these basic types of displays.

Figure 6.4. Sample Bar Chart with Summary Scores for Main Content Areas.

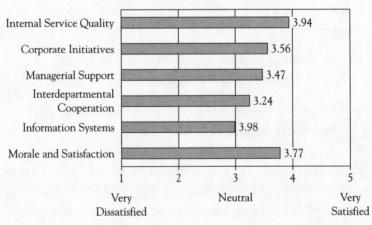

Figure 6.5. Sample Item-Level Chart with Comparative Data Provided.

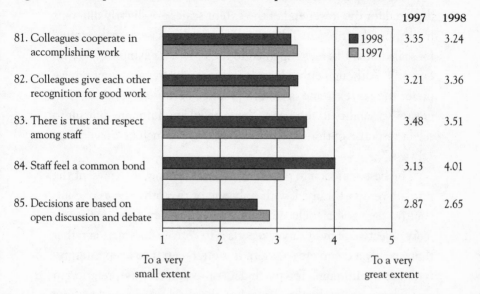

Figure 6.6. Sample Chart Comparing Responses for Two Specific Groups.

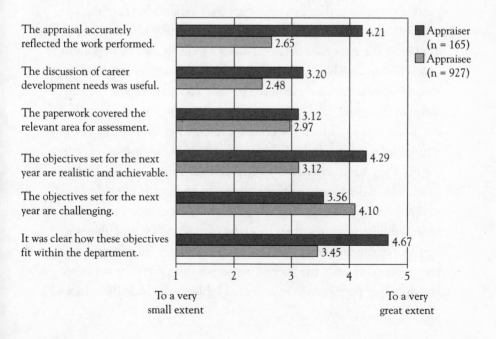

In reviewing these examples, it is useful to note that the anchors depicted for the lower end of the extent scales are slightly different from those described in Table 2.4. We used "To a very small extent" for scale point 1 here, as opposed to the previous example of "To no extent"). Although either form is an acceptable response option, we prefer the less extreme option in practice because it tends to yield greater variability in responses. Some people find it more difficult to select response options with absolutes in them such as "never" and "always."

The best approach to providing detailed findings is to present the primary results obtained, with only one or two other types of comparative data points included if absolutely necessary. Because the primary objective of most survey reports is to convey information rather than specify a complete solution, it is often better to keep interpretation to a minimum. Too much data or too much interpretation in this section can make the results less clear and subsequently diffuse their impact. Although these points have already been made in the data analysis and interpretation process in Step Five, it is worth repeating them here; they can also affect the overall delivery of the survey findings. Similarly, although at times it may be tempting to display all the responses obtained using a series of cuts by important demographic variables such as region, gender, function, or ethnicity, the survey practitioner is required to take a stand here and concentrate on the results as much as possible. Focusing on these types of detailed cuts too early in the process presents two problems: (1) potential isolationistic and subsequent dismissal of various sets of findings if they tend to hold for only certain groups, and (2) data overload and disengagement with the main findings. If the objectives of the survey are to assess the impact of some set of interventions on several different groups, then this type of approach is probably warranted. For the sample data displayed in Figure 6.6, for example, it is preferable to provide the average responses from both the appraisee and appraiser perspectives in order to highlight the clear differences in perspectives on the usefulness of the appraisal process between the two groups of users.

Because the purpose of the survey effort in Figure 6.6 was to assess and respond to these discrepancies, providing a total summary score of both sets of responses would probably have obscured these results (particularly given the differences in sample sizes). In most cases, however, this level of comparative information is best left to future analyses and then as a summary of general trends only; at the least it should be a low-key listing in the appendix so that the overall findings and trends can be fully examined, understood, and acted on before people move into the more detailed and complex data.

In some cases, however, such as with items of varying degrees of nonresponse or when working with an organization whose culture is steeped in data analysis, it may be necessary to err on the side of providing more rather than less information. Figure 6.7 provides an example of this type of approach based on a satisfaction survey conducted for an executive leadership program.

This format emphasizes direct comparisons among *response percentages* for various categories rather than on *mean scores* as in Figure 6.5 and 6.6. Although only two groups are shown here side-by-side (workshop "A" and "B"), this format can accommodate multiple subgroups of this nature. In the end, the choice of the appropriate chart type depends on (1) the type of data being presented, (2) the nature of the key findings, (3) the ease of interpretation of these findings, (4) the client's or the survey consultant's familiarity with a specific format, and (5) personal appeal.

Conclusions and Recommendations

Now that the data have been described in great detail, the end user is ready to consider your insightful interpretive comments, conclusions, and any potential recommendations for action you might have. This is the place to highlight the main themes, trends, and relationships that resulted from the data analysis stage.

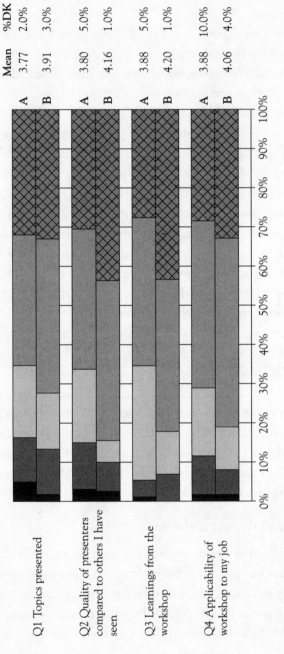

Figure 6.7. Satisfaction with Executive Leadership Workshop.

(1) Very dissatisfied
(2) Somewhat dissatisfied
(3) Neither
(4) Somewhat satisfied
(5) Very satisfied

Examples of this type of information might look something like this:

Summary of differences—direct customer contact versus internal staff:

• Employees with direct customer contact indicated greater understanding of the mission and goals of the change effort. They also rated senior leadership more positively.

• However, these employees rated the company's structure, employee support systems, and their managers' behavior more negatively.

Summary of differences—length of service:

• Employees who have been working in the company for two years or less are far more likely to be optimistic about positive change occurring as a result of the organization survey. Employees working five years or more are more likely to be pessimistic.

• Although all three categories of leadership (senior management team, region-division senior management, and area directors) are rated highly by new employees, a clear difference in the ratings given to area directors and other senior management develops quickly after that and persists throughout each length-of-service category. Ratings of leadership are lowest among employees who have worked in the company for a longer period of time (three years or more).

• Employee morale and feelings of empowerment and satisfaction decline as length of service increases. Ratings of the job itself remain relatively consistent, however, lending weight to the validity of external causes for the drop in satisfaction.

Besides highlighting key trends, conceptual models and advanced statistics often influence the contents of this section as well, although this may or may not be made apparent to the reader. Figure 6.8 and Table 6.2 provide examples of how one of these more complex analyses based on the results of a multiple regression procedure can be used to describe key levers for change in a report. As you will see, the numerics involved in this analysis are not presented (compare this presentation, for example, to the more complete but perhaps less easily understood model detailed in Figure 5.5).

Regardless of the level of complexity used in the analysis process, however, this section also provides the survey team (and ultimately the sponsor as well) with the opportunity to recommend various alternative courses of action as a result of the issues identified. There is often some repetition of highest and lowest ratings—areas that were mentioned most often or most aggressively in the write-in responses or those pertaining to specific content areas of interest. The only other main elements that might be included in this section are some additional information regarding future roll-out plans for lower levels in the organization as well as possible opportunities for future research or study.

Here are some sample recommendations that can be included in this type of report:

Structure: implement a series of devices to enhance marketing and sales integration:

- Integrate annual business plans so that there are overlapping objectives.
- Involve marketing in the sales planning process.

Figure 6.8. Key Levers for Change.

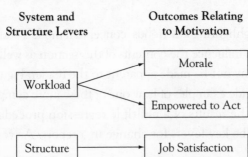

Table 6.2. Key Levers for Change:
Individual Performance and Motivation.

Because the motivation section of the survey contains a number of different questions pertaining to various aspects such as morale and feelings of empowerment, these specific items were examined independently to identify key levers for change. The following graphics represent the primary levers (that is, the single most important predictors) for enhancing each aspect of employee motivation.

Workload	Structure
Q91. Branches have sufficient staff support during peak periods.	Q48. Structure is decentralized; people are encouraged to take initiative and have authority to act.
Q92. Information gets to the right people at the right time.	
Q93. People are rewarded for serving their customers to a very great extent.	Q49. Structure helps business performance.
Q98. I do far less paperwork than I used to 12 months ago.	Q50. The current organizational structure helps different departments cooperate and work together effectively.
Q99. Formal systems and processes enhance our ability to work effectively.	
	Q51. Employees have the authority and latitude they need to serve their customers.

Source: Adapted from Rea and Parker, 1992.

- Negotiate quarterly the objectives and priorities of the functions together.
- Institute and promote joint training and development workshops.
- Involve sales staff more in key marketing processes (for example, product brainstorming, marketing strategies, quarterly merchandise planning).
- Periodically conduct cross-functional team-building exercises.

- Use temporary or permanent marketing and sales task forces to get work done.

- Reinforce marketing and sales integration whenever possible and reflect it in criteria for succession planning.

Of all the sections in a survey report, however, the recommendations probably change the most depending on when it occurs in the roll-out process and to whom the results are being presented. The first preliminary sharing of the results with the survey sponsor, for example, probably provides for the most open and uninhibited series of conversations regarding the results. But when presenting a set of survey findings to senior management for the first time, it is often prudent to avoid overemphasizing this section because this group often wants to think about and reflect on the implications and recommendation of the results themselves. The conclusions and recommendations presented to this group are likely to be very different in tone (and perhaps even in content) from what this group might want communicated to all employees in some type of corporatewide document. Similarly, in many individual reporting situations such as departmental or functional groupings, the purpose of a feedback presentation may be to develop a series of recommendations and action planning steps based on a joint discussion and interpretation of the data displayed in the detailed survey results section. However, we have seen departments in some organizations take a completely analyzed and fully interpreted set of survey results for their specific area, and create a totally independent communication piece with their own conclusions and recommendations for distribution to their people.

Appendix

The final element to a standard survey report is the appendix (or if more than one, the appendixes). The appendix is probably the easiest section to write (after the cover page), and it is likely to be large. This is where the practitioner provides any and all additional materials that might be relevant to the survey effort. The appendix usually contains the following kinds of items:

- A sample copy of the survey instrument used (if no hard copy was used, then a listing of the specific items and associated scales would be substituted)

- Copies of all important communications (for example, cover letter mailed with survey, reminder and follow-up letters, e-mails, postcards, print screens of Web pages, information sheets provided, and on-line instructions)

- List of key contributors to various stages of the process (for example, task force members, survey sponsor and team members, or participants in the item-design focus group or interviews)

- Content analysis information about write-in comments (if not included in the detailed survey results section or if more detail is warranted)

- Any other supplementary documents such as additional listings of numbers by specific groups

Balancing Expectations and Reality

The presentation and delivery of feedback results is in and of itself a relatively straightforward process. Assuming that most of the issues and components described are adequately addressed, one more set of issues needs to be discussed. These pertain primarily to the ethics and responsibilities inherent in the survey feedback process itself.

First, survey practitioners and the survey team should realize that any data collection process, regardless of the content to which it is directed, has the potential to raise anxiety and fear on the part of re-spondents and end users, and even the survey sponsor. Between the formal costs and resources associated with the conduct of a survey effort and the emotional energy and heightened awareness and ex-pectations of a response to organizational concerns among respon-dents, it is very likely that the results will be met with some resistance and anxiety when presented and even further on in the process. For example, most individuals go through a four-stage process commonly known as S-A-R-A when receiving any kind of feedback. Based loosely on the well-known writings of Elisabeth Kübler-Ross (1970) regarding the grieving process, in survey work S-A-R-A is meant to represent the four stages of Shock, Anger, Rejection (or Resistance), and Acceptance. (Some practitioners also include an H in the model for Hope.) Presenting survey recipients with this simple framework at the outset of a feedback delivery meeting often helps them through the initial stages of the process by showing them that their initial reactions are normal. To this end the survey practitioner needs to help manage and work the client, sponsor, or end users through these concerns in a productive manner. This means creating survey reports that temper negative findings and areas for change with positives and strengths, even when there may appear to be few or none. It also means preparing the client for difficult ratings and helping the client accept the results for what they are rather than allowing them to defensively dismiss the ratings as being invalid, unimportant, or beyond management's ability to respond.

A second issue here regarding professional conduct concerns the extent to which the survey practitioner maintains his or her integrity in the delivery process regarding (1) the reality and validity of the interpretation of the data obtained and (2) adherence to the original contract regarding the confidentiality of responses. It should be clear from the discussion here and in Step Five that there is never a perfectly correct interpretation for any given set of survey data (you're trying to communicate a compelling story after all), but it is possible for people to completely misinterpret, intentionally obscure, and even falsify certain types of findings and outcomes based on their own idiosyncratic view of the results. The latter is probably not too common in practice, nevertheless people often put their own spin on a set of survey results when preparing to convey them to others in the organization, particularly in situations where a powerful group other than the survey team (or practitioner) takes control of the communication and action planning process. In these situations, the onus is on the survey professional to ensure that end users and employees receive an appropriate set of findings and interpretation that accurately reflect the data obtained, at least on some level. It is only fair that everyone who participated should receive some acknowledgment and feedback for their efforts and that the feedback should be accurate, meaningful, and easy to understand.

Similarly, it is the ethical responsibility of the survey practitioner to protect the level of confidentiality of the individual responses obtained, regardless of the pressures placed on them by the client or other powerful groups interested in exploiting the survey results. For example, if respondents were promised confidentiality at the level of a twenty-person minimum per individual report, then all requests exceeding this limit (for example, for a department with eleven responses) from the client, survey sponsor, or even senior management should be rejected. The only solution here would be to provide the data in question, combined with some other smaller set to reach the minimum allowed. Once again, this is one of the benefits of using an external agent to collect and analyze the survey responses because it provides a buffer between senior management and the data protection mechanisms. For many external survey experts, the only way their raw survey data may be obtained is through a successful legal action.

Checklist for Step Six

1. Determine the roll-out process; decide on the method and sequence by which the results are to be presented to all those involved (see Table 6.1 for a sample survey roll-out plan). Usually rolling-out results include some kind of cascading process. At a minimum, however, the following elements should be considered in any roll-out plan:
   - What target group will receive the survey results?
   - What is the timeframe from the close of administration to reporting?

- What are the objectives and issues involved in rolling-out survey results?

2. Prepare the survey report. A completed survey report should contain each of the following elements:
   - Cover page: name of survey, date of survey, creator(s) of survey
   - Executive summary: brief narrative of findings in summary form
   - Introduction to the study: who participated, when and why the survey was conducted
   - Review of preliminary research: background information, methods overview, research
   - Method of research: how the survey was designed and how the results were collected
   - Detailed survey results: exact findings of survey, usually by item or summary dimension
   - Conclusions and recommendations: recommended actions based on findings
   - Appendix: cover letters, the survey instrument itself, list of contributors

3. Balance expectations and reality.
   - Always remember that any data collection process has the potential to raise anxiety and fear on the part of respondents, end users, and even the survey sponsor.
   - Maintain your integrity in the delivery process regarding (1) the reality and validity of the interpretation of the data obtained and (2) adherence to the original contract concerning the confidentiality of responses.
   - Protect the confidentiality of the individual responses obtained, regardless of the pressures by the client or other powerful groups interested in exploiting the survey results.

7

Step Seven: Learning into Action

Knowledge must come through action.

Sophocles

Despite the continued popularity of consultants promoting change management initiatives in organizations, there is considerable evidence to suggest that most such efforts fail to have any noticeable, let alone lasting, impact on the company. A 1992 survey of three hundred electronics companies, for example, indicated that 63 percent of those organizations implementing new TQM efforts had failed to yield improvements in their level of product defects (Schaffer and Thomson, 1992). Similarly, poor outcomes have been reported for other types of large-scale interventions such as reengineering, business process improvement, and culture change efforts (Kotter, 1995; Spector and Beer, 1994; Trahant and Burke, 1996). There are probably many contributing factors to this high failure rate, but one is the extent to which the organization truly embraces and supports the process or methodology of choice.

Many organizations undertake a variety of large-scale corporate initiatives, including survey assessments, in an effort to stay current with the latest management fad, without having put enough time or thought into how or why a particular change or process might be beneficial to the system. These haphazard approaches to change management often result in the communication of a "new strategic

direction" every year or two and, in some cases, potentially conflict-
ing initiatives and messages within a few months of each other.
Termed *flavor of the month* by some of the more cynical commenta-
tors in the field (Adams, 1996; Micklethwait and Wooldridge, 1996),
these efforts often confuse employees; frequent changes often prevent
these initiatives from taking hold in the larger culture as well. In fact,
the tendency to follow suit, as in "Let's get some of that 360-degree
feedback stuff," is one reason many employees today approach most
new corporate initiatives or directives with apathy or cynicism. In
short, there is often insufficient follow-through to make change happen and to make it endure.

Not surprisingly, these same issues and concerns are mirrored in
organizational survey efforts, particularly in this final phase of the
process of transferring ownership and taking action based on the results obtained. Many people, including some survey practitioners,
consider the delivery of the results in and of themselves to be the
end point in the process. In fact, this step is critical to determining
how much impact a survey will have on an organization but does
not create change in and of itself.

At this point in the process, our discussion, approach, and implicit
values tend to diverge from many other types of survey practitioners
(and management consultants for that matter) in the field. In this
chapter, our emphasis is on using organizational surveys for organization development and change. All the other components discussed
in Steps One to Six may be common to many survey approaches and
will most certainly have an effect on the quality of the survey, the results obtained, and how these are received by the end users. These
components alone will not, however, guarantee a successful end result—lasting organizational change and improvement. The action
planning and utilization process is the key to creating any type of significant impact in the way things are done in the organization. Figure 7.1 presents a graphic depiction of the change in emphasis at this
final stage between the more tactical aspects of the survey process and
organizational transformation.

Figure 7.1. Using Surveys for Change.

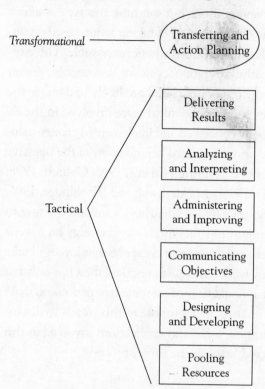

Transformational ——————— Transferring and Action Planning

Delivering Results

Analyzing and Interpreting

Tactical

Administering and Improving

Communicating Objectives

Designing and Developing

Pooling Resources

Even if the survey construction, administration, communication, analysis, and delivery are conducted with the utmost competence, if the survey results are not absorbed and ultimately used by organization members to make key decisions, the survey cannot be considered to have been *maximally* effective. Regardless of the goals and objectives of the assessment itself, it is of paramount importance that managers and employees take ownership of the findings and make changes happen as a result. A survey might be intended primarily to assess the morale of employees, but if the information obtained is not used in some manner (perhaps communicating to employees that people are generally positive about working for the organization or saying that significant issues and concerns need to be dealt with), it cannot have much of an effect. This may be an acceptable outcome for some practitioners and some survey sponsors, but we think this type of effort, that is, when there is no clear intention of taking action based on survey results, should probably be avoided whenever possible. These situations often lead to apathy, frustration, cynicism, and negative energy on the part of the survey respondents and are likely to damage the credibility of the survey sponsor and all who are involved in the effort. Moreover, such poorly conceived and implemented change management initiatives are primary reasons behind many of the negative perceptions of the field of consulting (Adams, 1996; Church, 1998; Church and Waclawski, 1998b; Micklethwait and Wooldridge, 1996; Pinault, 2000), and deservedly so. Clearly, if someone is going to spend a significant amount of time, money, and energy on a well-constructed and implemented survey and expects employees to take time out from their busy work schedule to respond, then it is only fair that the results obtained should be used for some type of decision making or organizational change. The purpose of this step is to discuss some of the most important issues and applications involved in this final, and often neglected, stage in the survey process.

Using Surveys to Create Lasting Change

In our opinion, a substantial portion of the perceived failure of surveys to create lasting change is due to faulty or nonexistent action planning or survey follow-up. Unfortunately, many survey practitioners today still consider the delivery of results to be the end point in the survey process. This could not be farther from the truth. Although from the survey practitioner's perspective, delivering the results is a significant project milestone that marks the completion of a great deal of the data-based work (it represents the culmination of the first six phases) for the client organization and end users of the survey (managers and executives), it is just the beginning! This is the first true point at which the survey results can actually be used to create positive change at the organization, department, and even individual levels. In short, focusing only on the results themselves and how they are delivered (not to mention how they are received) is not enough to guarantee successful change.

For these reasons, the action planning process is the key to creating any type of significant impact in the way things are done in an organization. Increasingly, practitioners are realizing the importance of this phase in the survey process and calling for more attention to surveys for change (for example, Kraut and Saari, 1999). Moreover, the importance of action planning in survey work is becoming a popular topic at professional association conventions as well (Kraut, 2000). Although we have been advocating this issue for years, based on the OD approach to the use of data feedback, recently we had the privilege of participating in two important events focused exclusively on the issue of survey action planning: (1) an invited presentation to the Mayflower Group and (2) participation in a practitioner forum at the annual meeting of the Society for Industrial and Organizational Psychology. These experiences have not only served to reinforce our belief in the importance of this phase of the survey process, which is grounded in our training and experience as OD practitioners and organizational psychologists, but have also helped us refine some of our thoughts about the action planning process itself, which will be discussed throughout this chapter.

Barriers to the Transfer of Ownership

It is certainly no secret to the experienced survey practitioner that surveys are often a source of significant anxiety and trepidation for end users (for example, your clients, such as the survey sponsor, survey champion, key senior management members, or other professionals such as those in HRD, OD, or I-O-psychology-related functions). As the time of disclosure and reporting draws near, the end user or client in question often may become reluctant to embrace or own the data. This is due to the less-than-stellar findings on some variables measured by the survey. When the ethics and integrity of senior leaders receive the lowest ratings overall from employees, for example, it can be difficult giving this feedback to the very same executives who were rated poorly at the start of the roll-out process.

Some organizations conduct employee opinion surveys annually as a part of their ongoing HR or OD strategy, but in many cases surveys are undertaken for diagnostic purposes by organizations that are experiencing significant problems or changes. These latter companies will look for an outside or external survey provider to help them design, administer, analyze, and report the survey results. When this process has been well thought out, coordinated, and implemented, it can flow amazingly smoothly. Even seasoned survey professionals, however, can have trouble in the final phases of reporting and action planning. This is when the proverbial rubber meets the road; often the end users of the survey results are not ready, willing, or able to deal with the ramifications of less-than-favorable findings.

Before moving on, an important issue needs to be addressed regarding the types of survey-related service and support that are available to organizations—that is, the difference between a *survey consultant* and a *survey vendor*. Although we have used the terms *consultant* and *vendor* interchangeably, some important distinctions should be highlighted between these two roles (and in some cases associated types of practitioners), particularly because those in the roles can have a significant impact at this stage, the most change-focused one of the survey effort.

Generally speaking, the difference is as follows: *consultants provide expertise on a given topic or area of knowledge, whereas vendors provide needed goods and services.* Although perhaps obvious at first, the emphasis and appropriateness of each type of role to a given stage in the survey process is key. For example, a survey consultant would probably be most useful in the stages of pooling resources, designing the instrument, and conducting the analysis, whereas a survey vendor might be preferable when complex administration methods and massive report production requirements must be dealt with. Moreover, these roles are not mutually exclusive; some survey consultants can also serve effectively as vendors, and vice versa. Having said this, how-ever, there is a potential danger in treating all potential survey prac-titioners as one type or the other. Many vendors firms, for example, are capable at data processing but poorly equipped (with respect to the OD, HRD, and I-O-related skills or resources needed) to provide appropriate levels of follow-up consulting, action planning support, and implementation following a large-scale survey effort. Similarly, to assume that all survey consultants are equally interchangeable ven-dors capable of the same level of service and expertise—which we have termed the *vendor-mindset* (Church and Waclawski, 1998b)—can also be dangerous. Some consultants, for example, have little ex-perience in linking survey content to strategic objectives or change initiatives, using advanced data analysis methods, developing surveys for organizations with global constituents, or using cutting-edge data collection techniques. Thus, when choosing an external survey prac-titioner to either conduct a survey effort or consult to an internal team on one being done in-house, it is critical that each be examined for unique strengths and weaknesses relative to the goals and objec-tives of the survey effort.

Needless to say, this very important time in the survey process must be handled with a mixture of sensitivity and assertiveness on the part of the consultant or survey practitioner. Remember that the level of interest in the results tends to vary considerably with the amount of time taken by the survey team to communicate the findings. Tim-ing is important during this final stage as well. At this juncture, the survey practitioner must be especially sensitive to the anxieties and fears of the client or end user, while guiding the survey sponsor through the process of disseminating information and action planning in a timely manner. At this phase in the survey cycle, some of the most reasonable and sensible end users and survey sponsors can be blinded by their own fears and rendered virtually unwilling or inca-pable of taking action. There are many ways in which this anxiety can manifest itself; for the purposes of this step we will limit our discussion to the following two forms we have experienced most frequently: paralysis and denial.

Paralysis

The first mechanism for the expression of anxiety comes from a term often used by one of our professors in graduate school who was an experienced consultant and survey practitioner. What he affectionately called *analysis paralysis* refers to a person's inability to get beyond the analysis stage (Step Five) when working with survey data. If you are struggling with a survey sponsor to put the finishing touches on a survey report that you have been toiling over for weeks and have gone through endless iterations of edits and your client keeps asking you for "one more set of analyses, just to be sure we have got it all right," then you probably are on the receiving end of an analysis paralysis situation.

However, this may not be serious. Often in these cases if your client is at all reasonable, some simple nudging will suffice. Gently let your client know that what he or she is experiencing is normal but counterproductive. Remind him or her of your original agreements regarding content and delivery timetables. Point out the implicit agreement with the survey respondents to provide a valid and legitimate set of results. Be supportive of your client and walk him or her through the issues. It is at this point in the survey process that you will have to be acutely aware of your client's emotional and psychological states vis-à-vis the survey effort. Be patient and remember that even though you may have seen this paralysis happen many times before, your client probably has not. If all else fails, use the data to help your client move beyond his or her anxieties. In most cases there will be ample write-in commentary expounding on the necessity to report out results to all involved and take action. Sometimes the words of coworkers can be more convincing than any argument made by the survey practitioner or survey team.

Denial

Another possible manifestation of anxiety that may not be so benign is that of outright denial of the results. This is a convenient defense mechanism, for if the client rejects the findings of the survey, then he or she does not have to do anything (take any action) about them. If not rectified, this can render your survey useless. Denial can take several forms:

- Flat rejection of the survey findings ("these data are inaccurate," "people didn't understand the question," "people didn't understand the scales," "this is not what's really going on here")

- Placing blame on or finding fault with the survey team or process ("your sample is bad," "you didn't ask the right questions," "you surveyed people at the wrong time")

- Requests for additional external points of comparison (usually those intended to be used to demonstrate that the organization is not doing that poorly after all)

- Attempts to whitewash the data (for example, completely taking control of and rewriting the survey findings to the point where the "official" communication of the results to others is obtuse or inaccurate)

Of these forms of denial, the fourth is the most serious; although this does not occur often, it is an unpleasant reality of the survey process, particularly for those who have invested significantly in the effort.

As with paralysis, denial can be overcome but requires some skill and shrewdness on the part of the survey practitioner or team. Experience tells us that reporting the results of a survey can be fraught with political complications, which are veritable land mines to the transfer and action planning processes. Denial often occurs as a result of the sponsor's or senior management's fear of delivering bad news to the organization. It often seems as if the end user is blaming the survey team for the content and issues identified in the results. Despite conventional wisdom, the messenger often does get shot. If you find yourself on the receiving end of a denial situation, it is often due to a combination of (1) this very rational fear or concern of exposure in conjunction with (2) the fact the client does not feel adequate ownership of the survey process, which in turn is often due to a lack of involvement in the process from the beginning. As a survey practitioner, it is your job at this point to facilitate and engender a sense of ownership in the data in order to transfer the results to action on the part of the end user. This is not an easy task at the eleventh hour, especially if you are asking the client to own something that is not particularly positive (and most surveys do have their share of positives and negatives). Nevertheless, if this denial is not overcome, you can go no further with the results, however wonderfully analyzed and prepared they may be. Several actions can be taken to avert this problem:

- Keep the key end users (the survey sponsor and senior management members) fully briefed during all phases of the survey process. If this is not possible, work very closely with the appropriate staff members to ensure joint ownership. The goal here is to pass the baton.

- Encourage the client to put his or her signature on as many documents and memos as possible regarding the survey process (both before and after administration).

- Have the survey sponsor commit to reporting the results (in a way that he or she is comfortable with) to everyone who participated in the survey process.

- Arrange for the survey sponsor to commit, in advance of the administration, to an action plan.

- Go back to the original contract; remind the sponsor of his or her commitment to action.

- Don't give up!

In the end it is your job to help your client see the light at the end of the tunnel.

A Commitment to Action

As we mentioned, one of the first and most important elements in ensuring that a survey effort will result in organizational change is a commitment to action on the part of the survey champion, client, or senior management of the organization. Just as a highly visible, active, and respected promoter of the survey effort is very important at the beginning of the process when laying the groundwork for organizational participation and commitment (as discussed in Step One), so too is this role immensely important before, during, and after the delivery and communication of the findings throughout the organization. Having the support of senior individuals lends credibility and importance to survey results that otherwise simply would not be there. With the plethora of information coming into people's lives on a daily basis, survey findings are likely to be treated as another distraction that is not particularly (or seemingly) related to one's day-to-day job if they are not associated with positive change by someone of stature. A commitment to action, expressed in terms of the survey champion's own reaction and response to the results obtained, is key to building energy to use the results in decision making.

The example in Exhibit 7.1 demonstrates one way to obtain senior leadership's stamp of approval. A letter or memo of this type is frequently included as the introduction to survey findings and sets the stage for action planning. Written communications alone are not sufficient to create the energy needed for successful change as a result of a survey, but they are important and set the tone for future

Exhibit 7.1. Sample CEO Communication Regarding Survey Results.

Dear Colleague,

We are constantly striving to become a better organization—more productive, profitable, service-oriented, and better managed. The latter includes being more attuned and responsive to your needs. This is why we chose to examine the way we run our organization by conducting an organization survey. During the past two months we asked every Company XYZ employee to take part in our first organizationwide survey. We wanted to know what you think of XYZ as a place to work, as well as your views about our future direction, the way we manage, and how you regard your job and working environment.

We were very pleased that over 5,000 employees completed the survey process. As a result we now have a great deal of useful information that we will use to improve the company. Your responses show areas where we are strong as well as those we need to improve. This report contains a summary and analysis, followed by a full and detailed presentation of all the results. Some of these results may be surprising or may confirm what you already knew. In any case, as you read through the report, I expect you will get a better view of Company XYZ, as I have.

By raising our own awareness of the issues that influence our performance, I believe we are taking an important step. Starting now we will explore these results and together develop a series of actions to address your needs and concerns.

In the weeks and months ahead, I hope that you and your managers will be discussing how this can be accomplished. We will report to you on survey-related actions by a special newsletter. I hope all of you will take an active role in using the survey results. Finally, I wish to thank all of you for your participation and therefore invaluable contribution to Company XYZ.

Jane Doe

CEO, Company XYZ

communications, particularly when written and signed by the CEO or another highly visible figure.

Four Approaches to Survey Action Planning

As we have discussed, there are several barriers to effective action planning using organizational survey results. However, once these have been overcome or minimized, the survey practitioner must then turn to the process of action planning—using the survey findings with his or her client for determining next steps and targeting areas for improvement and intervention. In the ideal situation, action planning will have been discussed and planned for (both in terms of the overall survey strategy and the level of resources required) well in advance. Unfortunately, this is not always the case. Many consultants, survey practitioners, and client organizations do not think about the appropriate use of survey results through an action planning process until the very end, that is, after the data have been analyzed and the reports delivered. Moreover, some survey "specialists" will not even get involved at this stage, claiming it is a role for another type of consultant; this can lead to the client being frustrated if this not expressed up-front. Thus, formulating a strategy for taking actions based on survey results should be discussed and decided on early in the survey process (preferably during contracting and objective setting in Step One). The need to do something with the results should not be a sudden realization that just "comes up" during feedback delivery or a topic that gets avoided in the hope the client won't need it. In order to ensure maximum utility and impact from the survey results, a discussion of the expected outcomes of the survey should always include the plan for using the results for organization change and improvement.

We have found that four broad strategies for action planning can be undertaken, based on survey results: *traditional cascade*, *leader development*, *incentive based*, and *strategic change*. Before discussing each approach in detail, however, it is important to emphasize three key points.

First, although the approaches are different, they are not mutually exclusive. In fact, they are often used in combination in order to achieve maximum benefit from the survey results. Second, the approaches will have varying degrees of success, depending on the quality of implementation and on the organizational context. Third, the strategies vary on two important characteristics: (1) level of integration and (2) level of intervention (see Figure 7.2). By *level of integration* we mean that these approaches range along a continuum regarding the extent to which they are linked, connected, or embedded in other organizational programs.

Are the survey content and the use of the results tied to the organization's strategic planning process? Or perhaps they are tied to that new LDL (leaders developing leaders [Tichy, 1997]) initiative that was started in another part of the business. By *level of intervention* we mean that action planning processes vary as to which outcomes and changes initiated from them are aimed at affecting individuals, groups (teams, divisions, functions, or business units) or the organization as a whole—in short, the level of impact desired. For example, does the action planning effort focus more on changing senior management style or specific promotions or reassignments (individual level); improving working relationships, communications, and processes across

Figure 7.2. Four Types of Action Planning Strategies.

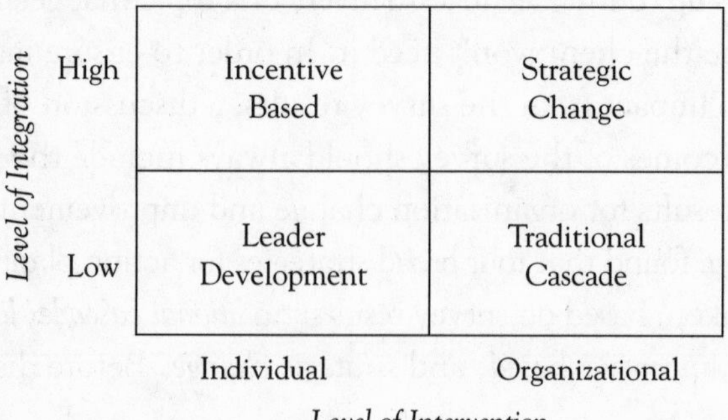

	Individual	Organizational
High (*Level of Integration*)	Incentive Based	Strategic Change
Low	Leader Development	Traditional Cascade

Level of Intervention

different teams, functions, or units (group level); or on changing the organizational culture, the entire information technology superstructure, the strategic direction, or the mission and vision for the future (organizational level)?

The following section outlines each of the four approaches to making the most of organizational survey efforts through the action planning process. The relative strengths and weaknesses of each approach are also discussed.

The Traditional Cascade Approach

This is the approach with which most organizations and survey vendors (as opposed to survey consultants) are likely to be familiar. The cascading method of delivery is a straightforward means for promoting a higher level of understanding of the key themes identified in a survey effort and gaining commitment to some form of action in the organization. Generally speaking, the more significant the amount of management's time that is allotted to discuss and explore the survey results, the greater the understanding and commitment (up to a point). Moreover, the most common use of this type of survey planning approach is to combine the survey reporting with a discussion (sometimes managed interactively in a problem-solving format) of broader organizational issues. These types of working sessions, if they are facilitated correctly and are actively and visibly supported by significant senior leaders, can send a message to the rest of the organization that the survey process is indeed (1) worth the effort, (2) being taken seriously by management, and (3) going to result in some tangible outcomes.

Although it is often complex and laborious, the cascading process can be invaluable in getting the level of commitment necessary among the senior- and middle-management ranks for successfully implementing the various changes planned, based on the survey results. Thus, as might be expected, this type of top-down approach requires the support of senior leadership and key players in the organization very early on in the survey reporting stage. In the best-case scenario, by using this method of working with the results, the survey practitioner or team will have the commitment of the survey sponsor and senior leadership. Perhaps some initial actions will be undertaken before the majority of middle management and employees are even aware that the data analysis process has been completed, giving the practitioner a much-needed head start.

The Roll-Out Process

Generally, the reporting of results starts with a series of meetings with the survey sponsor to inform him or her about the key findings and themes from the survey (see Chapter Six [Step Six] for additional information about this process). Usually, an executive summary is reported at this time. The purpose of this meeting is two-fold: (1) to provide the immediate client (for example, the survey sponsor or perhaps the survey champion) with the findings before the rest of the organization (including the rest of senior leadership) has a chance to see them, and (2) to allay any last-minute fears or anxieties about what to expect after the results have been released.

These preliminary meetings are not only a point of courtesy to the primary survey client but a way to manage the process and flow of information, as well as any personal concerns, while reaffirming the importance of a sincere commitment to action. Given the level of anxiety and sometimes resistance that is often present at the delivery of survey findings, the importance of the meetings cannot be overemphasized.

Once these meetings have been conducted, the survey results are presented to succeeding levels of management (usually the vice presidential or division levels will follow) in a top-down fashion. In this manner results cascade down from the top to the bottom of the organization in waves of communication and action planning sessions. As the results get reported to each successive level in the management hierarchy, the specificity of the results also increases. For example, division heads would not only receive a report containing the organizationwide survey results but also the results that are specific to their own division. Likewise, department managers would receive a report profiling the organizationwide results, their division results, and their own department-specific results (see Step Six for examples).

Typically, as part of this data roll-out process, issue-driven task forces and steering committees are put in place to develop action plans to address the organizationwide issues that arise from the survey (see Church, Margiloff, and Coruzzi, 1995). The task forces are usually made up of members from various functional units and organizational levels in order to ensure adequate representation of different organizational "pockets" and a diversity of perspectives. Typically, these groups are charged with the goal of driving strategic planning at the organization, unit, and department levels, and developing timelines and systems for the measurement of change. Often at the conclusion of the cascade process, a series of focus groups is conducted to debrief survey perceptions, revisit and fine-tune the action plans generated, and discuss the impact of the survey and potentially redirect other organizational efforts and initiatives.

The Communication Process

The organization can cascade survey results in different ways, including town meetings, video presentations, corporate newsletters, printed brochures and booklets, and even on-line reporting on intranets or Web sites. In general, the same communication outlets discussed in Step Three apply here as well. Regardless of how the results and the organization's commitment to action are conveyed, however, it is important to remember that surveys raise employees' awareness of issues, and in turn, their expectations for action and improvement. If management refuses to acknowledge or address these factors, frustration and cynicism toward future change initiatives are likely consequences. Moreover, in some situations (for example, following a massive downsizing effort, a restructuring, or a series of mergers and acquisitions) conditions such as employee morale can be negatively affected when a survey effort is ignored or buried by management. Thus, it is the survey practitioner's role and responsibility to help the decision makers in the organization ensure that a formal and tangible response is generated. This response should consist of the following:

- Giving considerable thought to and having discussions about what the survey results mean

- Determining how the survey results should be communicated to others

- Planning for what actions should be taken

- Taking action

- Following up on the success or failure of these actions

Only by adhering to all of these will the survey results be capable of having a meaningful impact on the organization.

Benefits and Shortcomings

The benefits of the traditional approach are that

- It is an effective means for communicating results to different levels of the organization quickly.

- It emphasizes communication of results at all levels.

- The hierarchical roll-out design allows time for commitment from senior management (vis-à-vis) action planning before presenting results to lower levels in the organization.

- The approach can be very effective if used in conjunction with one of the other four types of action planning strategies.

The shortcomings of this approach are that

- If used alone, it is the least effective means for creating change (this approach is heavily oriented toward communication only).

- The approach reinforces the top-down (as opposed to more bottom-up) approach to problem solving and creating change in organizations.

- This approach is not easily integrated into other organizational initiatives, given that its primary focus is on communication.

- It can lead to delays in communicating results if roadblocks appear between levels (for example, senior management wants to delay reporting to lower levels).

The Leader Development Approach

In many organizations the use of the traditional cascade approach as a stand-alone method for survey action planning has produced less-than-stellar results, given its emphasis on communication (as opposed to action) and its lack of focus on individual ownership and accountability. The leadership development approach has been developed largely in response to the inadequacies of the traditional cascade method as a solo intervention. Moreover, the structure of the leader development approach has added benefits, as it is designed to foster individual accountability, not only for organizational change based on the survey results but for developing leaders within the organization. Thus its purpose and content tend to be very personal and specific in nature.

The Roll-Out Process

As in the traditional cascade approach, organizationwide survey results are typically delivered first to the CEO and senior leadership at an off-site meeting. During this meeting there is a preview of the organization's major issues that, if done well, should integrate with the firm's objectives. Directly following this meeting a series of facilitated, off-site workshops is held for leaders and managers to receive and work with their business unit, division, and departmental results. Typically, these workshops last for several days, and participants are grouped by organizational level. Workshops are usually scheduled so that the senior leaders attend earlier than middle managers. In this way the results cascade in a top-down manner.

In addition to receiving their specific survey results at the workshops, leaders and managers often receive other types of individualized data such as multisource (or 360-degree) feedback (MSF; see Bracken, Timmreck, and Church, 2001) and personality assessments. An example of the latter is the Myers-Briggs Type Indicator (Hirsh and Kummerow, 1990), which helps identify areas for improvement, as well as how to build leadership skills in the organization. Small-group and one-on-one coaching sessions are used to focus on the convergence and diagnostic nature of all these data on the manager's leadership style. The inputs here include survey feedback, MSF, personality, observations, team ratings, and so on. During these one-on-one coaching sessions, individuals are pushed to develop plans for making changes and improvements based on the themes in their data. These action plans are normally designed to address a balance of areas for personal, departmental, and even organizational change (depending on the level of the manager or leader in the organization). These action plans are typically offered in the form of "drafts" to be taken back to the workplace, pending clarification and commitment from the manager's work unit (for example, direct reports and a supervisor). This is an important step, as the process is designed to include direct reports and others, not only in providing feedback (on the survey and multisource feedback instruments) but in the action planning process itself. No single individual can change an organization, except perhaps the CEO. The rest of us need the support of coworkers, colleagues, and supervisors, not to mention parallel changes in systems, technology, culture, and structure.

These managers, who have been inundated with personalized survey and behavioral feedback, are expected to return to their workplace and conduct meetings with their work unit to begin taking action. These meetings are usually conducted with four objectives in mind: (1) for the manager to share his or her specific learnings about being a leader and how this affects the department and other areas of the business, (2) to help the manager gain clarity or resolve any questions about the survey and multisource feedback received (for example, "Does anyone have some ideas as to why this item was rated so poorly?"), (3) for the manager to present and get help in revising his or her initial action plan, and (4) to get work unit members involved in the actions to be taken by assigning roles and responsibilities and determine how change will be measured.

Benefits and Shortcomings

The benefits of the leader development approach are that it

- Promotes individual commitment to change

- Fosters action at the work-unit level using intact teams, not task forces

- Involves direct reports (research shows that conversations with direct reports lead to improvements (Walker and Smither, 1999)

- Provides a context for understanding survey results, that is, focuses on the link between leadership behavior and work unit and organizational outcomes

- Fosters leadership development and improvement, which is good for the organization as a whole

- Use of extensive resources required for this approach demonstrates organizational commitment to improvement

Potential shortcomings are that the approach

- Can have little organizational support for change, particularly if supporting processes and resources are not in alignment

- Relies heavily on the commitment, energy, and proactive nature of individual managers and leaders

- Is not usually well integrated into other organization initiatives, given the strong focus on individual accountability and development

- Does not lend itself to sample survey approaches so is likely to require a more costly census approach

The Incentive-Based Approach

The third type of approach to survey action planning reflects the use of incentives. This approach is different from the preceding two in that it emphasizes accountability through performance measurement and potential adjustments to compensation levels. The most common use of this approach is to create individual change and improvement. If done well (that is, is based on the right core competencies, as measured by a reliable and valid behaviorally based survey instrument), it can be a powerful process for ensuring real change. However, it is more complicated to implement and requires additional and considerable internal organizational support of the kind that is often politically volatile in nature. For example, in order to take advantage of such an approach, it requires being able to link individual-level survey results (let's say the department manager level) with individual-level internal metrics. Because these data often reside in different departments in the organization, it can be difficult to cross these boundaries. Moreover, if such information is misused, it can result in serious employment or legal problems for the employee and the organization. Nonetheless, some organizations do use this approach.

The Roll-Out Process

This approach can be delivered through either the traditional cascade approach or through the leadership development process. The emphasis here, however, is not typically on the method of communication but on creating enhanced and meaningful individual accountability by linking survey results to individual performance metrics. These metrics often include such indicators as individual and departmental productivity, quality audits, formal performance appraisals, customer service ratings, staffing levels, and turnover. In this way survey results are formally and inextricably tied into the individual manager's or leader's annual performance objectives. Thus, improvements based on future survey results (which assumes repeated assessments) are linked to the manager's or leader's per-formance appraisal and management system, and in the end are used to make individual compensation adjustments as well. This can be galvanizing with respect to focusing on improvement.

One way to implement a more integrated, incentive-based ap-proach is through the creation of a management performance profile (MPP). Similar to the notion of a balanced scorecard (Kraut and Saari, 1999), the MPP provides a means for comparing individuals using a combination of different types of information. Here is how it works. First, a customized model or equation is developed that serves to differentiate between higher- and lower-performing individuals. This model is generated statistically and is based on prior data; the model uses a host of internal and external performance metrics. Typ-ically, these metrics consist of key performance measures that are both important and linked to existing initiatives for the organization—measures such as sales, productivity, turnover, and ratings of customer satisfaction; individual survey results and multisource feedback data may be used as well (Church and Waclawski, 1998a). When the MPP model has been completed and validated, each key performance met-ric in the equation will have a corresponding weight that indicates its relative contribution to the total score that can be generated. Thus, survey results might have more weight in one organization and less in another, based on their predictive power. Of course, raw empiricism need not always drive such models. In some situations weights may be adjusted either up or down, depending on prevailing priorities, needs, or values. In any case when the model is ready, as part of the assessment process, data for each leader or manager involved are input into the equation, and the results are used to develop a composite pic-ture of each individual's unique index of performance.

This performance profile can then be used both at the individual and organizational levels. At the individual level, it provides a way to asses specific leadership capabilities, which can feed into personnel decisions like leadership succession planning, promotions, and assignments. At the organizational level, it can provide a holistic snapshot of the organization's leadership capabilities, a diagnostic tool for assessing training needs, and a database for the organization to make informed policy decisions (see Figure 7.3). Regardless of the level at which it is most used, the right performance measures must be selected and used in the model. Moreover, the indexing equation should be customizable, depending on the focal manager's function, job type, job responsibilities, development plan, and performance objectives.

Benefits and Shortcomings

Benefits of the incentive-based approach are that it

- Fosters a maximum level of individual accountability through individual performance metrics and personnel decision-making processes

Figure 7.3. Managerial Performance Profile.

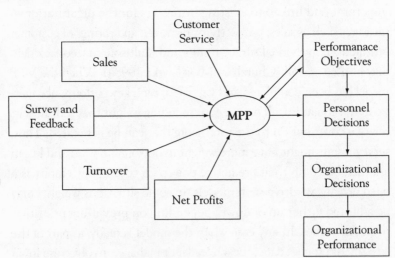

Source: Church and Waclawski, 1998a, p. 88. Copyright © 1998 by the American Society for Quality. Reprinted with permission.

- Provides better integration with other organizational initiatives, especially those related to personnel decisions

- Offers a means for understanding different levels of contribution of the various measures (surveys versus other metrics) without over- or underemphasizing any one

- Demonstrates and quantifies the link between behavior and performance

Potential shortcomings are that the approach

- Can be overly punitive, as opposed to developmental in nature, if not done properly

- Complex and costly to develop and validate

- May be met with resistance

- Requires much documentation and assurance of the "right" metrics (or legal compliance and validation, depending on how it is used)

- Is extremely focused on individual (and sometimes team) assessment and diagnosis, as opposed to organization development and change

- Does not lend itself at all to sample survey approaches; requires a more costly census approach

The Strategic Change Approach

The fourth and final category of action planning is the strategic change approach to using organizational surveys. It is most commonly used in conjunction with large-scale organization development and change initiatives. Moreover, it often involves a strong commitment from the entire management and leadership body of measurement, intervention, and improvement over time. Thus, with some rare exceptions, it is unlikely that any survey effort limited to a single administration would fall under this category.

The main objective of this type of survey-based action planning effort is to place an equal and concurrent amount of emphasis on individual behavior change *and* organization change. This is accomplished by ensuring the close alignment of the individual managerial behaviors being assessed and rewarded (using a variety of different types of measures) with the mission, vision, strategic objectives, and core competencies of the organization for the purpose of creating significant and lasting large-scale transformation.

Similarly, there is an equal emphasis on individual and organizational metrics. In this approach numerous sources of performance data that span multiple levels of analysis (for example, innovations and patents, customer service, turnover, industry awards and recognition, speed to market, profitability, appraisals, public image and business-based rankings, market share, strength of new hires, and ROI) are used to examine the impact of various changes and interventions and to track progress toward some new direction, mission, or vision for the organization.

Given this description, it should come as no surprise that many data-driven OD practitioners find surveys to be an important tool in their internal and external consulting work, both for conducting organizational diagnoses and driving organizational culture change. To this end, when surveys are (1) linked strategically to the primary organizational purpose and direction (both in terms of the content being assessed and the process of delivery) and (2) the approach to action planning is focused on creating large-scale systemic change using a multilevel approach to performance metrics and measurement, these methods become more than just tools for understanding and diagnosis. They can serve as an effective means for helping organizations transform themselves. Of course, it is unlikely that a survey effort (no matter how well conceived and implemented) can achieve all this alone. As is probably apparent, the strategic change approach to survey action planning is typically embedded in a more fundamental large-scale initiative over time; these initiatives usually originate with high energy (or significant need) at the seniormost echelons of an organization.

For example, as noted earlier, surveys can be useful for organizations going through mergers and acquisitions (M&A) (Burke and Jackson, 1991). In these situations surveys can serve as important tools for helping the merging organizations better understand and cope with the similarities and differences between them. More specifically, the entire survey effort—from development to action planning—in such a setting can be intentionally focused on important factors such as the nature of their respective cultures, disparate supporting structures, the mission and strategy driving each organization, and the systems that support work (for example, communication, IT, and training and development). These measures can be used to evaluate individual and team performance, as well as the day-to-day practices and behaviors of each set of senior and middle managers—in short, the way both companies do business. Thus, surveys undertaken for the purpose of strategic change enable organizations that are planning to be merged (or even already in process) to understand the nature of their similarities and differences and ultimately to help plan for the future of the new composite organization.

The Roll-Out Process

Organizational survey efforts undertaken for the purpose of creating strategic change can be approached (in terms of the action planning stage) through the use of the cascade or leadership development approach or a combination of both. Again, the key issue here (and the primary distinction from other approaches to survey action planning) is to ensure that the organization's mission and strategy are used to drive the survey content and that survey results are linked to both individual and organizational measures of performance. This link to the objectives and performance measures of the individual and the organization as a whole, with an emphasis on repeated measurements and the evaluation of change over time, makes the survey and the action planning process associated with it truly strategic in nature (see Figure 7.4).

Aside from these distinctions, one that we have not mentioned is the use of predictive modeling to guide change. This is often the hallmark of survey action planning efforts that are used in a strategic change context. We are talking here about a process that can be far more rigorous, complex, and ultimately significant to the future of an organization than the more standard regression procedures for framing relationships in a dataset for interpretative purposes (see Step Five). Although these approaches are certainly appropriate for a general analysis of survey results, the models that result do not even approximate the predictive power of an equation based on multiple sources of data (individual and organizational) collected across different times, levels, and units, and before and after a variety of change initiatives have been undertaken. And the analysis of such datasets can be extremely time consuming, complex, and indeed problematic for a whole host of reasons. Some of these will

Figure 7.4. Example of the Strategic Change Approach.

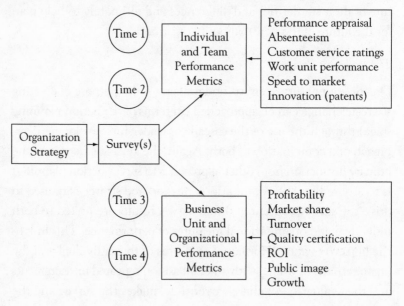

be discussed in detail later, but for now, imagine the complexities of creating the initial MPP model expanded tenfold, once a predictive model is generated (for example, via structural equation modeling and related techniques), its benefit to the organization can be enormous. In short, these techniques better inform decision making at both the individual and organizational levels (ranging from strategic planning to compensation and benefits to structural resign) by extracting maximum benefit from the data collected.

In short, this approach to working with and using survey data represents the best of all worlds. Unfortunately, it can also be extremely difficult (and therefore somewhat rare in practice) to implement with all elements, factors, players, systems, and measures in alignment.

Benefits and Shortcomings

The benefits of the strategic change approach are that

- When done correctly it represents the best approach to survey utilization
- The greatest impact is at the individual and organizational levels
- The survey becomes "transformational," as opposed to tactical in nature
- The approach integrates well into organizational strategy, initiatives, systems, and culture
- The approach provides important data that drive organizational change
- Truly predictive models can be generated

Potential shortcomings are that it

- Can be met with much resistance
- Requires the collection of vast amounts of specific data at all levels in the organization

- Can be expensive, complex, and time consuming to implement

- Does not lend itself to sample survey approaches so is likely to require a more costly census approach

- Requires significant and continued commitment and resources from senior and middle levels of the organization

Five Critical Factors That Determine the Success of Survey Action Planning

Regardless of which of the four approaches an organization takes, in our experience five factors are critical to the success of any survey action planning process. We have alluded to or mentioned them, but because taking action from surveys is such a critical component to their success, we summarize them here as well.

1. *Resources needed for action planning must be "built-in" during initial project contracting.* This means that action planning is not an afterthought but is thoroughly considered beforehand (in Step One). Resources to support actions that result from the survey must be considered and, to the extent possible, allocated in advance. This is essential; action planning efforts often fail because survey projects are inappropriately budgeted ("We don't have enough money left in the survey budget to implement any of these recommendations").

2. *Action planning intentions (and commitment) must be communicated early and to everyone.* The fact that managers and executives are expected to take action as a result of their survey findings should not come as a surprise to anyone in the organization. Many times, however, employees are not convinced of this notion—often because of prior failures. Thus, a "message of commitment to action" needs to be communicated early and often (see Step Three). In addition, mutual expectations between line management and the survey team need to be negotiated in advance of the survey delivery.

3. *Action planning possibilities must be given strong consideration during item development.* More specifically, whether a survey tool is purchased off-the-shelf or developed for a given situation, the content therein should be biased toward containing behaviorally based and action-oriented items, as opposed to items solely focused on attitudes and opinions (see Step Two). Action-oriented items by their very nature suggest solutions to problems.

4. *There must be strong organizational support and accountability for taking action based on the survey results.* Typically, this means that the survey sponsor or survey champion has the power, resources, and executive-level clout to ensure appropriate follow-through on the survey results (Steps One and Seven). This must also involve some level of formal accountability for improvement on the part of managers and executives.

5. *Senior-level commitment to taking action and reassessing progress must be strong.* In our experience, and as we have been arguing strongly throughout this book, without buy-in (financially, intellectually, and emotionally) from the top-most ranks of the organization, *all action planning efforts are doomed to failure.* This is a simple reality because of the organizational commitment of time, effort, and resources that are required to implement significant action based on a set of survey results. In short, the first four critical factors will not be met without senior-level commitment to taking action.

The Action Planning Process

We have said throughout our discussion that for a survey effort to be considered effective, it should contribute to important decision-making processes and result in some action. However, we have not described how this works and what these actions and outcomes might be. The identification and selection of possible alternatives following a survey effort are driven largely by the outcome of the data analysis and interpretation phase. As we discussed in Step Five, the use of conceptual models, theoretical frameworks, trends, grouping analyses, and other types of corporate directives can be useful in providing a view of the bigger picture and showing where efforts for change might be best directed.

If, for example, the analysis indicates that ratings of employee satisfaction are highly related to perceptions of poor management information systems, then it is clear that management needs to make changes to these systems. This might mean updating the system itself, replacing it with an entirely new one, or providing more training on how to maximize the use of the system currently in place. Whatever the outcome, management needs to proceed through the following steps:

1. Recognize that this is a problem and that it has consequences.

2. Show their recognition to employees through some form of communication.

3. Prepare a plan for improving or replacing the technology employed.

4. Make a commitment to acting on this plan.

If the content analysis and interpretation of the write-in comments indicate a significant lack of management emphasis on developing employees and preparing them for the future, this is an area that probably needs to be addressed as well. Depending on the situation, however, the required response might be anywhere from ensuring that all available developmental opportunities are effectively communicated to employees as they become available, to designing an entirely new training and development system aimed at giving managers the appropriate skills to train and mentor their direct employees.

Besides using larger, more complex frameworks and models, some survey questionnaires have their own (albeit somewhat simplistic) action planning prioritization process built into the items. For example, based on a mean ranking of what employees consider to be their most important benefits (as described in Figure 7.5), it would be relatively easy to determine what types of follow-up interventions should be made about modifying an existing benefits plan. If the data analysis and interpretation have been completed with an attention to detail and the involvement of key players and constituents in the organization, the types of outcomes and actions necessary should be relatively easy to determine.

Specifying the types of outcomes, interventions, and actions that might result from a large-scale survey effort would be never-ending. Just as the content of the data can reflect issues at the work unit, department, or organization level, so too can the interventions and actions taken as a result of the analysis be directed at different levels, where appropriate (see Figure 7.6).

Figure 7.5. Mean Ranking of Most Important Employee Benefits.

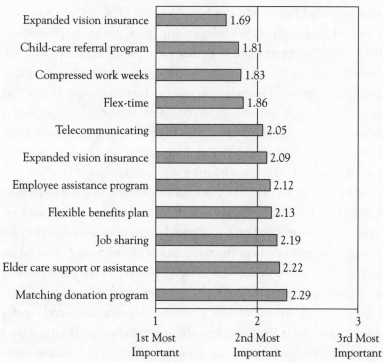

Figure 7.6. Levels of Data and Intervention.

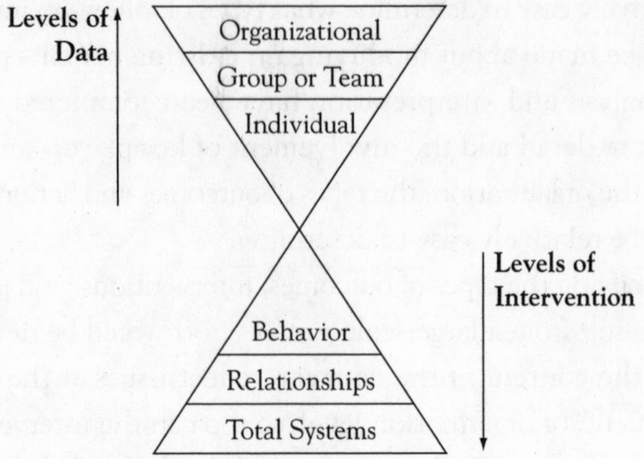

In this way, multiple interventions can be used concurrently to achieve a better, more integrated impact. For example, a possible intervention at the individual level directed at changing managerial behaviors might consist of a multisource (360-degree) feedback initiative. Similarly, at the relationship level, group-on-group feedback might be appropriate or perhaps team-building efforts and the introduction of cross-functional task forces designed to integrate roles and responsibilities across groups. Interventions directed at achieving a total systems-level change in the organization might consist of a multitude of coordinated efforts across different areas (for example, restructuring, changing reward and benefit systems, hiring new leadership, or making a culture change).

The only real constraints are those existing in the quality and quantity of the data. It would probably not make sense to pursue a restructuring effort based on recommendations from a survey effort for a large department where the responses obtained were not based on a random sample and reflected only 15 percent of the total number of employees in that area. If, on the other hand, 80 percent of employees agreed that the current structure is dysfunctional and creates conflict and inefficiencies, then some set of changes in this regard might be warranted. This is one reason an effective and successful survey effort is more than just a simple series of questions (and the reason for the existence of this book and others like it).

Although certainly not exhaustive, Table 7.1 provides a sampling of some of the major types of interventions and follow-up actions

Table 7.1. Potential Interventions Following a Survey Effort.

Intervention	Issues Intended to Address
Assessment centers and training needs assessment	To assess employee (typically managers') skill levels in key areas to identify specific training needs.
Skills training	To provide employees with the requisite skills to perform their jobs effectively.
Team-building sessions and interpersonal relationships	Opportunities for teams or work groups to enhance group processes, as well as working and interpersonal relationships.
Leadership development	To identify and develop leaders within the organization; to orient current and potential leaders to the values and performance standards of the organization; to provide a venue for networking and relationship building among leaders in different organizational functions or units.
Restructuring	To reapportion resources according to need and business performance in an effort to maximize productivity and minimize waste.
Business process	To work "smarter" and more efficiently with reengineering existing resources; to maximize performance and streamline existing ways of doing things.
Multisource (360-degree) feedback	To create self-awareness among leaders and managers through the process of giving and receiving feedback; to provide a unit of measurement on which leaders and managers can measure their performance and the accomplishment of goals and objectives; culture change through common practices.

that can result from a large-scale survey effort and the types of issues these are typically intended to address. Readers interested in finding out more about specific interventions, as well as additional options, should look to the organization development and change management literatures (for example, Beckhard and Pritchard, 1992; Berger, Sikora, and Berger, 1994; Bracken, Timmreck, and Church, 2001; Burke, 1994; Church and Waclawski, 1998a; Hornstein and others, 1971; Howard, 1994; Kanter, Stein, and Jick, 1992; Tichy, 1983; Tichy, 1997).

In some cases, particularly when working at lower levels in the organization, it can be beneficial for end users to identify and work through specific issues in their data or in conjunction with a survey consultant rather than identify these issues up-front. As we discussed in Step Six, this process of collaboration can lead to greater commitment regarding the intended outcomes, as well as greater specificity in the types of interventions identified and ultimately implemented.

Exhibit 7.2 is a sample step-by-step set of instructions and accompanying worksheets that can be used to help people work through specific survey-related issues. Of course, the implementation of this approach to using and working with survey results needs to have been decided long before the questionnaire is administered. Once again, this brings us back to one of the issues (discussed in Step One) behind establishing a plan and concrete objectives at the outset. If the survey practitioner and sponsor know how deep in the organization and to what ends the data will be delivered (for example, senior management only for general trend analysis versus work group levels for every manager with fifteen or more direct reports), the appropriate individuals can be involved and the right demographic information needed for cutting the data included in the instrument. Once the data have been collected, however, and even if managers are ready and willing to use their individual results, if the demographic information was not included it is probably impossible to obtain the results needed for effective action planning at this level.

Exhibit 7.2. Sample Survey Worksheets and Action Planning Guide.

Developing Action Plans

1. *Move from your reactions to the data to next steps.*

   Meet with your team and go over the results of the survey. Discuss how you will use the data to improve what you do and how you will do it. What might be some areas you want to work through as a team?

   The following worksheets provide a place for you to record what you have learned from the survey. Use the first worksheet to identify areas of strength and those that need improvement. Then use the second worksheet to summarize in three to five points the most important issues for your team to work on. What did you learn and what do you need to work on as a result?

Areas of strength	Areas for improvement
Communicating with direct reports	Confronting my superiors when necessary
Giving my direct reports timely feedback	Fostering communication between my department and others
Rewarding and recognizing high performers	Providing a clear direction for my department

Most important issues

1. As a team, we need to integrate our work processes with other departments in Company XYZ.

2. As a team, we need to determine our future direction and objectives.

3. As a leader, I need to challenge my supervisors when appropriate instead of being silent.

4. As a leader, I need to provide strong leadership and help my team reach its objectives.

5. As a leader, I need to take a more hands-on approach to management.

(continued on the next page)

Exhibit 7.2. Sample Survey Worksheets and Action Planning Guide.
         (continued)

2. *Establish a contract for working on the data.*

Set up a timeline of activities and decide who will do what. Schedule your next meeting to communicate expectations for what each member will bring to the next meeting.

Contract to my team

As our team leader, I promise to actively work on addressing the key issues for our team that resulted from the Company XYZ survey. I promise to hold monthly meetings to review our objectives and progress on these issues. Also I promise to be open and receptive to honest feedback regarding our progress.

3. *Check your group process.*

End your meeting with a check on the group's process. How did the meeting go? What went well and what didn't go well? How can you do things differently in the future? Make sure that everyone understands the main issues, is comfortable with plans you developed to address these issues, and is clear about his or her responsibility in the change process.

4. *Follow up on your commitments.*

Measure the success or failure of your efforts by setting systems in place to evaluate progress. This can occur through group discussions or resurveying on key issues.

5. *Conduct periodic meetings to evaluate your team's progress.*

These follow-up meetings can be incorporated into your staff meetings or can occur independently. Whatever the case, these meetings should occur frequently and on a regular basis to ensure maximum commitment to the change process.

The following worksheet can be used as a starting point for recording your team's action plans and charting your progress.

Exhibit 7.2. Sample Survey Worksheets and Action Planning Guide.
(continued)

Issue	Point person	Intervention	Deadline	Results expected
Intergroup relations	Mai Reeport	Team building exercise and work-sharing program		Elimination of duplication of effort, better relationships outside department
Challenging up	Jane Manager	Regular meeting with my supervisor to discuss key issues		Voicing issues of my department to leadership
Setting direction	Jane Manager and all team members	Department mission statement with specific objectives and timelines		Gaining clarity about where we are going and why; alignment with corporate strategy

Linking Survey Results to Other Measures of Performance

Given the rise in survey use to drive strategic organizational change, the emphasis on linking survey results to other measures of performance has never been greater. Therefore, the administration of organization assessment surveys has become an increasingly important and popular part of many change efforts. As noted in the strategic change approach to action planning, surveys can be particularly useful when their results are linked to other measures of performance (for example, customer service ratings, financial performance indicators, measures of turnover and attrition). Linking survey results to these hard measures enables organizations to identify relationships between various aspects of organizational functioning (leadership, company values, management practices, and policies and procedures) and desired performance outcomes. Figure 7.7 provides an example of how various issues and item-related content areas might be linked to hard performance indicators. In this way survey results can be used to target areas for change, which will enhance organizational effectiveness as well as demonstrate the importance and relevance of survey findings

Figure 7.7. Linking Survey Results to Performance Measures.

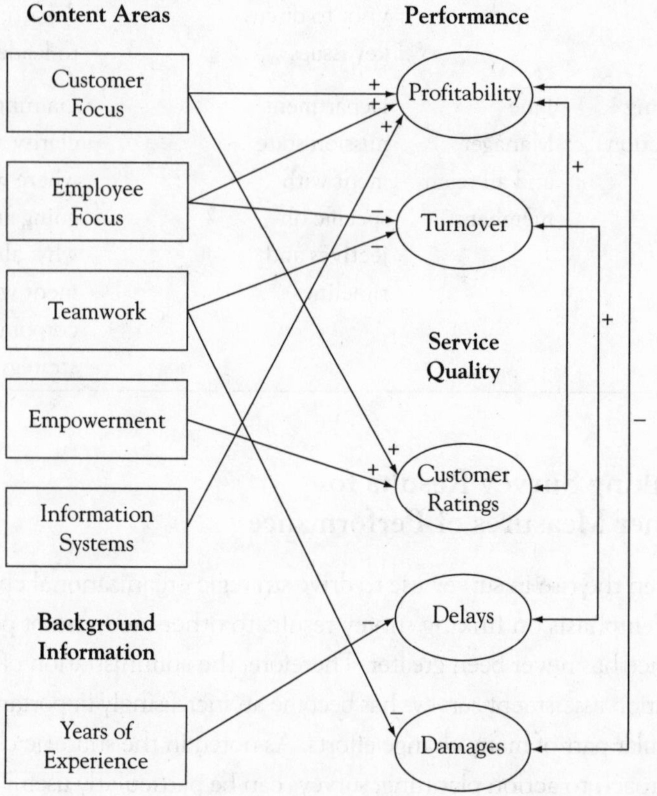

Source: Church, 1995, p. 28. Used by permission of MCB University Press.

to people's day-to-day work activities. Not surprisingly, a plethora of issues must be considered when linking survey results to other measures of performance. These can be broken down into three broad categories: theoretical, political, and technical.

Regarding theoretical considerations, the main objective here is to determine relevant indices of comparison. For example, linking a survey that measures managers' opinions about the company's dental plan to ratings of external customer service does not make sense. Why would anyone expect satisfaction with a dental plan to translate directly to the quality of customer service provided? The nature of managerial behaviors in the work group, however, is likely to have an impact in this regard. In determining linking variables one must identify the appropriate measures of performance that can be logically and empirically merged with the survey data. This will necessitate, at the very least, a thorough review of relevant literature regarding the variables to be linked and a solid research design. Organizations that plan on linking variables to survey data will be best served by considering these types of issues in advance of the survey design. Such consideration and planning will allow specific issues and complexities related to the research questions of interest to be built into the survey process a priori.

Considering the possible political implications and the true availability of linking survey data to hard performance measures is also advisable. Many people would perceive the need to work the political process in this regard as a necessary evil. However, aligning rather than alienating key players in the organization is essential to the success of any survey-related effort. For example, if the results of a survey are intended to be linked to individual or departmental performance measures (for example, sales, revenue, customer satisfaction, turnover, innovations and patents, or repeat business), going through the proper channels to obtain the necessary data and explaining its uses will be of paramount importance. The last thing the survey team wants to do is alienate respondents by overburdening them in this process. Further, if the data are obtained through inappropriate means, the resulting chaos and backlash when discovered could easily destroy the perceived integrity and validity of the survey data. It is an unfortunate fact that other people in the organization who are not directly involved in the survey process may not be interested in sharing their data with another professional, regardless of the intended uses and potential benefits of the information. These types of situations make the process of linking survey data to other measures seem almost impossible. Once again, we are back to the issue of obtaining appropriate senior-level commitment and setting the right objectives during the contracting stage.

A consideration of technical computability is also required. In order to link the results to other measures, it is imperative to ensure that the level of analysis between the various datasets is consistent. Again, this should be determined before the survey plan and design is complete. The appropriate demographic or background variables must be included in the instrument from the start to provide the opportunity for adequate level matching among datasets. For example, if the desire is to link external customer service ratings collected at the department level to ratings of empowerment obtained from a survey effort at the department level, then the practitioner needs to make sure that the survey data will (1) include this variable with the same departmental categories and (2) that the data will be capable of being averaged and subsequently analyzed at this level as well. The analyses will ultimately be limited by the greatest level of specificity of the data collected on both measures, that is, the lowest available point. So going back to our previous example, if either of the measures to be linked is not specific enough (for example, the data have been collected at the divisional but not the departmental levels), the specificity of the analyses will be hampered. Other technical considerations include the ability to link databases, which will necessitate the use of compatible statistical packages or spreadsheets. Although not impossible to do, linking different datasets can be complex and time consuming. Again, the advice or consultation of an experienced data analyst is invaluable here.

Building Systems for Evaluating Success

Measuring the progress of survey efforts is an important part of demonstrating commitment to the survey and also ensuring that things are changing for the better. Informal "How are we doing?" conversations are useful in gauging progress, but they are not enough. Serious evaluation must be undertaken to solidify commitment and ensure continued efforts in the right direction. Many organizational surveys and survey-related interventions are implemented in the context of ongoing organizational change or development initiatives, and it may be difficult to parse out the effects of such interventions. Nevertheless, without such attempts, proof of change and the importance of surveying in general will be lacking.

One of the main difficulties in evaluating the success of any organizational survey effort is that a valid and reliable instrument is necessary but not sufficient for affecting change. As we have discussed in this chapter, many factors are involved in creating meaningful organizational change through surveys, not all of which are under anyone's control, including the survey practitioner or the survey sponsor. For evaluation purposes, however, the difficulty can be to determine exactly which was the principal factor in causing the success or downfall of any given set of interventions following a survey effort.

One way to examine the effectiveness of an intervention is to use comparative groups. This process involves finding a group of different departments, functions, regions, or work groups in the same organization that went about the communication and use of their results through different methods. Some groups, for example, may have provided more general communication of the findings; others may have delivered the results to every manager and had them work through the findings with their teams. Because these quasi-experimental groups would typically share the same organizational culture, the survey practitioner is likely to find useful insights into the process of working with survey data in their organization. These insights, then, may also be applicable to other troubled areas or future survey efforts.

One final note: the evaluation of interventions aimed at development and change (such as organizational surveys) is historically weak. In fact, the research methods employed in past evaluations of OD- and HRD-related interventions in particular have repeatedly come under serious scrutiny (Ledford and Mohrman, 1993; Roberts and Robertson, 1993; Robertson, Roberts, and Porras, 1993; Terpstra, 1981). More specifically, researchers have found evidence of a negative relationship between the methodological rigor of evaluations of these types of interventions and their reported success (Golembiewski and Sun, 1990; Roberts and Robertson, 1993; Terpstra, 1981). Known as *positive-findings bias*, this disturbing relationship has been hypothesized to stem from the evaluator's unconscious desire to prove the efficacy of his or her interventions (Terpstra, 1981). This finding can have serious implications for the survey practitioner who wishes to evaluate interventions that arise from his or her own survey findings. Therefore, it is probably better to work with an objective third party who can help devise an impartial way of measuring progress. Some of the most common and useful ways of measuring progress are (1) resurveying at a later date, (2) conducting focus groups or interviews to assess change, and (3) measuring changes in absenteeism, turnover, and productivity rates. In the end, however, the survey sponsor, champion and, indeed, the entire client organization decide whether the effort was a success.

The Evolving Role of the Survey Practitioner

We want to close our discussion with an important topic that deserves more attention in the literature, namely, the evolving role of today's survey practitioner. Given the inherent complexities involved in designing, conducting, and analyzing surveys, and in action planning, it should come as no surprise that the role of the survey practitioner is expanding. Surveying is no longer just throwing a questionnaire together and dropping it in the mail to a few employees. The twenty-first century is one of telecommuting, intranets, chaos theory, e-commerce, news bytes, discontinuous strategic change, PDAs and Palm Pilots, global economy, B2B, genetic reengineering, and just about e-everything (including "e-surveys"). In short, this is not your parents' (or your grandparents') survey world.

In the past, survey practitioners were often thought of as survey content or process experts whose contribution lay primarily in constructing, administering, and analyzing the results of relatively straightforward employee attitude and opinion surveys. As such, the essential skills of the "first generation" of survey practitioner, if you will, centered primarily around item design and instrument development, the pros and cons of various data collection methods, and numerous statistical techniques and reporting procedures—in short, all of the areas that make up the tactical elements or the nuts and bolts of the survey process.

Over time, as the types and applications of organizational surveys have became more diverse and sophisticated (moving away from satisfaction surveys toward customer service applications and surveys for organization change and development) and as more advanced statistical analysis techniques have emerged (for example, structural equation modeling), additional skill sets are now required of the practitioner. As before, he or she must remain a content expert in guiding the process of survey development and delivery through its administration but is now expected to possess a mastery over other areas as well. Some of these include the appropriate use of more advanced data analysis techniques, including linkage-related procedures. In other words, today's survey practitioner must also be, for lack of a better term, a data guru.

Unfortunately, there is little time to learn this role as more and more organizational members expect analyses and results to be delivered instantly and without error. To make the situation even more complex, it is often the case that clients (internal or external) want to be actively involved (sometimes to their own detriment if they are unfamiliar with such procedures) in the data analysis process; they want desperately to guide the exploration of key relationships. In some cases this is only a minor distraction, but in others it can prove difficult to be continually responsive to what might be termed offbeat requests while trying to focus on the big picture analysis.

Moreover, even if one is able to master all of these skills and balance the complexities and competing pressures inherent in the process, the skills are generally considered as merely a baseline for assessing proficiency in survey work and not as a competitive advantage. In some cases they are not seen as a specialized area of expertise. In short, they simply get you to the table. What you do from there will make all the difference both in terms of being an effective survey consultant and in implementing a world-class survey effort.

Today it takes more than a data guru to make a survey successful. Other skills include such previously unheard-of consulting skills as contracting, communicating with people in business (in nontechnical terms, which is antithetical to the understanding of advanced statistics), effective platform abilities, the capability to deliver the results in an engaging manner to all types of people, and the ability to create a compelling story from what amounts to a pile of numbers (see Step Five).

But it doesn't stop there. Most clients today are very well educated about the possible types of action planning strategies available to them. This is based in large part on the popularity and prevalence of surveys in many large (Fortune 500) organizations and the familiarity most have with some form of survey process. For many clients in search of a survey consultant (in this case rather than a vendor), their decision will be based on who can help them best use the survey results for positive change. Therefore, in order to survive and be effective in today's competitive survey marketplace, survey consultants and vendors must be *change agents*. This role is the end state of our evolution as a survey practitioner (see Figure 7.8).

Given that we have spent a significant amount of effort throughout this book emphasizing the use of surveys for strategic purposes, this point should come as no surprise. More important though, increasing numbers of organizations are attempting to use their surveys

Figure 7.8. Evolving Role of the Survey Practitioner.

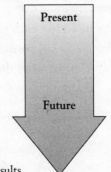

- **Content and Process Expert**
  - Timing, administration, confidentiality
  - Working, core items, background information

- **Data Guru**
  - Advanced analysis, data modeling
  - Report writing

- **Change Agent**
  - Strategic approach to surveys
  - Facilitating understanding and action
  - Partnering and coaching beyond delivering the results

for the express purpose of organizational transformation and change, as opposed to the more traditional tactical concerns such as assessing employee attitudes or measuring customer satisfaction. Books such as *First, Break All the Rules* (Buckingham and Coffman, 1999) and *Employee Surveys That Make a Difference: Using Customized Feedback Tools to Transform Your Organization* (Folkman, 1998), which showcase the survey as a tool for organizational change, are evidence of this new direction.

This means that today's practitioner must possess a strategic mindset and accompanying toolkit for designing, implementing, and using surveys to create lasting change. In the role of change agent then, the survey practitioner must be able to help his or her client understand not only what the survey results mean but how to use them to drive the organization to achieve its mission and meet its objectives. This means influencing behavior change at the individual, team, function, division, and organization levels. Thus, the role requires even greater expertise in a variety of skills in addition to those already mentioned.

Perhaps the most important skill is that of facilitation. This means being able to partner with the client to help him or her reach conclusions about how to interpret results and take meaningful action based on them. This type of facilitation can be done one-on-one (with a CEO, HR director, internal consultant, or line manager) or in groups such as during strategic planning sessions, business-process reengineering teams, top management meetings, or issue-focused task forces. In the end, today's survey practitioner must be a facilitator, change agent, consultant, data guru, content expert, and confidant. Who knows what the future will bring!

Checklist for Step Seven

1. Minimize barriers to the transfer of ownership.
   - Be sensitive to the anxieties of the client while guiding them through the process of disseminating information and action planning.
   - Work with the client to get beyond analysis paralysis. Help the client visualize the finished product and commit to hard deadlines for roll-out.
   - Minimize possible causes for denial by keeping key end users fully briefed during the survey process and getting the client to commit to reporting the results.

2. Get a commitment to action.
   - Start by meeting with the survey sponsor to inform him or her of the main findings from the survey.
   - Set a process in place for a formal and tangible management response that helps the client (1) discuss what the survey results mean, (2) determine how the survey results should be communicated, (3) plan for what actions should be taken, (4) take action, and (5) follow up on the success or failure of actions taken.

3. Begin the action planning process.
   - Help the end user (1) recognize there is a problem and that it has consequences, (2) show their recognition of this to employees through communication, (3) prepare a plan for improvement, and (4) make a commitment to acting on this plan.

4. Choose the best and most effective action planning approach available, given the existing resources and commitment.
   - Target areas for change that will enhance organizational effectiveness such as productivity, sales, quality measures, and customer satisfaction.
   - Link survey results whenever possible to other measures of performance.

5. Build systems for measuring progress and evaluating success.
   - Get client organization to record actions taken as a result of the survey and to measure the impact of actions taken.
   - Contract with client to resurvey six months to one year later.
   - Help the client set up an internal survey process for long-term data collection and measurement of results.

References

Adams, S. *The Dilbert Principle.* New York: HarperBusiness, 1996.

Atwater, L. E., and Yammarino, F. J. "Does Self–Other Agreement on Leadership Perceptions Moderate the Validity of Leadership and Performance Predictions?" *Personnel Psychology,* 1992, *45,* 141–164.

Babbie, R. E. *Survey Research Methods,* Belmont, Calif.: Wadsworth, 1973.

Bauman, R. P., Jackson, P., and Lawrence, J. T. *From Promise to Performance: A Journey of Transformation at SmithKline Beecham.* Boston: Harvard Business School Press, 1997.

Beckhard, R., and Harris, R. T. *Organizational Transitions: Managing Complex Change.* (2nd ed.) Reading, Mass.: Addison-Wesley, 1987.

Beckhard, R., and Pritchard, W. *Changing the Essence: The Art of Creating and Leading Fundamental Change in Organizations.* San Francisco: Jossey-Bass, 1992.

Berger, L. A., Sikora, M. J., and Berger, D. R. (eds.). *The Change Management Handbook: A Road Map to Corporate Transformation.* Burr Ridge, Ill.: Irwin, 1994.

Berk, R. A. "Applications of the General Linear Model to Survey Data." In P. H. Rossi, J. D. Wright, and A. B. Anderson (eds.), *The Handbook of Survey Research.* San Diego, Calif.: Academic Press, 1983, pp. 495–546.

Block, P. *Flawless Consulting: A Guide to Getting Your Expertise Used.* San Diego, Calif.: University Associates, 1981.

Booth-Kewley, S., Rosenfeld, P., and Edwards, J. E. "Computer-Administered Surveys in Organizational Settings: Alternatives, Advantages, and Applications." In P. Rosenfeld, J. E. Edwards, and M. D. Thomas (eds.), *Improving Organizational Surveys.* Newbury Park, Calif.: Sage, 1993, pp. 73–101.

Bracken, D. W., Timmreck, C. W., and Church, A. H. (eds.). *The Handbook of Multisource Feedback.* San Francisco: Jossey-Bass, 2001.

Breisch, R. E. "Are You Listening?" *Quality Progress*, 1996, 29(1), 59–62.

Buckingham, M., and Coffman, C. *First, Break All the Rules: What the World's Greatest Managers Do Differently*. New York: Simon & Schuster Trade, 1999.

Bunker, B. B., and Alban, B. T. *Large Group Interventions: Engaging the Whole System for Rapid Change*. San Francisco: Jossey-Bass, 1997.

Burke, W. W. *Organization Development: A Process of Learning and Changing*. (2nd ed.) Reading, Mass.: Addison-Wesley, 1994.

Burke, W. W., Coruzzi, C. A., and Church, A. H. "The Organizational Survey as an Intervention for Change." In A. I. Kraut (ed.), *Organizational Surveys: Tools for Assessment and Change*. San Francisco: Jossey-Bass, 1996, pp. 41–66.

Burke, W. W., and Jackson, P. "Making the SmithKline Beecham Merger Work." *Human Resource Management*, 1991, 30, 69–87.

Burke, W. W., Javitch, M. J., Waclawski, J., and Church, A. H. "The Dynamics of Midstream Consulting." *Consulting Psychology Journal: Practice and Research*, 1997, 49(2), 83–95.

Burke, W. W., and Litwin, G. H. "A Causal Model of Organizational Performance and Change." *Journal of Management*, 1992, 18, 523–545.

Camp, R. C. *Business Process Benchmarking: Finding and Implementing Best Practices*. Milwaukee, Wisc.: ASQC Quality Press, 1995.

Church, A. H. "Estimating the Effect of Incentives on Mail Survey Response Rates: A Meta-analysis." *Public Opinion Quarterly*, 1993, 57(1), 62–79.

Church, A. H. "Managerial Self-Awareness in High Performing Individuals in Organizations." Doctoral dissertation, Columbia University, *Dissertation Abstracts International*, 55–05B, 1994a, 2028.

Church, A. H. "The Character of Organizational Communication: A Review and New Conceptualization." *International Journal of Organizational Analysis*, 1994b, 2(1), 18–53.

Church, A. H. "Linking Leadership Behaviours to Service Performance: Do Managers Make a Difference?" *Managing Service Quality*, 1995, 5(6), 26–31.

Church, A. H. "Giving Your Organizational Communication C-P-R." *Leadership and Organizational Development Journal*, 1996, 17(7), 4–11.

Church, A. H. "Managerial Self-Awareness in High Performing Individuals in Organizations." *Journal of Applied Psychology*, 1997, 82(2), 281–292.

Church, A. H. "Dilbert and Organizational Change: Friend or Foe?" *Performance in Practice*, Summer 1998, 1–2.

Church, A. H. "Do Better Managers Actually Receive Better Ratings? A Validation of Multi-Rater Assessment Methodology." *Consulting Psychology Journal: Practice and Research*, 2000, 52(2), 99–116.

Church, A. H., and Bracken, D. W. "Advancing the State of the Art of 360-Degree Feedback: Special Issue Editors' Comments on the Research and Practice of Multirater Assessment Methods." *Group and Organization Management,* 1997, *22*(2), 149–161.

Church, A. H., Margiloff, A., and Coruzzi, C. A. "Using Surveys for Change: An Applied Example in a Pharmaceuticals Organization." *Leadership and Organization Development Journal,* 1995, *16*(4), 3–11.

Church, A. H., and Waclawski, J. "Making Multirater Feedback Systems Work." *Quality Progress,* 1998a, *31*(4), 81–89.

Church, A. H., and Waclawski, J. "The Vendor Mind-Set: The Devolution from Organizational Consultant to Street Peddler." *Consulting Psychology Journal: Practice and Research,* 1998b, *5*(2), 87–100.

Church, A. H., and Waclawski, J. "The Impact of Leadership Style on Global Management Practices." *Journal of Applied Social Psychology,* 1999, *29*(7), 1416–1443.

Church, A. H., and Waclawski, J. "Is There a Method to Our Madness? Survey and Feedback Method Effects Across Five Different Settings." Paper presented at the 15th Annual Meeting of the Society for Industrial and Organizational Psychology. New Orleans, Apr. 15, 2000.

Church, A. H., Waclawski, J., and Burke, W. W. "Multisource Feedback for Organization Development and Change." In D. W. Bracken, C. W. Timmreck, and A. H. Church (eds.), *The Handbook of Multisource Feedback.* San Francisco: Jossey-Bass, 2001.

Church, A. H., Waclawski, J., McHenry, J., and McKenna, D. "Organization Development in High Performing Companies: An In-Depth Look at the Role of OD in Microsoft." *Organization Development Journal,* 1998, *16*(3), 51–64.

Edwards, J. E., Thomas, M. D., Rosenfeld, P., and Booth-Kewley, S. *How to Conduct Organizational Surveys: A Step-by-Step Guide.* Thousand Oaks, Calif.: Sage, 1997.

Fink, A. *The Survey Handbook.* Thousand Oaks, Calif.: Sage, 1995.

Folkman, J. *Employee Surveys That Make a Difference: Using Customized Feedback Tools to Transform Your Organization.* Provo, Utah: Executive Excellence, 1998.

Frankel, M. "Sampling Theory." In P. H. Rossi, J. D. Wright, and A. B. Anderson (eds.), *The Handbook of Survey Research,* San Diego, Calif.: Academic Press, 1983, pp. 21–67.

Furnham, A., and Stringfield, P. "Congruence of Self and Subordinate Ratings of Managerial Practices as a Correlate of Supervisor Evaluation." *Journal of Occupational and Organizational Psychology,* 1994, *67,* 57–67.

Golembiewski, R. T., and Sun, B. C. "Positive Findings Bias in QWL Studies: Rigor and Outcomes in a Large Sample." *Journal of Management,* 1990, *16,* 665–674.

Higgs, A. C., and Ashworth, S. D. "Organizational Surveys: Tools for Assessment and Research." In A. I. Kraut (ed.), *Organizational Surveys: Tools for Assessment and Change.* San Francisco: Jossey-Bass, 1996, pp. 19–40.

Hirsh, S. K., and Kummerow, J. M. *Introduction to Type in Organizations.* (2nd ed.). Palo Alto, Calif.: Consulting Psychologists Press, 1990.

Hornstein, H. A., Bunker, B. B., Burke, W. W., Gindes, M., and Lewicki, R. J. (eds.). *Social Intervention: A Behavioral Science Approach.* New York: Free Press, 1971.

Howard, A. H. *Diagnosis for Organizational Change: Methods and Models.* New York: Guilford Press, 1994.

Johnson, R. H. "Life in the Consortium: The Mayflower Group." In A. I. Kraut (ed.), *Organizational Surveys: Tools for Assessment and Change.* San Francisco: Jossey-Bass, 1996, pp. 285–309.

Jones, J. E., and Bearley, W. K. *Surveying Employees: A Practical Guidebook.* Amherst, Mass.: HRD Press, 1995.

Kanter, P. M., Stein, R. A., and Jick, T. D. *The Challenge of Organizational Change: How Companies Experience It and Leaders Guide It.* New York: Free Press, 1992.

Katz, D., and Kahn, R. L. *The Social Psychology of Organizations.* (2nd ed.) New York: Wiley, 1978.

Kotter, J. P. "Leading Change: Why Transformation Efforts Fail." *Harvard Business Review,* 1995, *73*(2), 59–67.

Kraut, A. I. "An Overview of Organizational Surveys." In A. I. Kraut (ed.), *Organizational Surveys: Tools for Assessment and Change.* San Francisco: Jossey-Bass, 1996a, pp. 1–14.

Kraut, A. I. "Planning and Conducting the Survey: Keeping the Strategic Purpose in Mind." In A. I. Kraut (ed.), *Organizational Surveys: Tools for Assessment and Change.* San Francisco: Jossey-Bass, 1996b, pp. 149–176.

Kraut, A. I. "Want Favorable Replies? Just Call! Telephone Versus Self-Administered Surveys." Poster presented at the annual convention of the Society for Industrial and Organizational Psychology, Atlanta, 1999.

Kraut, A. I. "Meaningful Action Can Follow Organizational Surveys: Some Success Stories." Symposium conducted at the annual convention of the Society for Industrial and Organizational Psychology, New Orleans, 2000.

Kraut, A. I., Oltrogge, C. G., and Block, C. J. "Written vs. Telephone Surveys of Employees: Are the Data Really Comparable?" Poster presented at the annual convention of the Society for Industrial and Organizational Psychology, Dallas, 1998.

Kraut, A. I., and Saari, L. M. "Organization Surveys Coming of Age for a New Era." In A. I. Kraut and A. K. Korman (eds.), *Evolving Practices in Human Resource Management: Responses to a Changing World of Work.* San Francisco: Jossey-Bass, 1999, pp. 302–327.

Kübler-Ross, E. *On Death and Dying.* New York: Macmillan, 1970.

Kuhnert, K., and McCauley, D. P. "Applying Alternative Survey Methods." In A. I. Kraut (ed.), *Organizational Surveys: Tools for Assessment and Change.* San Francisco: Jossey-Bass, 1996, pp. 233–254.

Ledford, G. E., Jr., and Mohrman, S. A. "Self-Design for High Involvement: A Large-Scale Organizational Change." *Human Relations,* 1993, 46(1), 143–173.

Lehmann, D. R. *Market Research and Analysis.* (3rd ed.) Homewood, Ill.: Irwin, 1989.

Lewin, K. "Group Decision and Social Change." In E. E. Maccoby, T. M. Newcomb, and E. L. Hartley (eds.), *Readings in Social Psychology,* New York: Holt, Rinehart and Winston, 1958, pp. 197–211.

Macey, W. H. "Dealing with the Data: Collection, Processing, and Analysis." In A. I. Kraut (ed.), *Organizational Surveys: Tools for Assessment and Change.* San Francisco: Jossey-Bass, 1996, pp. 204–232.

Micklethwait, J., and Wooldridge, A. *The Witch Doctors: Making Sense of the Management Gurus.* New York: Times Business, 1996.

Nadler, D. A. *Feedback and Organization Development: Using Data-Based Methods.* Reading, Mass.: Addison-Wesley, 1977.

Nadler, D. A., and Tushman, M. L. "Designing Organizations That Have Good Fit: A Framework for Understanding New Architectures." In D. A. Nadler, M. S. Gerstein, R. B. Shaw, and Associates (eds.), *Organizational Architecture: Designs for Changing Organizations.* San Francisco: Jossey-Bass, 1992, pp. 39–59.

Paul, K. B., and Bracken, D. W. "Everything You Always Wanted to Know about Employee Surveys." *Training and Development,* 1995, 49(1), 45–49.

Pedhauzer, E. J. *Multiple Regression in Behavioral Research: Explanation and Prediction.* (2nd ed.) New York: Holt, Rinehart and Winston, 1982.

Pinault, L. *Consulting Demons: Inside the Unscrupulous World Of Global Corporate Consulting.* New York: HarperBusiness, 2000.

Rea, L. M., and Parker, R. A. *Designing and Conducting Survey Research: A Comprehensive Guide,* San Francisco: Jossey-Bass, 1992.

Rea, L. M., and Parker, R. A. *Designing and Conducting Survey Research: A Comprehensive Guide.* (2nd ed.) San Francisco: Jossey-Bass, 1997.

Roberts, D. R., and Robertson, P. J. "Positive-Findings Bias, and Measuring Methodological Rigor, in Evaluations of Organization Development." *Journal of Applied Psychology,* 1993, 77(6), 918–925.

Robertson, P. J., Roberts, D. R., and Porras, J. I. "Dynamics of Planned Organizational Change: Assessing Empirical Support for a Theoretical Model." *Academy of Management Journal,* 1993, 36(3), 619–634.

Rogelberg, S. G. "Surveys and More Surveys: Addressing and Dealing with Oversurveying." Symposium conducted at the annual convention of the Society for Industrial and Organizational Psychology, Dallas, 1998.

Rogelberg, S. G., and Waclawski, J. "Instrument Design." In D. W. Bracken, C. W. Timmreck, and A. H. Church (eds.), *The Handbook of Multisource Feedback.* San Francisco: Jossey-Bass, 2001.

Rossi, P. H., Wright, J. D., and Anderson, A. B. "Sample Surveys: History, Current Practice, and Future Prospects." In P. H. Rossi, J. D. Wright, and A. B. Anderson (eds.), *The Handbook of Survey Research,* San Diego, Calif.: Academic Press, 1983, pp. 1–20.

Rucci, A. J., Kirn, S. P., and Quinn, R. T. "The Employee-Customer Profit Chain at Sears." *Harvard Business Review,* 1998, 76(1), 83–97.

Sashkin, M., and Kiser, K. J. *Putting Total Quality Management to Work.* San Francisco: Berrett-Koehler, 1993.

Schaffer, R. H., and Thomson, H. A. "Successful Change Programs Begin with Results." *Harvard Business Review,* 1992, 70(1), 80–89.

Schein, E. H. *Process Consultation,* Vol. 1: *Its Role in Organizational Development.* (2nd ed.) Reading, Mass.: Addison-Wesley, 1988.

Schumacker, R. E., and Lomax, R. G. *A Beginner's Guide to Structural Equation Modeling.* Mahwah, N.J.: Erlbaum, 1996.

Schuman, H., and Kalton, G. "Survey Methods." In G. Lindzey and E. Aronson (eds.), *The Handbook of Social Psychology.* Vol. 1. (3rd ed.) New York: Random House, 1985, pp. 635–697.

Schuman, H., and Presser, S. *Questions and Answers in Attitude Surveys: Experiments on Question Form, Wording, and Context.* Thousand Oaks, Calif.: Sage, 1996.

Spector, B., and Beer, M. "Beyond TQM Programmes." *Journal of Organizational Change Management,* 1994, 7(2), 63–70.

Spendolini, M. J. *The Benchmarking Book.* New York: AMACOM, 1992.

Stanton, J. M. "An Empirical Assessment of Data Collection Using the Internet." *Personnel Psychology,* 1998, 51(3), 709–725.

Stolzenberg, R. M., and Land, K. C. "Causal Modeling and Survey Research." In P. H. Rossi, J. D. Wright, and A. B. Anderson (eds.), *The Handbook of Survey Research*, San Diego, Calif.: Academic Press, 1982, pp. 613–675.

Sudman, S. "Applied Sampling." In P. H. Rossi, J. D. Wright, and A. B. Anderson (eds.), *The Handbook of Survey Research*, San Diego, Calif.: Academic Press, 1983, pp. 145–194.

Tabachnick, B. G., and Fidell, L. S. *Using Multivariate Statistics*. (2nd ed.) New York: Harper & Row, 1989.

Terpstra, D. E. "Relationship between Methodological Rigor and Reported Outcomes in Organization Development Evaluation Research." *Journal of Applied Psychology*, 1981, 66, 541–543.

Tichy, N. M. *Managing Strategic Change: Technical, Political and Cultural Dynamics*. New York: Wiley, 1983.

Tichy, N. M. *The Leadership Engine: How Winning Companies Build Leaders at Every Level*. New York: HarperCollins, 1997.

Trahant, B., and Burke, W. W. "Creating a Change Reaction: How Understanding Organizational Dynamics Can Ease Reengineering." *National Productivity Review*, Autumn, 1996, 37–46.

Tse, A., Ching, R., Ding, Y. B., Fong, R., and Yeung, E. "A Comparison of the Effectiveness of Mail and Facsimile as Survey Media on Response Rate, Speed And Quality." *Journal of the Market Research Society*, 1994, 36(4), 349–355.

Ulrich, D. *Human Resource Champions: The Next Agenda for Adding Value and Delivering Results*. Boston: Harvard Business School, 1997.

Van Velsor, E., Taylor, S., and Leslie, J. B. "An Examination of the Relationships among Self-Perception Accuracy, Self-Awareness, Gender, and Leader Effectiveness." *Human Resource Management*, 1993, 32(2,3), 249–263.

Waclawski, J. "Using Organizational Survey Results to Improve Organizational Performance." *Managing Service Quality*, 1996a, 6(4), 53–56.

Waclawski, J. "Large-Scale Organizational Change and Organizational Performance." Doctoral dissertation, Columbia University, 1996b. *Dissertation Abstracts International, 57–05B*, 3443 (University Microfilms No. AAG9631797).

Waclawski, J. "The Real World: The E-Business Revolution—Faster Than a Speeding Bullet." *The Industrial-Organizational Psychologist*, 2000, 37(3), 70–80.

Waclawski, J., and Church, A. H. "Learning into Action Planning." Presentation delivered at the quarterly meeting of the Mayflower Group, Colorado Springs, Colorado, May 6, 1999.

Waclawski, J., and Church, A. H. "Survey Lessons from the Consulting Realm: Strategies for Action Planning." Practitioner Forum held at the 15th Annual Meeting of the Society for Industrial and Organizational Psychology, New Orleans, April 15, 2000.

Walker, A. G., and Smither, J. W. "A Five-Year Study of Upward Feedback: What Managers Do with Their Results Matters." *Personnel Psychology*, 1999, 52, 393–423.

Weisbord, M. R. *Organizational Diagnosis: A Workbook of Theory and Practice*. Reading, Mass.: Addison-Wesley, 1978.

Weisbord, M. R. *Future Search: An Action Guide to Finding Common Ground in Organizations and Communities*. San Francisco: Berrett-Koehler, 1995.

Wiley, J. W. "Linking Survey Results to Customer Satisfaction and Business Performance." In A. I. Kraut (ed.), *Organizational Surveys: Tools for Assessment and Change*. San Francisco: Jossey-Bass, 1996, pp. 330–359.

Yost, P. R., and Homer, L. E. "Electronic Versus Paper Surveys: Does the Medium Affect the Response?" Poster presented at the annual convention of the Society for Industrial and Organizational Psychology, Dallas, 1998.

Index

DATE DUE

DEMCO 38-297